WOMEN AND JUDAISM

GARLAND REFERENCE LIBRARY
OF SOCIAL SCIENCE
(VOL. 316)

WOMEN AND JUDAISM
A Select Annotated Bibliography

Inger Marie Ruud

GARLAND PUBLISHING, INC. • NEW YORK & LONDON
1988

Library of Congress Cataloging-in-Publication Data

Ruud, Inger Marie.
　Women and Judaism.

　(Garland reference library of social science ;
v. 316)
　Includes index.
　1. Women in Judaism—Bibliography.　2. Women,
Jewish—Bibliography.　I. Title.　II. Series.
Z796.3.J4R88　1988　016.296′088042　87-29109
[BM729.W6]
ISBN 0-8240-8689-9 (alk. paper)

Printed on acid-free, 250-year-life paper
Manufactured in the United States of America

CONTENTS

PREFACE

This bibliography is about women in Judaism. The main
purpose is to provide access to all sorts of works dealing
with as many aspects as possible of women's life from
ancient to modern times: women in religion, education and
employment, marriage and family, politics, and society. I
have tried to find materials on Jewish women in all
countries with a Jewish population of any importance. The
majority of the entries are about women in Israel and the
United States. Many of the entries included are studies
which have their origins in the contemporary feminist
movement. This movement has forced a reconsideration of
women's place in cult and society and a redefinition of
women's role in religious literature.

The bibliography is a selective one. The basis of
selection centers on providing for scholars and the general
public an annotated bibliography of materials on women in
Jewish religion and societies in the form of monographs,
journal articles, chapters of monographs, essays and
articles from collections, and doctoral dissertations, in
English, German, French, and the Scandinavian languages.
Due to language problems, materials in Hebrew are not
included.

The coverage of the bibliography is not limited to a
definite span of years, but the majority of the items
included are works published in this century. The materials
have been collected in libraries in Oslo, Copenhagen,
London, and New York. All possible works have been checked
in the original for accuracy of citation. In the case of a
few monographs and dissertations not available for personal
examination, they have been verified in the Library of
Congress catalogues, and in *Dissertation Abstracts*.

Each citation is as bibliographically complete as possible. The following information is given:

a) Monographs:

Author, title, place and date of publication, publisher, number of pages, and series (if any).

b) Articles:

Author, title, title of publication (periodical, Festschrift, symposium, etc.), number of pages, place and date of publication, and publisher.

The bibliography is arranged alphabetically by author and the entries are numbered serially. The index is divided into three parts: a topographical index, a subject index, and an author index. The items in the subject index are listed under a few broad headings. The author index is included because many of the entries in the bibliography have more than one author. Each entry is only cited once, and there are no cross-references.

Most entries are annotated. The annotations may vary from a single sentence to a full paragraph. In some cases the mere title is so informative that an annotation is omitted. The main purpose with each annotation is to give a short, concise, and informative summary of the contents without any valuation of the quality.

An attempt has been made to assure accuracy in the bibliographical data by repeated rechecking and proofreading. However, I have never come across a bibliography totally without errors, and they are doubtless present also in this one. I hope the errors are few and ask for the reader's indulgence.

ACKNOWLEDGMENTS

I wish to express my appreciation to all those who have made this project possible. My acknowledgments go to the following organizations and libraries: The Norway-America Association for awarding me a Thanks to Scandinavia Scholarship for the academic year 1982/83; The Thanks to Scandinavia, Inc., by Mr. Richard Netter; International Federation of University Women, Geneva; and the Ministry of Consumer Affairs and Government Administration, Directorate of Personnel, Oslo, for making it financially possible for me to spend three months in the United States in the autumn of 1982; the library of the Jewish Theological Seminary of America in New York; the library of the Hebrew Union College--Jewish Institute of Religion in Cincinnati and New York; The Institute for Advanced Studies of World Religions, State University of New York at Stony Brook; British Library in London, and the Royal Library in Copenhagen.

I would also like to acknowledge my colleagues at the Royal University Library of Oslo for all kind assistance, particularly the Interlending Section for supplying books and articles from many parts of the world, and the management of the library for granting me leaves and supporting me financially.

Finally, my sincere thanks go to the editors of Garland Publishing, Inc., for accepting this book.

Oslo, Norway
The Royal University Library
19 August, 1987
Inger Marie Ruud

REFERENCES

Acta Cytologica; The Journal of Clinical Cytology and Cytopathology, 2 Jacklynn Court, St. Louis, MO 63132.

Adolescence; An International Quarterly Devoted to the Physiological, Psychological, Psychiatric, Sociological, and Educational Aspects of the Second Decade of Human Life, Libra Publishers, Inc., 3089C Clairemont Dr., Ste. 332, San Diego, CA 92117.

American Academy of Religion, Journal, Scholars Press, Box 1608, Decatur, GA 30031-1608. (Formerly: Journal of Bible and Religion)

American Anthropologist, American Anthropological Association, 1703 New Hampshire Ave., N.W., Washington, DC 20009.

American Behavioral Scientist, Sage Publications, Inc., 275 S. Beverly Dr., Beverly Hills, CA 90212.

American Historical Review, American Historical Association, 400 A St. S.E., Washington, DC 20003.

American Jewish Archives; Devoted to the Preservation and Study of American Jewish Experience, Hebrew Union College-Jewish Institute of Religion, 3101 Clifton Ave., Cincinnati, OH 45220.

American Jewish Congress. Congress Monthly; A Journal of Opinion and Jewish Affairs, American Jewish Congress, 15 E. 14th St., New York, NY 10028. (Formerly: American Jewish Congress. Congress Bi-Weekly)

American Jewish History; American Jewish Historical Society,
Two Thornton Rd., Waltham, MA 02153. (Formerly, until
Sept. 1978: American Jewish Historical Quarterly)

American Journal of Comparative Law, American Association
for the Comparative Study of Law, School of Law (Boalt
Hall), University of California, Berkeley, CA 94720.

American Journal of Education, University of Chicago Press,
5801 S. Ellis Ave., Chicago, IL 60637. (Formerly, until
vol. 88, 1979, School Review)

American Journal of Orthopsychiatry, American
Orthopsychiatric Association, 19 W. 44th St., New York, NY
10036.

American Journal of Public Health, American Public Health
Association, 1015 15th St., N.W., Washington DC 20005.
(Formerly: American Journal of Public Health and the
Nation's Health)

American Quarterly, University of Pennsylvania, 303 College
Hall/CO, Philadelphia, PA 19104.

Andover Newton Quarterly, Andover Newton Theological School,
Newton Center, MA 02159. (Formerly: Andover Newton
Bulletin)

Anima; An Experiential Journal, Anima Publications,
1053 Wilson Ave., Chambersburg, PA 17201.

Anthropological Quarterly, Catholic University of America
Press, 620 Michigan Ave., N.E., Washington, DC 20064.

Asian and African Studies, Haifa University, Institute of
Middle Eastern Studies, Mount Carmel, Haifa, Israel.

Atlantis; A Women's Studies Journal, Mount Saint Vincent
University, 166 Bedford Highway, Halifax, N.S. B3M 216,
Canada.

Berkeley Journal of Sociology; Critical Review, University
of California, Berkeley, Sociology Department, 410 Barrows
Hall, Berkeley, CA 94720. (Formerly, Vols. 1-4, 1955-58:
Berkeley Publications in Society and Institutions)

Biblica, Biblical Institute Press, Piazza della Pilotta 35, 00187, Rome, Italy.

Biblical Archaeologist, American School of Oriental Research, 4243 Spruce St., Philadelphia, PA 19104.

Biblical Theology Bulletin, Biblical Theology Bulletin, Inc., c/o Theology Department, St. John's University, Jamaica, NY 11439.

Brethren Life and Thought; A Quarterly Journal Published in the Interest of the Church of Brethren, Brethren Press, Butterfield and Meyers Rds., Oak Brook, IL 60521.

Bucknell Review; A Scholarly Journal of Letters, Arts and Science, Bucknell University Press, c/o Associated University Presses, 440 Forsgate Dr., Cranbury, NJ 08512.

Canadian Journal of Psychiatry, Canadian Psychiatric Association, 225 Lisgar St., Ste. 103, Ottawa, Ont. K2P OC6, Canada. (Formerly: Canadian Psychiatric Association Journal)

Catholic Biblical Quarterly, Catholic Biblical Association of America, Catholic University of America, Washington, DC 20064.

Centennial Review, Michigan State University, College of Arts & Letters, 200 Linton Hall, East Lansing, MI 48824-1036. (Formerly: Centennial Review of Arts and Science)

Center Magazine, Santa Barbara. (Formerly: Center Diary)

Child and Family, National Commission on Human Life, Reproduction and Rhythm, Box 501, Oak Park, IL 60303.

Christian Century; An Ecumenical Weekly, Christian Century Foundation, 407 S. Dearborn St., Chicago, IL 60605.

Commentary, 165 East 56th St., New York, NY 10022.

Commonweal, Commonweal Publishing Co., Inc., 232 Madison Ave., New York, NY 10016.

Communio Viatorum; A Theological Quarterly, Comenius Faculty of Protestant Theology, Jungmannova 9, 110 00 Prague 1, Czechoslovakia.

Congress Monthly; See: American Jewish Congress

Conservative Judaism, Rabbinical Assembly, 3080 Broadway, New York, NY 10027.

Contemporary Jewry; A Journal of Sociological Inquiry, Transaction Periodicals Consortium, Rutgers University, New Brunswick, NJ 08903.

Crisis; International Journal of Suicide and Crisis Studies, C.J. Hogrefe, Inc., 12-14 Bruce Park Ave., Toronto, Ont. M4P 2S3, Canada.

Culture, Medicine and Psychiatry; An International Journal of Comparative Cross-Culture Research, D. Reidel Publishing Co., Box 17, 3300 AA Dordrecht, Netherlands.

Demography, Population Association of America, Box 14182, Benjamin Franklin Station, Washington, DC 20044.

Dialectical Anthropology, Elsevier Scientific Publishing Co., P.O. Box 211, 1000 AE Amsterdam, Netherlands.

Dine Israel; An Annual of Jewish Law: Past and Present, Tel Aviv University, Faculty of Law, Tel Aviv, Israel.

Dispersion and Unity, Jerusalem, Israel.

Dissent, Foundation for the Study of Independent Social Ideas, Inc., 521 Fifth Ave., New York, NY 10017.

Economic Development and Cultural Change, University of Chicago Press, 5801 S. Ellis Ave., Chicago, IL 60637.

Ecumenical Review, World Council of Churches, 150 Route de Ferney, 1211 Geneva 20, Switzerland.

Ethnicity; An Interdisciplinary Journal of the Study of Ethnic Relations, Academic Press, Inc., Journal Division, 111 Fifth Ave., New York, NY 10003.

European Judaism, Foundation for European Judaism, Kent House, Rutland Gardens, London S.W. 7, England.

Evangelische Theologie, Christian Kaiser Verlag, Isabellastr. 20, 8000 Munich 40, W. Germany.

Expository Times, T. & T. Clark Ltd., 59 George St., Edinburgh EH2 2LQ, Scotland.

Feminist Review, London, England.

Fertility and Sterility, American Fertility Society, 2131 Magnolia Ave., Ste. 201, Birmingham, AL 35256.

Foundations; A Baptist Journal of History and Theology, Rochester, NY.

Frontiers: A Journal of Women's Studies, University of Colorado, Women's Studies Program, Boulder, CO 80309.

Gerontologist, Gerontological Society of America, 1411 K St., N.W., Suite 300, Washington, DC 20005.

Gratz College Annual of Jewish Studies, Philadelphia, PA.

Harvard Theological Review, Harvard Divinity School, 45 Francis Ave., Cambridge, MA 02138.

Hebrew Annual Review; A Journal of Studies of Hebrew Language and Literature, Ohio State University, Department of Judaic and Near Eastern Language and Literatures, 1841 Millikin Road, Columbus, OH 43210.

Hebrew Studies; A Journal Devoted to the Hebrew Language, the Bible and Related Areas of Scholarship, National Association of Professors of Hebrew, 1346 Van Hise Hall, 1220 Linden Dr., University of Wisconsin-Madison, Madison, WI 53706.

Hebrew Union College Annual; Hebrew Union College-Jewish Institute of Religion, 3101 Clifton Ave., Cincinnati, OH 45220.

Humanity and Society, Association for Humanist Sociology, Department of Sociology, Howard University, Washington, DC 20059.

Iliff Review, Iliff School of Theology, 2201 S. University Blvd., Denver, CO 80210.

Imagination; Cognition and Personality, Baywood Publishing Co., 120 Marine St., Box D, Farmingdale, NY 11735.

In the Dispersion, See: Dispersion and Unity.

Informationen für die Frau, Deutscher Frauenrat, Augustastr. 42, 5300 Bonn-Bad Godesberg, W. Germany.

International Journal of Comparative Sociology, Karnataka University, Department of Social Anthropology, Dharwad 580003, Karnataka, India.

International Journal of Middle East Studies, Cambridge University Press, Edinburgh Bldg., Shaftesbury Rd., Cambridge CB2 2RU, England.

International Journal of Social Psychiatry, Avenue Publishing Co., 55 Woodstock Ave., London NW11 9RG, England.

International Journal of Sociology of the Family, c/o Man Singh Das, Ed., Northern Illinois University, Department of Sociology, De Kalb, IL 60115.

International Journal of Women's Studies, Eden Press Women's Publications, 4626 St. Catherine St., W., Montreal, P.Q. H3Z IS3, Canada.

International Review of Education, Martinus Nijhoff Publishers, Spuiboulevard 50, 3311 GR, Dordrecht, Netherlands.

International Review of Modern Sociology, Northern Illinois University, Department of Sociology, De Kalb, IL 60115.

Israel Digest, World Zionist Organization: Information Division, Jerusalem, Israel.

Israel Journal of Psychiatry and Related Disciplines, Israel Science Publishers Ltd., Box 3115, Jerusalem 91030, Israel. (Formerly: Israel Annals of Psychiatry and Related Disciplines)

Israel Law Review, Israel Law Review Association, c/o Hebrew University, Faculty of Law, P.O. Box 24100, Mount Scopus, Jerusalem, Israel.

Israel Magazine, Philadelphia, PA.

Jewish Journal of Sociology, World Jewish Congress, 55 New Cavendish St., London W1M 8BT, England.

Jewish Observer and Middle East Review, London, England.

Jewish Quarterly Review, Dropsie University, Broad and York Sts., Philadelphia, PA 19132.

Jewish Social Studies, Conference on Jewish Social Studies, Inc., 2112 Broadway, Rm. 206, New York, NY 10023.

Jewish Spectator, New York.

The Jewish Woman. Official Organ of the Council of Jewish Women, New York, NY.

Journal for the Study of Judaism in the Persian, Hellenistic and Roman Period, E.J. Brill, P.O. Box 9000, 2300 PA Leiden, Netherlands.

Journal for the Study of the Old Testament, JSOT Press, Department of Biblical Studies, University of Sheffield, Sheffield, S10 2TN, England.

Journal of Biblical Literature, Scholars Press, University of Montana, Missoula, MT 59801.

Journal of Clinical Psychology, Clinical Psychology Publishing Co., Inc., 4 Conant Square, Brandon, VT 05733.

Journal of Contemporary History, Sage Publications Ltd., 28 Banner St., London EC1Y 8QE, England.

Journal of Divorce, Haworth Press, Inc., 12 W. 32nd St., New York, NY 10001.

Journal of Ecumenical Studies, Temple University, Philadelphia, PA 19122.

Journal of Educational Psychology, American Psychological Association, 1200 17th St., N.W., Washington, DC 20036.

Journal of Ethnic Studies, Western Washington University, College of Ethnic Studies, Bellingham, WA 98225.

Journal of Family Law, University of Louisville, School of Law, Louisville, KY 40292.

Journal of Feminist Studies in Religion, Scholars Press, Chico, CA.

Journal of Gerontological Social Work, Haworth Press, Inc., 12 W. 32nd St., New York, NY 10001.

Journal of Jewish Studies, Oxford Centre for Postgraduate Hebrew Studies, Oriental Institute, Pusey Lane, Oxford OX1 2LE, England.

Journal of Marriage and the Family, National Council on Family Relations, 1910 West County Rd. B, Ste. 147, St. Paul, MN 55113. (Formerly: Marriage and Family Living)

Journal of Political Economy, University of Chicago Press, 5801 S. Ellis Ave., Chicago, IL 60637.

Journal of Psychology and Judaism, Human Sciences Press, Inc., 72 Fifth Ave., New York, NY 10011.

Journal of Religion and Health, Human Sciences Press, Inc., 72 Fifth Ave., New York, NY 10011.

Journal of Religious Studies, Cleveland State University, Department of Religion, Cleveland, OH 44115. (Formerly: Ohio Journal of Religious Studies)

Journal of Sex and Marital Therapy, Brunner-Mazel, Inc., 19 Union Sq. W., New York, NY 10003.

Journal of Social Issues, Plenum Publishing Corp., 233 Spring St., New York, NY 10013.

Journal of Social Psychology, Heldref Publications, 4000 Albemarle St., N.W., Washington, DC 20016.

Journal of Social Psychology, The Journal Press, Provincetown, MA.

Journal of Urban History, Sage Publications, Inc., 275 S. Beverly Dr., Beverly Hills, CA 90212.

Journal of Youth and Adolescence; Multidisciplinary Research Publication, Plenum Press, 233 Spring St., New York, NY 10013.

Judaica; Beiträge zum Verständnis des jüdischen Schicksals in Vergangenheit und Gegenwart, Judaica Verlag, Etzelstr. 19, CH-8038 Zürich, Switzerland.

Judaism; A Quarterly Journal of Jewish Life and Thought, American Jewish Congress, 15 E. 84th St., New York, NY 10028.

Keeping Posted, Union of American Hebrew Congregations, 838 Fifth Ave., New York, NY 10021.

Khamsin; Journal of Revolutionary Socialists of the Middle East, Ithaca Press, 13 Southwark St., London SE1 1RQ, England.

Kidma; Israel Journal of Development, Society for International Development, Israel Chapter, 3 Moshe Wallach St., P.O. Box 13130, Jerusalem 94385, Israel.

Labor History, Tamiment Institute, Ben Josephson Library, New York University, Bobst Library, 10th Fl., 70 Washington Sq. South, New York, NY 10012.

Lancet, Lancet Ltd., 7 Adam St., London WC2N 6AD, England.

Leo Baeck Institute, Bulletin, Athenaeum Verlag, Postfach 1220, D-2640 Konigstein, W. Germany.

Leo Baeck Institute, Year Book, Secker & Warburg, 54 Poland St., London W1V 3DF, England.

Lexington Theological Quarterly, Lexington Theological Seminary, 631 S. Limestone St., Lexington, KY 40508. (Formerly: College of the Bible Quarterly)

Lilith; The Jewish Women's Magazine, Lilith Publications, Inc., 250 W. 57th St., Ste. 1328, New York, NY 10019.

Marriage and Family Living, See: Journal of Marriage and the Family.

Memoria; rivista di storia delle donne, Rosenberg & Sellier, Via Andrea Doria 14, 10123, Turin, Italy.

Mennonite Quarterly Review, Mennonite Historical Society, Goshen College, Goshen, IN 46526.

Michigan Jewish History, Jewish Historical Society of Michigan, 21721 Parklawn, Oak Park, MI 48237.

Midstream; A Monthly Jewish Review, Theodor Herzl Foundation, Inc., 515 Park Ave., New York, NY 10022.

Midwest Quarterly; A Journal of Contemporary Thought, Pittsburg State University, Midwest Quarterly, Pittsburg, KS 66762.

Montana; The Magazine of Western History, Montana Historical Society, 225 N. Roberts St., Helena, MT 59620.

Ms; The New Magazine for Women, Ms Magazine Corporation, 119 W. 40th St., New York, NY 10018.

New German Critique; An Interdisciplinary Journal of German Studies, University of Wisconsin-Milwaukee, Department of German, Box 413, Milwaukee, WI 35201.

New Outlook; Middle East Monthly, Tazpiot Ltf., 2 Rehov Karl Netter, Tel Aviv, Israel.

New Testament Studies, Cambridge University Press, Edinburgh Bldg., Shaftesbury Rd., Cambridge CB2 2RU, England.

Off Our Backs; A Women's News Journal, Off Our Backs, Inc., 1841 Columbia Rd., N.W., Rm. 212, Washington, DC 20010.

Ohio Journal of Religious Studies, See: Journal of Religious Studies.

Parliamentary Affairs; Devoted to All Aspects of Parliamentary Democracy, Oxford University Press, Walton St., Oxford OX2 6DP, England.

Population and Environment; Behavioral and Social Issues, Human Sciences Press, Inc., 72 Fifth Ave., New York, NY 10011. (Formerly: Journal of Population)

Present Tense; The Magazine of World Jewish Affairs, American Jewish Committee, 165 E. 56th St., New York, NY 10022.

Psychology of Women Quarterly, Cambridge University Press, Edinburgh Bldg., Shaftesbury Rd., Cambridge CB2 2RU, England.

Psychology Today, Ziff Davis Publishing Co., Consumer Division, One Park Ave., New York NY 10016.

Publications of the Jewish Historical Society, See: American Jewish History.

Religion and Reason; Method and Theory in the Study and Interpretation of Religion, Walter de Gruyter & Co., Mouton Publishers, Postfach 110240, D-1000 Berlin 11, W. Germany.

Religion in Life, See: United Methodist Board of Higher Education and Ministry Quarterly Review.

Religious Education; A Platform for the Free Discussion of Issues in the Field of Religion and Their Bearing on Education, Religious Education Association, 409 Prospect St., New Haven, CT 06510.

Religious Studies Review; A Quarterly Review of Publications in the Field of Religion and Related Disciplines, Council on the Study of Religion, Wilfrid Laurier University, Waterloo, Ont., N2L 3C5, Canada.

Response; A Contemporary Jewish Review, Jewish Educational Ventures, Inc., 610 W. 113th St., New York, NY 10025.

Revue de l'Histoire des Religions, F. Presses Universitaires de France, 108 bd. Saint Germain, 75279 Paris Cedex 6, France.

Revue Francaise d'Etudes Politiques Méditerranéennes,
Société Africaine d'Edition, B.P. 1877, Dakar, Senegal.

Rhode Island Jewish Historical Notes, Rhode Island Jewish
Historical Association, 130 Sessions St., Providence, RI
02906.

Sammlung Gemeinverständlicher Vorträge und Schriften aus dem
Gebiete der Theologie und Religionsgeschichte, Tübingen,
W. Germany.

School Review, See: American Journal of Education.

Semitica, Institut d'Etudes Semitiques, Adrien Maisonneuve,
11 Rue St. Sulpice, 75006 Paris, France.

Sex Roles; A Journal of Research, Plenum Press, 233 Spring
St., New York, NY 10013.

Signs; Journal of Women in Culture and Society, University
of Chicago Press, 5801 S. Ellis Ave., Chicago, IL 60637.

Social Problems, Society for the Study of Social Problems,
Inc., HB 208, State University College at Buffalo, 1300
Elmwood Ave., Buffalo, NY 14222.

Social Science and Medicine, Pergamon Press, Inc., Journals
Division, Maxwell House, Fairview Park, Elmsford, NY
10253.

Social Science Quarterly, University of Texas Press,
Box 7819, Austin, TX 78713.

Social Work, National Association of Social Workers,
Publications Department, 257 Park Ave. South, New York, NY
10010.

Sociological Focus, North Central Sociological Association,
University of Cincinnati, Department of Sociology,
Cincinnati, OH 45221.

Sociological Inquiry, University of Texas Press, Box 7819,
Austin, TX 78712.

Sociological Review, Routledge & Kegan Paul PLC, Broadway House, Newton Rd., Henley-on-Thames, Oxon RG9 1EN, England.

Sociology of Work and Occupations, See: Work and Occupations.

Southern Economic Journal, University of North Carolina at Chapel Hill, Southern Economic Association, Hanes Hall 019A, Chapel Hill, NC 27514.

Studies in American Jewish Literature, State University of New York Press, State University Plaza, Albany, NY 12246.

Svensk Teologisk Kvartalskrift, Liber Forlag, S-205 10, Malmö, Sweden.

Temenos, Finnish Society for the Study of Comparative Religion, Henrikinkatu 3, 20500 Turku, Finland.

Theologische Quartalschrift, Erich Wewel Verlag, Anzingerstr. 1, D-8000 München 80, W. Germany.

Theologische Zeitschrift, Friedrich Reinhardt Verlag, Missionsstr. 36, CH-4012 Basel, Switzerland.

Theology Today, Princeton Theological Seminary, Box 29, Princeton, NJ 08542.

Tradition (New York); A Journal of Orthodox Jewish Thought, Human Sciences Press, Inc., 72 Fifth Ave., New York, NY 10011.

Transactional Analysis Journal, International Transactional Analysis Association, 1772 Vallejo St., San Francisco, CA 94123.

Union Seminary Quarterly Review, Union Theological Seminary, 3041 Broadway, New York, NY 10027.

United Methodist Board of Higher Education and Ministry. Quarterly Review; A Scholarly Journal for Reflection on Ministry, United Methodist Publishing House, Box 871, Nashville, TN 37203. (Formerly: Religion in Life)

USA Today, Society for the Advancement of Education, 1860 Broadway, New York, NY 10023.

Vetus Testamentum, E.J. Brill, P.O. Box 9000, 2300 PA Leiden, Netherlands.

Western States Jewish Historical Quarterly, See: Western States Jewish History.

Western States Jewish History, Western States Jewish Historical Association, 2429 23rd St., Santa Monica, CA 90405. (Formerly: Western States Jewish Historical Quarterly)

Women's Studies International Forum; A Multidisciplinary Journal for the Rapid Publication of Research Communications and Review Articles in Women's Studies, Pergamon Press, Inc., Journals Division, Maxwell House, Fairview Park, Elmsford, NY 10253. (Formerly: Women's Studies International Quarterly)

Work and Occupations; An International Sociological Journal, Sage Publications, Inc., 275 S. Beverly Dr., Beverly Hills, CA 90212. (Formerly, until 1982: Sociology of Work and Occupations)

Worship Concerned with the Problems of Liturgical Renewal, Liturgical Press, St. John's Abbey, Collegeville, MN 56321.

Yad Vashen Bulletin, Jerusalem, Israel.

Zeitschrift für die Alttestamentliche Wissenschaft und die Kunde des Nachbiblischen Judentums, Berlin, W. Germany.

Zeitschrift für Religions- und Geistesgeschichte, E.J. Brill GmbH, Antwerpenerstr. 6, 5000 Köln 1, W. Germany.

Women and Judaism

BIBLIOGRAPHY

1. Abramowitz, Naomi Ruth. "The Investigation of Family
   Size Decisions in the Context of Marital Interaction:
   An Analysis of the Responses of Fifteen Jewish
   Couples Interviewed Conjointly About Their Decision
   to Terminate Childbearing." Ed.D. diss., Columbia
   University, 1976. 187 pp.

   An examination of the dynamics that are significant
   for a couple when they decide that their family is
   complete. The categories for analysis were: the
   decision to stop; premarital ideas about family size;
   relationship with extended family; pregnancy and
   childbirth experience; experience in parenthood; use of
   contraception; sexual relationship; and marital
   relationship. Thinks that the insights reached by the
   study "are in the direction of formulating a
   developmental theory of family-size preference and will
   require longitudinal study for empirical testing."

2. Abu-Saba, Mary Bentley, Judith Plaskow, and Rosemary
   Radford Ruether. "Women Responding to the Arab-
   Israeli Conflict." In *Women's Spirit Bonding*,
   edited by Janet Klaven and Mary I. Buckley, 221-33.
   New York: Pilgrim Press, 1984.

3. Adelman, Penina V. *Miriam's Well: Ritual for Jewish
   Women Around the Year*. New York: Biblio Press,
   1986. 175 pp.

4. Adler, Rachel. "The Jew Who Wasn't There: *Halakhah*
    and the Jewish Woman." In *On Being a Jewish
    Feminist: A Reader*, edited by Susannah Heschel,
    12-18. New York: Schocken Books, 1983.

    Asserts that Jewish women's problems stem from the
    fact that they are viewed in law (*halakhah*) and
    practice as peripheral Jews. Women are generally
    placed in the same category as children and Canaanite
    slaves. Members of these categories are exempt from
    all positive commandments. Demands that the *halakhic*
    scholars must examine women's problems anew and make
    it possible for women to claim their share in the
    Torah and have the chance to do the things a Jew was
    created to do.

5. Adler, Rachel. "A Mother in Israel: Aspects of the
    Mother Role in Jewish Myth." In *Beyond
    Androcentrism. New Essays on Women and Religion*,
    edited by Rita M. Gross, 237-55. Missoula, Mont.:
    Scholars Press, 1977.

    Using evidence from Biblical myth, rabbinic and post-
    rabbinic *Midrash*, Adler tries to trace a strain within
    Jewish tradition which subtracts the creative aspects
    from the mother role in order to augment the power of a
    patriarchal deity and of the human father. Mentions
    Lilith, Adam's first wife who rebelled against
    patriarchal power. Lilith is extravagantly fecund,
    bearing hundreds of demons a day. This is seen as
    terrifying, the outpouring of an alien and
    uncontrollable energy. Finds it significant that the
    children produced by an autonomous female power are
    demons. In Jewish tradition man is endowed with the
    primary creative role. A virtuous and God-fearing
    woman is one who gracefully accedes her creative role
    to the Deity, applauding His fertility when she is
    miraculously endowed with a child.

6. Adler, Rachel. "*Tuman* and *Taharah*: Ends and
    Beginnings." In *The Jewish Woman: New Perspectives*,
    edited by Elizabeth Koltun, 63-71. New York:
    Schocken Books, 1976. A slightly abridged reprint
    from *The First Jewish Catalog: A Do-it-Yourself Kit,*

edited by Richard Siegel, Michael Strassfeld and
Sharon Strassfeld, 167-71. Philadelphia: The Jewish
Publication Society of America, 1973, and from
Response, no. 18 (Summer 1973): 117-27.

The laws of *tumah* and *taharah* are the laws of ritual
impurity and purity. Describes how these many and
strict laws are related to menstruation (*niddah*).

7. Adler, Ruth Pomerance. *Women of the Shtetl: Through
the Eyes of Y.L. Peretz.* New Jersey: Fairleigh
Dickinson University Press, 1980. 144 pp.

A sociological study of Jewish women in Eastern
Europe.

8. Aguilar, Grace. *The Women of Israel; or, Characters
and Sketches from the Holy Scriptures and Jewish
History. Illustrative of the Past History, Present
Duties, and Future Destiny of the Hebrew Females, as
Based on the Word of God.* 2 vols. London:
R. Groombridge, 1845-51.

Urges the importance of imbuing Jewish girls with
pride in their religion so that they do not become
indifferent and leave their faith because others
promise more.

9. Agus, Arlene. "This Month is for You: Observing
Rosh Hodesh as a Woman's Holiday." In *The Jewish
Woman: New Perspectives*, edited by Elizabeth
Koltun, 84-93. New York: Schocken Books, 1976.

Rosh Hodesh, the Festival of the New Moon, is
celebrated eleven times a year. The ceremony is a
celebration of divine creation and of those
characteristics which women share with the moon: the
life cycle, rebirth, renewal.

10. Albeck, Plea. "The Status of Women in Israel."
The American Journal of Comparative Law 20
(Fall 1972): 693-715.

A comprehensive review of the legal status of
women in Israel. Many laws are quoted, interpreted,
and discussed, for instance, laws dealing with
marriage, divorce, family life, right to property
and inheritance, employment, abortion, contraception,
etc. The responsibilities of the state combined with
those of religion are pointed out. It is also noted
that Israeli law has much of its background in English
Common Law.

11. Allen, Christine Garside. "Who was Rebekah? On Me
    Be the Curse, My Son!" In *Beyond Androcentrism.
    New Essays on Women and Religion*, edited by Rita M.
    Gross, 183-216. Missoula, Mont.: Scholars Press,
    1977.

    Tries to find a new approach to Rebekah since most
    interpreters of Genesis have considered Sarah,
    Rebekah, and Rachel to be minor figures in the
    revelation of God's call to Abraham, Isaac, and Jacob.
    Asserts that Rebekah was an extraordinarily profound
    person in her own right and can be seen as the first
    woman saint.

12. Aloni, Shulamit. "Israel: Up the Down Escalator."
    In *Sisterhood is Global. The International Women's
    Movement Anthology*, edited by Robin Morgan, 363-67.
    Harmondsworth, England: Penguin Books, 1984.

    Thinks that equality between men and women in Israel
    is an illusion. There is no equality in the armed
    services or in kibbutzim. Women have reverted to
    their traditional roles. In religion many things are
    closed to women. Concludes, however, with optimism:
    women in Israel have started becoming aware both of
    their rights and their lack of rights.

13. Aloni, Shulamit. "Israel's Women Need Women's Lib."
    Israel Magazine 3 (April 1971): 58-64.

14. Aloni, Shulamit. "The Status of the Woman in Israel."
    Judaism 22 (1973): 248-56.

15. Alper, Robert Abelson. "A Support Group for Parents of Intermarried Jewish Children." D. Min., Princeton Theological Seminary, 1984. 105 pp.

   This thesis is based on the assumption that parents of intermarried Jewish children have special problems that are worthy of attention. The idea of establishing support groups turned out to be a positive experience for the participating parents.

16. Amado Lévy-Valensi, Eliane. "L'urgence des questions posées par l'histoire." In *L'autre dans la conscience Juive. Le sacré et le couple. Données et débats*, edited by Jean Halpérin and Georges Lévitte, 165-72. Paris: Presses Universitaires de France, 1973.

   Discusses women's status in Genesis.

17. Appleman, Solomon. *The Jewish Woman in Judaism: The Significance of Woman's Status in Religious Culture.* Hicksville, N.Y.: Exposition Press, 1979. 141 pp.

   Points out what he sees as prevalent misconceptions concerning woman's status in Jewish religious life and tries to answers them. Lists nine misconceptions and shows how, even within these misconceptions, there exist further misconceptions: 1) Women are not counted toward the Minyan; 2) Women are not allowed to be called to the Torah (*aliya*); 3) Women do not wear the *tallis* or *t'fillin*; 4) Women are not allowed to lead the congregation in prayer as a Chazan (cantor); 5) Women are not allowed to pronounce the kaddish; 6) How much more degrading can it be than to open the Siddur (prayer book) and find that there actually exists a blessing that men say every morning thanking God that they were not made (created) as a woman! 7) Women must sit separately from the men in the Synagogue (proving without question how unimportant women are in Judaism); 8) Women have only three precepts to perform: Nidah, Challah, *Hadlakes Hanair*. Also, would it make any difference if a woman were pious? 9) The woman rabbi.

   Each of the nine topics is discussed.

18. Archer, Leonie J. "The Role of Jewish Women in the
     Religion, Ritual and Cult of Graeco-Roman
     Palestine." In *Images of Women in Antiquity*,
     edited by Averil Cameron and Amélie Kuhrt, 273-87.
     London: Croom Helm, 1983.

     Wants to examine to what extent women were permitted
     to give public expression, through participation in
     the nation's religion, ritual, and cult, to the piety
     which governed their lives in Hellenistic Palestine
     (300 B.C.-A.D. 200). Concludes that about the only
     privilege left to women was that of weeping: their
     one official position was that of publicly mourning
     the dead at funerals. They were excluded from all
     official means of religious expression, and their
     lives were reckoned to be half the value of men's
     lives. Refers to many verses in the Old Testament
     to show this.

19. Arendt, Hannah. *Rahel Varnhagen: Lebensgeschichte
     einer deutschen Judin aus der Romantik.* 6th ed.
     Münich: Piper, 1985. 298 pp.

     Biography of a Jewish woman living in Germany.
     Rahel Varnhagen, who lived from 1771 to 1833, is
     regarded as one of the great intellects of her time.

20. Aronson, David. "Creation in God's Likeness."
     Judaism 33 (Winter 1984): 13-20.

     Discusses the question of ordaining of women.
     Suggests a *takkanah* to make ordination of women legal
     according to *halakhah*. A *takkanah* is new legislation
     to modify previous *halakhic* traditions and has
     historically been used in situations where changes
     in the social, moral, and ethical insights have called
     for it, for instance, in situations dealing with the
     status of women.

21. Aronson, David. "Women in Jewish Life and Law."
     Jewish Spectator 45 (Summer 1979): 33-38.

     Describes many of the differences in men's and
     women's status in law. Asserts that the radical

social, economic, cultural, and familial changes in
the twentieth century have also greatly modified the
role and position of women in Jewish community.
Mentions different areas where women are supposed to
have the same rights as men. Admits, however, that
the gap between the ideal and the actual situation is
not readily bridged. Hopes that the new insights of
this century shall lead to a growing recognition in
Jewish community that woman, like man, is created in
the image of God and shall have equal rights with men.

22. Askenazi, Léon. "Le couple, créateur de l'histoire."
    In *L'autre dans la conscience juive: le sacré et le
    couple: données et débats*, edited by Jean Halpérin
    and Georges Lévitte, 267-80. Paris: Presses
    Universitaires de France, 1973.

    Analyses the concepts of "couple" and "history" with
    reference to several of the "couples" in the Old
    Testament. A debate follows the article, 281-89.

23. Askowith, Dora. "The Role of Women in the Field of
    Higher Jewish Education." *Judaism* 5 (Spring 1956)
    169-72.

    About American Jewish girls. States that the
    proportion of girls now pursuing elementary Jewish
    education has risen perceptibly within the last decade
    or two. Out of this growing reservoir there can be
    drawn potential aspirants to both Jewish scholarship
    and the rabbinate. What is required initially is a
    change in attitude on the part of the rabbinic bodies
    and the authorities at institutions of higher Jewish
    learning.

24. Avery, Evelyn Gross. "Fathers, Sons, and Lovers."
    In *Rebels and Victims. The Fiction of Richard
    Wright and Bernard Malamud*, 55-75. New York:
    Kennikat Press, 1979.

    Asserts that much of twentieth-century American
    fiction depicts a rapidly changing, highly
    competitive, materialistic society which challenges

traditional male-female relationships and family
allegiances.

25. Ayache-Sebag, Ginette. "Cultural Script of North
     African Jewish Women: The Making of an *Eshet-Hayil*."
     Transactional Analysis Journal 13 (1983): 231-33.

     A discussion of the sociocultural factors that
     shape the conditions of Jewish women in North African
     countries. Many of their problems are rooted in the
     conflicts between old and new, between ancestral and
     modern influences.

26. Bachelis, Faith G. "Regional Origin, Personality, and
     Mothers' Attitudes of Jewish Day School Students."
     Ph.D. diss., Yeshiva University, 1966. 266 pp.

27. Baile, David. "Masochism and Philosemitism: The
     Strange Case of Leopold von Sacher-Masoch."
     Journal of Contemporary History 17 (1982): 305-23.

     Leopold von Sacher-Masoch (1836-1906) presents, in
     novel after novel, the same beautiful Jewish heroine,
     expensively and luxuriously dressed, always degrading
     a much weaker male companion. Some critics have seen
     this as a sign of sympathy for the emancipation of
     women.

28. Bailey, Kenneth E. "Women in Ben Sirach and in the
     New Testament." In *For Me to Live: Essays in Honor
     of James Leon Kelso*, edited by Robert A. Coughenour,
     56-73. Winston-Salem, N.C.: Dillon-Liederbach,
     1973.

     Investigates Ben Sirach's understanding of women's
     nature and their place in the community. States that
     Ben Sirach's discussions of women in the
     Ecclesiasticus are always in the context of their
     relationship toward men. Examines the categories of
     mother, daughter, wife, women in general, married
     women, virgins, servant girls, widows, and harlots.
     Concludes that Ben Sirach describes women as inferior,
     useful only in the service of men. She is

responsible for the fact of sin in the world. She is
to be treated kindly, but never fully trusted.

29. Bakan, David. *And They Took Themselves Wives. The
    Emergence of Patriarchy in Western Civilization.*
    San Francisco: Harper and Row, 1979. 186 pp.

    About the notions of marriage and the family in the
    Bible and their bearing on some of the social problems
    of the contemporary world.

30. Bar-David, Molly L. *Women in Israel.* New York:
    Hadassah, Women's Zionist Organization, 1952.

    Presents a journalistic survey of the status of
    women in Israel after 1948. Offers brief biographical
    sketches of women prominent in agriculture, industry,
    science, art, literature, defense, politics, and the
    civil service. Mentions some legal and social
    discrimination against women in the late 1940s. Some
    have been corrected by legislation, but several
    discriminatory practices are still continuing.

31. Bar Yosef, Rivkah, and Ilana [Einhorn] Shelach. "The
    Position of Women in Israel." In *Integration and
    Development in Israel*, edited by S. Noah Eisenstadt,
    Rivkah Bar Yosef, and Chaim Adler, 639-73.
    New York: Praeger, 1970.

    Suggests that the main parameters for defining the
    relative position of women are those of similarity and
    equality. Combining the parameters, three status
    types are obtained: 1) "similar and equal"
    characterizes some of the basic laws, which define
    primary rights and duties in the main areas of role
    activity (the labor market, political activity,
    economic activity, and education); 2) "dissimilar
    and equal" was viewed as the basis for welfare laws
    which recognize a sex differentiation between men and
    women. As such, the differentiation is seen as a
    legitimate basis for differential treatment of men and
    women. The intention was to ensure women against
    possible losses incurred by their biologically

ascribed roles; 3) "dissimilar and unequal" defines
the status of women within the family and is
formalized by the religious legal systems.

32. Bar-Yosef, Rivka Weiss, and Dorit Padan-Eisenstark.
     "Role System under Stress: Sex-Roles in War."
     Social Problems 25 (1977): 135-45.

     Analyzes the effects of the Yom Kippur war on sex-
     roles in Israel. Although there is obligatory
     military service for both men and women, very few
     women got the chance to participate in the war.
     Civilian duties were also strictly limited for women
     during this crisis. Women were relegated to their
     traditional roles as wives and mothers.

33. Barnett, Larry D. "The Kibbutz as a Child-Rearing
     System. A Review of the Literature." *Journal of
     Marriage and the Family* 27 (1965): 348-49.

     A summary of existing literature concerned with the
     effects on the behavior of individuals reared in
     conjugal families and Israeli kibbutzim.

34. Bart, Pauline. "Depression in Middle-Aged Women."
     In *Woman in Sexist Society. Studies in Power and
     Powerlessness*, edited by Vivian Gornick and
     Barbara K. Moran, 99-117. New York: Basic Books,
     1971.

     A cross-cultural study of depression in middle-aged
     women where Jewish women play an important part.
     Finds that when ethnic groups are compared, Jews have
     the highest rate of depression. Thinks this is
     natural because in the traditional Jewish family the
     most important tie is between the mother and the
     children, and the cross-cultural study showed that
     depression is closely associated with maternal role
     loss.

35. Bart, Pauline. "How a Nice Jewish Girl Like Me
     Could." In *Nice Jewish Girls. A Lesbian Anthology*,

edited by Evelyn Torton Beck, 59-62. Trumansburg,
N.Y.: The Crossing Press, 1982.

Some reflections on being Jewish and lesbian.

36. Bart, Pauline. "Portnoy's Mother's Complaint:
     Depression in Middle-Aged Women." In *The Jewish
     Woman: New Perspectives*, edited by Elizabeth Koltun,
     72-83. New York: Schocken Books, 1976 (also pub-
     lished in *Response* no. 18 [Summer 1973]: 129-40.)

     Describes the problems of middle-aged women. Tries
     to find reasons why some get depressed. After
     examining the records of 533 women between the ages
     of forty and fifty-nine, Bart finds that Jews have the
     highest rate of depression. Much of the reason for
     this lies in the traditional female role. Thinks it
     is important that women actualize their own selves.

37. Bart, Pauline, and Patricia H. O'Brien. *Stopping
     Rape: Successful Survival Strategies*. New York:
     Pergamon Press, 1985. 200 pp.

     This book is based upon interviews with ninety-four
     assault victims; of whom fifty-one had avoided being
     raped, the others having been raped. Of the
     ninety-four women, eighteen were Jewish. Tries to
     identify factors associated with victim's avoidance.
     Physical strategies seem to be more effective than
     verbal ones. The findings indicate that Jewish
     women's aggressiveness is primarily verbal;
     consequently Jewish women are more vulnerable
     than women of other ethnic or religious origin.

38. Bartelt, Pearl Winter. "Women and Judaism." In *God,
     Sex, and the Social Project*, edited by James H.
     Grace, 53-92. New York: Edwin Mellen Press, 1978.

39. Barzilai, Sh., and A.M. Davies. "Personality and
     Social Aspects of Mental Disease in Jerusalem
     Women." *The International Journal of Social
     Psychiatry* 18 (1972): 22-28.

An investigation of 122 married Jewish women aged
fifteen to forty-four, hospitalized in mental
institutions in Jerusalem. Tries to find
relationships between mental disease on the one hand
and early marriage, low level of education, and
occupation, on the other.

40. Basker, Eileen. "Coping with Fertility in Israel: A
     Case Study of Culture Clash." *Culture, Medicine and
     Psychiatry* 7 (1983): 199-211.

     A study of the discrepancies between the view of a
     married Jewish woman who wants to interrupt an
     unwanted pregnancy and the clinical belief system of
     the medical authorities.

41. Baum, Charlotte, Paula Hyman, and Sonya Michel. *The
     Jewish Woman in America*. New York: New American
     Library, 1977. 290 pp.

     This book treats the position of Jewish women with
     different backgrounds: cultural, national and
     historical in American society. Describes who these
     women were, where they came from, and what they had
     been in the Europe they left behind.

42. Baum, Charlotte. "What Made Yetta Work? The Economic
     Role of Eastern European Jewish Women in the
     Family." *Response* no. 18 (Summer 1973): 32-38.

     In Early Eastern European Jewish communities women
     seem to have comprised a significant proportion of the
     Jewish labor force. Describes the different fields of
     labor where women were occupied. Most often they
     shared the burden of supporting the family because the
     males were not able to earn enough. In many
     instances, however, the women were the sole supporters
     of the family while the men studied *Torah*.

43. Bauman, Batya. "Women-identified Women in Male-
     identified Judaism." In *On Being a Jewish Feminist.
     A Reader*, edited by Susannah Heschel, 88-95.
     New York: Schocken Books, 1983.

Describes women as a part of an ecological whole.
Women have a common history of misogyny and a language
different from male language as well as a religion
that centers on the synchronicity of their bodies with
the cycles of nature. Traditional Jewish religion is
a religion for males by males. Jewish feminists
experience the conflict between being both a woman
and a Jew. Despite the patriarchal heritage, or
perhaps because of it, Jewish experience has taught
women the importance of feminist issues. And
"stripped of male dominance, the Jewish world view
may not be so different from the feminist world view."

44. Baumgarten, Joseph M. "4Q502, Marriage or Golden Age
    Ritual?" *Journal of Jewish Studies* 34 (1983):
    123-35.

    An examination of the extant fragments of the
    Quamran 4 Q 502 text. This has been interpreted as a
    ritual "for the marriage for Essenes living outside
    the community." The Quamran-Essene community has been
    regarded as the archetype of celibate monasticism, and
    this new text has aroused some interest and
    astonishment. Does not think that this text is a
    proof of marriage even if references are found to the
    assemblage of men, women, youths, and maidens. Thinks
    that the women present were aged women.

45. Baumgarten, Joseph M. "On the Testimony of Women in
    1QSA." *Journal of Biblical Literature* 76 (1957):
    266-69.

    An answer to Prof. H. Neil Richardson, who, in
    Journal of Biblical Literature 76, 108-22, presents a
    translation of the two additional columns of the
    Manual of Discipline designated 1QSA. Richardson, who
    follows Barthélemy in his interpretation, gives a
    woman the right to act as a witness against her
    husband in cases where he has violated the Law.
    Baumgarten thinks that his interpretation is
    completely wrong. Women had no such right.

46. Bearani, Hourieh Sha'ami. "Druze Women on the Move:
     Reflections of a Pioneer." *Kidma* 2, no. 3
     (1975): 34-35.

     There are eighteen Druze villages in Israel.
     According to the author the Druze community is the
     most conservative minority community in Israel.
     Asserts that the progress has been remarkable as far
     as women's status is concerned. In 1949 only a
     single Druze girl attended school. Today thousands
     of Druze girls receive a complete elementary education
     with many of them going to secondary schools and even
     to universities. Many professions are open for women.
     Believes that Druze women of Israel can surpass the
     progress of Druze women anywhere.

47. Beck, Evelyn Torton. "I.B. Singer's Misogyny." In
     Nice Jewish Girls. A Lesbian Anthology, edited by
     Evelyn Torton Beck, 243-49. Trumansburg, N.Y.:
     The Crossing Press, 1982.

     About the Nobel Prize winner in literature, Isaac
     Bashevis Singer, whose writing is claimed by Beck to
     represent a powerful assault on the Jewish woman.
     Asserts that women are depicted as stereotypes, and
     the most persistent one is woman as temptress.
     Singer sees the world as essentially male-centered
     and portrays women almost entirely as the sum total
     of their biological functions and as appendages or
     complements to men. Quotes from his writings to show
     this.

48. Beck, Evelyn Torton. "Next Year in Jerusalem?" In
     Nice Jewish Girls. A Lesbian Anthology, edited by
     Evelyn Torton Beck, 193-95. Trumansburg, N.Y.:
     The Crossing Press, 1982.

     Discusses modern anti-semitism and anti-Zionism.
     Asserts that lesbian-feminists from Israel are often
     attacked by women from other countries for living in
     Israel and being Israeli. Finds this to be an example
     of anti-semitism.

49. Beck, Evelyn Torton. *Nice Jewish Girls: A Lesbian Anthology.* Trumansburg, N.Y.: The Crossing Press, 1982. 286 pp.

    Twenty-nine contributions by different authors on being Jewish and lesbian. The contributions consist of essays, letters, autobiographies, fiction, and poetry.

50. Beer, G. *Die soziale und religiöse Stellung der Frau im israelitischen Altertum.* Sammlung gemeinverständlicher Vorträge und Schriften aus dem Gebiet der Theologie und Religionsgeschichte, no. 88. Tübingen: J.C.B. Mohr, 1919. 46 pp.

    Analyses different verses in the Bible dealing with the status of woman: her role as mother and wife and her ritual status. Concludes that Judaism gave a great deal of liberty to women in questions of daily life and religion and that Christianity consolidated and strengthened her favorable position.

51. Belkin, Samuel. "Levirate and Agnate Marriage in Rabbinic and Cognate Literature." *The Jewish Quarterly Review* 60 (1970): 275-329.

    Preservation of the family name and inheritance was obtained by means of levirate and agnate marriage. This paper seeks to probe, through an interpretative analysis, the fundamental reasons for the practice.

52. Bell, Robert R., and Leonard Blumberg. "Courtship Intimacy and Religious Background." *Marriage and Family Living* 21 (1959): 356-60.

    A study conducted at an Eastern metropolitan university. 90 percent of the respondents lived at home. A total of 410 questionnaires were used--250 female and 160 male respondents, 55 percent Jewish, 25 percent Protestant, and 20 percent Catholic. The picture suggests relatively early dating for Jewish young people. Going steady is perceived as further along the continuum toward engagement and

marriage than for Protestant or Catholic young people.
Also other differences show that religio-ethnic
differences are of importance in American courtship
relationships.

53. Bell, Robert R., and Jack V. Buerkle. "The Daughter's
     Role During the 'Launching Stage.'" *Marriage and
     Family Living* 24 (1962): 384-88.

     A study which indicates that the "launching stage"
     as perceived by mothers and their daughters of college
     age has a number of potential areas of disagreement
     and conflict. An analysis was done within three
     religious groups: Jews, Protestants and Catholics.
     The Jewish group had the greatest mother-daughter
     disagreements. Suggests that this may be due to the
     fact that many of the Jewish mothers are still
     "traditionally" oriented and the traditional power
     of the mother is being questioned and modified by the
     newly "emancipated" daughters.

54. Bell, Robert R., and Jack V. Buerkle. "Mother and
     Daughter Attitudes to Premarital Sexual Behavior."
     Marriage and Family Living 23 (1961): 390-92.

     Mothers are more "conservative" than their daughters
     in their attitudes to premarital sexual intercourse.
     This study indicates that this has little to do with
     religious affiliation but is a general attitude.

55. Bell, Robert R., and Jack V. Buerkle. "Mothers and
     Mothers-in-law as Role Models in Relation to
     Religious Background." *Marriage and Family Living*
     25 (1963): 485-86.

     A comparison between Jewish and Protestant wives
     regarding their relationship to their mothers and
     mothers-in-law. The findings indicate that the
     traditional function of the mother as a primary role
     model and influence has altered somewhat less in the
     Jewish family than in the Protestant family.

56. Bell, Robert R., Stanley Turner, and Lawrence Rosen. "A Multivariate Analysis of Female Extramarital Coitus." *Journal of Marriage and the Family* 37 (1975): 375-84.

This study is based on the responses of 2262 married women. 9 percent were Jewish. The published data do not correlate outcomes with religion.

57. Ben-Chorin, Schalom. "A Jewish View of the Mother of Jesus." In *Mary in the Churches*, edited by Hans Kung and J. Moltmann, 12-16. Minneapolis: Winston Press, 1983.

58. Ben-Porath, Yoram. "Fertility in Israel. An Economist's Interpretation: Differentials and Trends, 1950-1970." In *Economic Development and Population Growth in the Middle East*, edited by Charles A. Cooper and Sidney S. Alexander, 501-39. New York: American Elsevier, 1972.

An economic analysis of fertility. Explores the evidence in support of the hypothesis that the number of children families have depends on how many they want. The desires for children are analysed in terms of resources and on the price. The relationship between fertility and women's education and employment is given much attention.

59. Berenbaum, Michael. "Women, Blacks, and Jews: Theologians of Survival." *Religion in Life* 45 (1976): 106-18.

A study of similarities between Black, Jewish, and feminist theology. All three are accused of having altered their picture of God to fit their own policy.

60. Berkovits, Eliezer. "The Status of Woman within Judaism." In *Contemporary Jewish Ethics*, edited by Menachem M. Kellner, 355-74. New York: Hebrew Publishing Co., 1978.

61. Berman, Gerald S. "The Adaptable American Jewish
     Family: An Inconsistency in Theory." *Jewish Journal
     of Sociology* 18 (1976): 5-16.

     Finds inconsistency between two sets of attributes
     or themes: first, the close, intact family and kinship
     ties; and second, the extrafamilial orientation
     towards the economic structures of American
     society. In other words: How have Jews been so
     successful in economic matters and at the same time
     maintained the strong family ties? Concludes that it
     is the family solidarity which has produced
     economically successful individuals. The duality
     which characterizes the Jewish family does not reveal
     incompatible ideas but rather an adaptive balancing
     of opposites.

62. Berman, Louis Arthur. *Jews and Intermarriage: A Study
     in Personality and Culture.* New York: T. Yoseloff,
     1968. 707 pp.

     A sociological study of intermarriage.

63. Berman, Saul. "The Status of Women in Halakhic
     Judaism." In *The Jewish Woman: New Perspectives,*
     edited by Elizabeth Koltun, 114-28. New York:
     Schocken Books, 1976 (Reprinted and abridged from
     Tradition 14, no. 2 [1973]: 5-28).

     Jewish women are discontented with their role in
     religion, in matters of civil law as marriage and
     divorce, and their relegation to a service role in
     home and family. As a solution to these problems
     women should be encouraged to develop the forms they
     find necessary for their religious growth, for
     example, daily prayer and Torah study. Suggests also
     reforms in the position of women in matters of civil
     law and more freedom of choice as far as their role
     in society is concerned.

64. Bernstein, Deborah. "The Plough Woman Who Cried into
     the Pots: The Position of Women in the Labor Force
     in the Pre-State Israeli Society." *Jewish Social
     Studies* 45 (1983): 43-56.

An assessment and analysis of the status of women in the labor force of pre-state Jewish society in Palestine.

65. Bernstein, Fred. *Jewish Mothers' Hall of Fame.* New York: Doubleday and Co., 1986. 192 pp.

   On the relationship between the Jewish mother and her children.

66. Berrol, Selma. "When Uptown Met Downtown: Julia Richman's Work in the Jewish Community of New York, 1880-1912." *American Jewish History* 70 (1980): 35-51.

   About Julia Richman (1855-1912), a pioneer in educational questions and Jewish organizations working for school reforms, especially for women.

67. Bettelheim, Bruno. *The Children of the Dream.* New York: Avon Books, 1969. 363 pp.

   About communal child rearing with the focus on kibbutz children in Israel. Stresses the psychological anxieties of the women in the kibbutz. Most of these women have grown up with the Jewish "mamma" ideal. This ideal includes a single-minded devotion to family and children. Suggests that this ideal can be escaped in the kibbutz where women can free themselves from their fears for not being good mothers and place their children in the care of others.

68. Biale, Rachel. *Women and Jewish Law. An Exploration of Women's Issues in Halakhic Sources.* New York: Schocken Books, 1984. 293 pp.

69. Biberfeld, Marcel. "The Attitudes of Orthodox Jewish Mothers towards Their Mentally Retarded Children." D.S.W. diss., Yeshiva University, 1983. 166 pp.

An investigation examining the difference in
attitude between orthodox mothers of mentally retarded
children and orthodox mothers with no mentally
retarded children in their families. The
investigation was performed by questionnaires, and
responses were tabulated according to standard
statistical procedures.

70. Bird, Phyllis A. "Images of Women in the Old
     Testament." In *The Bible and Liberation: Political
     and Social Hermeneutics*, edited by Norman K.
     Gottwald, 252-88. New York: Orbis Books, 1983
     (Previously published in *Religion and Sexism.
     Images of Woman in the Jewish and Christian
     Traditions*, edited by Rosemary Radford Ruether,
     41-88. New York: Simon and Schuster, 1974).

     "The Old Testament is a man's book," the author
     asserts. Describes it as a collection of writings by
     males from a society dominated by males. However,
     the OT represents a great variety of viewpoints about
     woman. In some texts she is portrayed as a class of
     property; in others she is depicted as possessing a
     great measure of freedom. Concludes therefore that
     no single statement can be formulated concerning the
     image of woman in the OT. Tries to discover what
     unity and coherence may exist within this plurality
     of conceptions. Examines the different parts of the
     OT.: The Laws, The Proverbs, The Historical Writings,
     and The Accounts of Creation, describing the image
     of woman in the different parts.

71. Bird, Phyllis A. "Male and Female He Created Them.
     Gen. 1:27b in the Context of the Priestly Account
     of Creation." *Harvard Theological Review* 74
     (1981): 129-59.

     Examines literature on Gen. 1:26-28 focusing on the
     relationship between text-critical or historical-
     exegetical interpretation and constructive
     interpretation in theology. Thinks that Gen. 1:27
     must be understood within the context of vv. 26-28 and
     this complex within the large structure of the
     Priestly creation account. Thinks that the statement
     "male and female he created them" relates only to the

blessing of fertility, making explicit its necessary presupposition. It is not concerned with sexual roles, the status of relationship of the sexes to one another, or marriage. It describes the biological pair, not a social partnership; male and female, not man and wife.

72. Biren, Joan E. (JEB). "That's Funny. You Don't Look Like a Jewish Lesbian." In *Nice Jewish Girls. A Lesbian Anthology*, edited by Evelyn Torton Beck, 122-30. Trumansburg, N.Y.: The Crossing Press, 1982.

   Tells about how she struggled to be assimilated and not be taken for Jewish and how she now affirms both her Jewish identity and her lesbianism. Presents photographs of Jewish lesbians. "I look more like a Jewish lesbian every day."

73. Bitton, Livia E. "The Jewess as a Fictional Sex Symbol." *Bucknell Review* 21 (1973): 63-86.

   Asserts that the Jewess of fiction serves as the stereotyped sex-object par excellence. The fictional Jewess-image incorporated three aspects of feminine sexuality: virginity, eroticism, and motherhood. Discusses this image throughout the history of literature and in the Bible. Concludes that it has not disappeared.

74. Bitton-Jackson, Livia. *Madonna or Courtesan? The Jewish Woman in Christian Literature.* New York: The Seabury Press, 1982. 138 pp.

   A survey of English, French, German, Italian and American literature by Christian authors from the sixteenth through twentieth centuries. Wants to trace the ways in which the mythical image of the "wandering Jewess," the she-demon seductress or courtesan, and the silently suffering saint or madonna is manifested there.

75. Blau, Zena Smith. "The Jewish Prince: Some
    Continuities in Traditional and Contemporary Jewish
    Life." *Contemporary Jewry* 3, no. 2 (1977): 54-71.

    Analyses fiction by second-generation Jewish-
    American writers. Asserts that these writers tend to
    emphasize the concerns of the young son, the young
    male, to the exclusion of other concerns.

76. Blau, Zena Smith. "The Strategy of the Jewish
    Mother." In *The Jew in American Society*, edited by
    Marshall Sklare, 165-87. New York: Behrman, 1974.

77. Bloch, Alice. "Scenes from the Life of a Jewish
    Lesbian." In *On Being a Jewish Feminist. A Reader,*
    edited by Susannah Heschel, 171-76. New York:
    Schocken Books, 1983 (Reprint from *Dyke Magazine*
    1977).

    Tells about her life from her birth in 1947 up to
    adult age. Emphasizes how her Jewish background has
    affected her life as a lesbian. Is less interested
    in purity of feminist politics than in quality of
    woman-to-woman interaction.

78. Blumauer, Blanche. "Council of Jewish Women in
    Portland 1905." *Western States Jewish Historical
    Quarterly* 9 (1976): 19-20.

    The Council of Jewish Women of Portland was
    organized in 1895. In 1904 a Neighborhood House was
    established, and in 1905 two hundred children took
    advantage of the various schools and activities
    provided by the project.

79. Blumberg, Rae Lesser. "The Erosion of Sexual
    Equality in the Kibbutz." In *Beyond Intellectual
    Sexism: A New Woman, a New Reality*, edited by Joan
    Robers, 320-39. New York: David McKay, 1976.

    A structural interpretation of the erosion of sexual
    equality in the kibbutz. Suggests that the major
    variables responsible for the decline in women's

position in the kibbutz can be subsumed under four
dimensions of "subsistence environment"; 1)
subsistence technology; 2) environmental constraints,
including demographic factors; 3) nature of work and
division of labor; and 4) surplus capital, and
relations to means of production. Concludes that the
kibbutz ideology of sexual equality has proved
insufficient, despite good intentions, to save either
the best-regarded jobs or the high status of the
women. With the agrarian socialistic mode of
production chosen by the kibbutz founders, it has been
difficult to maintain female equality, as agrarian
production is incompatible with baby-care
responsibilities.

80. Blumberg, Rae Lesser. "From Patriarchy to Liberation?
    Today's Woman--United States and Worldwide." In
    Stratification: Socioeconomic and Sexual Inequality,
    99-117. Dubuque, Iowa: Wm. C. Brown Company Publ.,
    1978.

    One of the cases presented in this chapter is the
    question of what happened to women in the Israeli
    kibbutzim. The kibbutz movement was founded on the
    ideal of sexual equality. It has been in this area,
    however, that the kibbutz most visibly has fallen
    short of its founding principles. Analyses some of
    the reasons for this.

81. Blumberg, Rae Lesser. "Kibbutz Women: From the Fields
    of Revolution to the Laundries of Discontent." In
    Women in the World: A Comparative Study, edited by
    Lynne B. Iglitzin and Ruth Ross, 319-44.
    Santa Barbara: Clio Books, 1976.

    Describes the development of women's place in the
    kibbutz. Claims that women have lost many fields,
    mostly in occupation, politico-economic control and
    prestige; less in life options. They have lost
    nothing in formal rights but collectivization of
    domestic tasks have relegated women to service jobs
    in nurseries, kitchens, and laundries. They are no
    longer members of the productive labor force.

82. Blumberg, Rae Lesser. "The Women of the Israeli
     Kibbutz." *Center Magazine* 7, no. 3 (1974): 70-72.

     Describes the stages in the erosion of women's
     position and sexual equality in the kibbutz. The
     erosion occurs in five general phases which are
     described. It has resulted in a concentration of
     women (about 90 percent) in service jobs while the
     men hold decision-making positions. Hopes that women
     of the kibbutz may regain some of their lost status
     as industrialization advances.

83. Blumenthal, Aaron H. "An Aliyah for Women." In
     Conservative Judaism and Jewish Law, edited by
     Seymour Siegel, 265-80. New York: The Rabbinical
     Assembly, 1977.

     Aliyah (ascent) is the being called up for the
     reading of a portion of the *Torah* during the synagogue
     service. Analyses the history of right to *aliyah* and
     asserts that there is no *halakhic* objection to
     granting women this privilege. Concludes that in
     Tannaitic times a woman was accorded the privilege of
     an *aliyah*, but the practice was abolished some time in
     history, perhaps in the thirteenth century.
     Thinks that the time has come for someone to reverse
     the direction in which the *halakhah* has been moving
     for centuries and that it is proper to grant the
     privilege of *aliyah* to Jewish women.

84. Blumfield, Hanita F. "Jewish Women Sew the Union
     Label: A Study of Sexism and Feminism in the
     Emerging Unionization of the Garment Industry,
     New York City." *Humanity and Society* 6 (1982):
     33-45.

     The history of the unionization of Jewish women
     immigrant workers in the New York City garment
     industry at the turn of the century. Describes the
     conditions of the workers. They had to face many
     difficulties. Besides poor working conditions common
     to industrial workers at the time, they met particular
     problems as female workers in the form of sexism and
     discrimination. Describes the influence of Jewish
     union feminists on labor organizations.

85. Borowitz, Eugene B. *Choosing a Sex Ethic: A Jewish Inquiry.* New York: Schocken Books, 1969. 182pp.

   Rabbi Prof. Borowitz describes four alternative ethics: 1) healthy orgasm, 2) mutual consent, 3) love, and 4) marriage. In his own words: "Contemporary ethical discussion is, or should be, based on the principal of autonomy, or recognition of the independent value of each man's conscience." The history of Jewish sexual custom is discussed from Biblical and Rabbinic times and up to our time. In a final chapter, "speaking personally," he presents a summary of his own findings in the hope that it may help the reader test and integrate his own point of view and reach a thoughtful, autonomous conclusion.

86. Bortnick, David Marc. "Patterns of Interfaith Dating and Religious Observance among Jewish College Students in Florida." Ph.D. diss., The Florida State University, 1975. 115 pp.

   This study is based on data collected by means of a questionnaire mailed to six hundred students in Florida, males and females, freshmen and seniors. The findings suggest that patterns of dating behavior and religiosity are learned, particularly from parents.

87. Borts, Barbara. "Report on Women in the Rabbinate." *European Judaism* 15 (1981): 30-31.

   Thinks that the major question is: In what way does being a woman limit or enhance the work of a rabbi? Feels that, being a female rabbi, she can offer more in the area of female experiences connected with feelings, menstruation, and childbirth.

88. Bowes, Alison. "Women in the Kibbutz Movement." *Sociological Review* 26 (1978): 237-62.

   Examines the assumption that equality between the sexes should be possible in the kibbutz. Thinks that this assumption has proved invalid. The equality principle was founded on the presupposition that

women could perform the same social roles as men, but
the struggle for equality assumed only secondary
importance in the socialist-Zionist enterprise.

89. Brandow, Selma Koss. "Illusion of Equality: Kibbutz
     Women and the Ideology of the 'New Jew.'"
     International Journal of Women's Studies 2 (1979):
     268-86.

     Asserts that women in the kibbutz function in much
     the same ways as in other male-dominated societies.
     It seems as if women accept male dominance. Wonders
     if the idea of sexual equality was ever accepted in
     the kibbutz system. The emphasis put upon the
     creation of the "new Jew" carried a strongly masculine
     image with which both men and women appeared to
     identify. The "cult of masculinity" has dominated the
     life in kibbutz from the beginning. Concludes that
     probably future generations of kibbutz males will
     continue to evidence similar manifestations of this
     cult.

90. Brandow, Selma Koss. "The Role of Women in a
     Kibbutz." Ph.D. diss., Temple University, 1974.
     147 pp.

     Examines the assumption that there is no difference
     between men and women in the kibbutz. Uses the
     method of participant-observation in one kibbutz.
     This study indicates that both men and women
     subscribe to the original ideology of equality
     despite the fact that women are now working at the
     traditional female tasks.

91. Braude, Ann. "The Jewish Woman's Encounter with
     American Culture." In *The Nineteenth Century. A
     Documentary History*. Vol. 2 of *Women and Religion
     in America*, edited by Rosemary Radford Ruether and
     Rosemary Skinner Keller, 150-92. San Francisco:
     Harper and Row, 1981.

     Concludes the article with the assumption that
     Jewish women have often been criticized for trends
     toward Reform and Americanization. In the opinion of

the author the vital participation of women in all
degrees of Orthodoxy has been an essential creative
and sustaining tone throughout the history of American
Judaism.

92. Brav, Stanley R. "The Jewish Woman, 1861-1865."
    American Jewish Archives 17 (1965): 34-75.

    Describes activities and attitudes of Jewish women
    during the Civil War, 1861-65. The description is
    based on materials in contemporary journals and books.

93. Brayer, Menachem M. *The Jewish Woman in Rabbinic
    Literature.* 2 vols. Hoboken, N.J.: Ktav
    Publishing House, 1986.

    The first of these two volumes views the subject
    from a psychosocial perspective and the second from
    a psychohistorical one.

94. Breslauer, S. Daniel. "Literary Images of Women in
    the Jewish Tradition." *Hebrew Studies* 22 (1981):
    49-57.

    About selected images of women in Jewish literary
    sources, in the Bible, Rabbinic teachings, Hasidism
    and modern literature. Concludes that the different
    images of women are generated by different social and
    historical contexts.

95. Breslauer, S. Daniel. "Women, Religious Rejuvenation
    and Judaism." *Judaism* 32 (1983): 466-75.

    The question of Jewish self-renewal is connected
    with the question of women's claim for religious
    equality.

96. Brichta, Abraham, and Gabriel Ben Dor.
    "Representation and Misrepresentation of Political
    Elites: The Case of Israel." *Jewish Social
    Studies* 36 (1974): 234-52.

The political elite in Israel is predominantly male,
past fifty, East European in origin, and of either
urban or kibbutz background. Women are strongly
underrepresented. Thinks that this is due to the
prestige of pre-1948 elite, "The Founding Fathers."
Finds indications that a new generation of leadership
will emerge because of the lack of success in the
October war in 1973.

97. Brichta, Avraham. "Women in the Knesset, 1949-1969."
    Parliamentary Affairs 28 (1974-75): 31-50.

    Points to the fact that Israel is one of the few
    countries in the world which has a woman prime
    minister. The ratio of women in the Knesset is also
    high compared to representation in the parliament in
    other countries. The majority of the women in the
    Knesset are elected from socialist parties and of
    East European origin.

98. Bril, Jacques. *Lilith ou la Mère obscure.* Paris:
    Payot, 1981. 217 pp.

99. Brin, Ruth F. "Can a Woman Be a Jew?" In *A Coat of
    Many Colors. Jewish Subcommunities in the United
    States*, edited by Abraham D. Lavender, 243-51.
    Westport: Greenwood Press, 1977.

    Asserts that traditionally women were vicarious
    Jews. Today, however, in Western secular societies,
    women are frequently offered direct participation.
    The greatest discrimination against women today is to
    be found in the religious establishment. Women are
    excluded from many of the religious rights and duties
    of men. Women are also discriminated against in
    family life. Finds Jewish marriage and divorce laws
    unfair.

100. Broner, E.M. "Honor and Ceremony in Women's
     Rituals." In *The Politics of Women's Spirituality.
     Essays on the Rise of Spiritualist Power within the
     Feminist Movement*, edited by Charlene Spretnak,
     234-44. New York: Doubleday and Co., 1982.

101. Brooten, Bernadette J. "Jüdinnen zur Zeit Jesu: Ein Plädoyer für Differenzierung." In *Frauen in der Männerkirche*, edited by Bernadette Brooten and Norbert Greinacher, 141-48. München: Kaiser, 1982.

     Reacts against the negative valuation of Judaism at the time of Jesus, particularly concerning the status of women. Thinks this attitude has been typical for feminist theology. Polemicizes against some of her co-contributors in the anthology and asks for more detailed investigations in the question of women's rights at the time of Jesus.

102. Brooten, Bernadette. "Konnten Frauen im alten Judentum die Scheidung betreiben? Uberlegungen zu Mk 10, 11-12 und 1 Kor 7, 10-11." *Evangelische Theologie* 42 (1982): 65-80.

     A discussion about the ability of women to get a divorce at the time of Jesus. Most scholars on the New Testament deny that women could initiate divorce at that time. Finds divergencies in the five New Testament texts that treat this subject. In Matt. 5:32 and 19:3-12 and Luke 16:18 only the man is given the right to initiate divorce, while in Mark 10:11-12 and 1 Cor. 7:10-11 woman has this right as well. Mentions also other sources that give women the right to divorce.

103. Brooten, Bernadette J. *Women Leaders in the Ancient Synagogue: Inscriptional Evidence and Background Issues.* Brown Judaic Studies, vol. 36. Chico, Calif.: Scholars Press, 1982. 292 pp.

     Asserts that women served as leaders in a number of synagogues during the Roman and Byzantine periods. The main evidence for this view is based on nineteen Greek and Latin inscriptions from 27 B.C. to the sixth century A.D., where women bear the titles "head of the synagogue," "leader," "elder," "mother of the synagogue," and "priestess." The book is divided into two parts: 1) "the inscriptional evidence" and 2) "background questions."

104. Brooten, Bernadette J. "Zur Debatte über das
     Scheidungsrecht der Jüdischen Frau."
     Evangelische Theologie 43 (1983): 466-78.

     A reply to critics who disagree with her on the
     thesis that some women had the right to initiate
     divorce at the time of Jesus.

105. Brownmiller, Susan. "Riots, Pogroms and
     Revolutions." In *Against Our Will. Men, Women
     and Rape*, 114-39. London: Secker and Warburg,
     1975.

     In this study of rape, a portion of chapter 4 is
     about Jewish women and rape. Tells about how Jewish
     women were victims of rape during the pogroms in
     Poland and Russia, especially by the Cossacks.

106. Brueggemann, Walter. "Of the Same Flesh and Bone
     (GN 2, 23a)." *Catholic Biblical Quarterly* 39
     (1977): 532-42.

     Asserts that this text has not been appreciated by
     Biblical theology. It has been understood primarily
     in the context of tortuous discussions of a
     "metaphysical" kind about the physical constituency
     of the human person and sexual relationship. Thinks
     that it is rather an attempt to talk meaningfully
     about interpersonal relationships. Gen. 2:23a does
     not speak of derivation in a biological sense but
     about concern, loyalty, and responsibility.

107. Bull, Angela. *Anne Frank*. North Pomfret, Vt.:
     David and Charles, Inc., 1984. 64 pp.

     A biography of Anne Frank (1929-45).

108. Bullough, Vern L. "The Jewish Contribution." In
     Sexual Variance in Society and History, 74-87.
     New York: Wiley, 1976.

Discusses the influence of the ancient Hebrews on
the attitudes toward sexual behavior. Describes
women as quite active sexually, but on the whole
Judaism is regarded as male oriented in these
questions. Discusses also the status of
homosexuality and finds that one reason for the
increasing hostility against homosexuality has to
do with their struggle against being assimilated
into Greek society.

109. Bullough, Vern L., and Bonnie Bullough. *The
     Subordinate Sex. A History of Attitudes toward
     Women*. Urbana: University of Illinois Press,
     1973. 375 pp.

     Contains some materials on women in Judaism.

110. Burlage, Dorothy D. "Judaeo-Christian Influence on
     Female Sexuality." In *Sexist Religion and Women
     in the Church: No More Silence!* edited by Alice L.
     Hageman, 93-116. New York: Association Press,
     1974.

     Discusses Judaeo-Christian influences on marriage,
     divorce, and other sex-related behavior such as
     abortion, contraceptive methods, pre- and extra-
     marital sexuality. The laws and exhortations
     regarding women are much stronger than those
     regarding the behavior of men. Asserts that any
     extramarital sexual activity on the part of women
     threatens the patriarchal system by endangering
     the patrilinear succession as well as the concept
     of women as property.

111. Burrows, Millar. *The Basis of Israelite Marriage*.
     American Oriental Series, vol. 15. New Haven:
     American Oriental Society, 1938. 72 pp.

112. Camp, Claudia V. "The Wise Women of 2 Samuel: A
     Role Model for Women in Early Israel?" *Catholic
     Biblical Quarterly* 43 (1981): 14-29.

Asserts that the wise women of Tekoa (2 Samuel 14)
and Abel (2 Samuel 20) are representatives of at
least one significant, political role available to
women in the years preceding the establishment of the
kingship in Israel. This role which was firmly
rooted in the tribal ethos is classified as a
regularized set of functions. Asks what the source
and scope of the wise women's authority might have
been. Thinks the texts supply a clue in their use
of the image of the mother.

113. Cantor, Aviva. "Lilith Interviews Evelyn Torton
     Beck." *Lilith*, no. 10 (Winter 1983): 10-14.

     An interview with the editor of the anthology *Nice
     Jewish Girls: A Lesbian Anthology*. She is asked about
     some of the issues that led her to create the book.

114. Cantor, Aviva. "The Lilith Question." In *On Being
     a Jewish Feminist. A Reader*, edited by Susannah
     Heschel, 40-50. New York: Schocken Books, 1983
     (Reprint from *Lilith*, no. 1 [Fall 1976]).

     A discussion of Lilith as she appears in the
     Alphabet of Ben Sira and other sources. In the
     Alphabet she is an equal to Adam, to man, but Adam
     refused to accept her equality. Therefore, Lilith
     flew away from him and the Garden of Eden. After the
     escape Jewish tradition has characterized her as a
     demon. There are several legends of her vengeful
     activities to harm children and childbearing women.
     The demonic Lilith overshadowed Ben Sira's strong and
     independent Lilith. Cantor asserts that the traits
     attributed to Lilith after she lost her struggle for
     equality are tainted with male bias and fear, and
     connects her struggle with today's feminist struggle
     for equality.

115. Cantor, Aviva. "Power Plays: Breaking the Male
     Monopoly of Jewish Community Leadership."
     Lilith, no. 14 (Fall/Winter 1985-86): 7-13.

116. Carlebach, Julius. "The Forgotten Connection: Women and Jews in the Conflict between Enlightenment and Romanticism." *Leo Baeck Institute Year Book* 24 (1979): 107-38.

    About 1750 a social process of emancipation of Jews and women was going on. Both movements came to an end about the turn of the century. This might be seen as a victory of the German middle class and romanticism.

117. Carlisle, Thomas J. *Eve and After: Old Testament Woman in Portrait.* Grand Rapids, Mich.: William B. Eerdsman, 1984. 160 pp.

118. Carmody, Denise Lardner. "Judaism." In *Women and World Religions*, 92-112. Nashville: Abingdon, 1979.

    This survey article starts with the Biblical period (1200-200 B.C.). Bound together under the patriarchal God, the proto-Jews made stable family life one of their strongest pillars. The women are strictly under masculine control. However, we find many examples of strong women in the Bible: Deborah, Ruth, Esther, and Delilah. Charismatic office was open to women if God sent them his word. Women are mentioned as professional mourners, midwives, temple singers, and nurses. However, women were excluded from priesthood, mainly because they were considered unclean during considerable periods of their lives: i.e., during menstruation and after childbirth. The Talmudic period is from the time of the fall of the Temple in 70 A.D. and up to modern times. The word Talmud means "the teaching," and it centers on the meaning of *Torah*, God's law or guidance. The Talmudic view was that a wife's obligations to her husband were primarily to provide for his physical needs and enable him to study *Torah*. As in the Biblical period, Talmudic Judaism found sterility fearsome. Contraception was permitted if conception was thought likely to harm the mother. However, a misogynistic tendency raised its head. The women were considered to be men's temptresses. They were also regarded to be gluttonous eavesdroppers, lazy,

jealous, and garrulous. Carmody thinks that the only
way for women to obtain equal rights with men is to
participate on all levels of social life and in
production. In Israel today, however, fewer than
10 percent of the women work in the valued areas of
production.

119. Carroll, Elizabeth. "Kann die Herrschaft der Männer
      gebrochen werden?" In *Frauen in der Männerkirche*,
      edited by Bernadette Brooten and Norbert
      Greinacher, 57-73. München: Kaiser, 1982.

      About male dominance in the church. Sees this
      partly as based on the Jewish patriarchal tradition.

120. Cherlin, Andrew, and Carin Celebuski. "Are Jewish
      Families Different? Some Evidence from the General
      Social Survey." *Journal of Marriage and the Family*
      45 (1983): 903-10.

      Examination of the difference between Jewish,
      Protestant, and Catholic family patterns in the
      United States.

121. Christ, Carol P., Ellen M. Umansky, and Ann E. Carr.
      "Roundtable Discussion: What Are the Sources of My
      Theology?" *Journal of Feminist Studies in Religion*
      1, no. 1 (1985): 119-31.

122. Christ, Carol. "Women's Liberation and the
      Liberation of God: An Essay in Story Theology."
      In *The Jewish Woman: New Perspectives*, edited by
      Elizabeth Koltun, 11-17. New York: Schocken
      Books, 1976.

      Tells a story in which a woman wants to change
      places with God in order to force God to experience
      being a woman in a world shaped by God's covenant
      with man. The woman wants God to experience the
      suffering of women in a world where the mothers, the
      daughters, and the sisters do not exist--even for
      God. She hopes that after experiencing her
      suffering, God will change the world he has created.

According to Christ, the concept of God's liberation, which is alien to theological traditions in which God is conceived as all-powerful, is rooted in the Jewish mystical tradition. Kabbalistic and Hasidic stories say that God needs humans to free him from bondage.

123. Clapsaddle, Carol N. "Flight from Feminism: The Case of the Israeli Woman." In *The Jewish Woman: New Perspectives*, edited by Elizabeth Koltun, 202-13. New York: Schocken Books, 1976 (Reprinted from *Response*, no. 18 [Summer 1973]: 167-75).

Tells how until recently the Israeli women were counted among the most liberated women of the world, especially the kibbutz women. Asserts that they are now in full flight from feminism. The life in the kibbutz is very hard, and they want to enjoy the greater luxury and pampering of the Western housewife. Besides, because of past achievements, many women think they are fully liberated.

124. Clar, Reva. "First Jewish Woman Physician of Los Angeles." *Western States Jewish Historical Quarterly* 14 (1981): 66-75.

About Dr. Sarah Vasen (1870-1944) who was the first superintendent and resident physician of the Kaspare Cohn Hospital, forerunner of Cedars-Sinai Medical Center in Los Angeles.

125. Cohen, Benjamin Louis. "Constancy and Change in the Jewish Family Agency of Los Angeles: 1854-1970." D.S.W. diss., University of Southern California, 1972. 178 pp.

126. Cohen, Erik. "Mixed Marriage in an Israeli Town." *Jewish Journal of Sociology* 11 (1969): 41-50.

A study focusing on Jewish-Arab relations in a mixed town. The study is based on very few cases since only about a dozen mixed unions were found in a population of several tens of thousands. Most of the unions are between an Arab man and a Jewish

woman, and usually they settle in an Arab community.
Since there is no legal way in which a Jew and an
Arab may marry in Israel, if neither becomes a
convert, there are various ways in which marriage
may be contracted. Very rarely an Arab man is
willing to be converted to Judaism. One way is to
enter into a civil union abroad. In some cases the
Jewish partner (most often the woman) embraces Islam.
Still another way is common-law unions. After seven
years they are considered legally valid by Israeli
courts, for example, in inheritance matters.

127. Cohen, Gerda L. "Family Planning in Israeli."
      Midstream 12, no. 6 (1966): 49-54.

      Asserts that the political and military leadership
      of Israel favors a high birth rate, partly because
      the immigration from other countries is decreasing.
      However, the Jewish birth rate steadily falls while
      the Arab rate steadily mounts. This fact is a bit
      frightening to the leadership of Israel. Discusses
      different Jewish views on abortion and contraception.

128. Cohen, Jessica Lynn. "A Comparison of Norms and
      Behaviors of Childrearing in Jewish and Italian
      American Mothers." Ph.D. diss., Syracuse
      University, 1977. 276 pp.

      A study of the norms and behaviors of childrearing
      and kinship solidarity of Italian American and Jewish
      women in Syracuse, New York. Many findings indicated
      that Italian American women exhibited significantly
      higher kinship solidarity than the Jewish women.
      They were also found to be more traditional in their
      methods of discipline, supervision, and patterns of
      authority. Jewish women favored endogamous marriages
      of their children to a higher degree than did the
      Italian American women and were significantly more
      involved in religious and ethnic organizations.

129. Cohen, Leah. "A Woman Reborn." *Keeping Posted* 17,
      no. 7 (1972): 7-8.

"Leah Cohen" is the pseudonym of an eighteen-year-old student at the Lubavitcher Seminary for Women in Brooklyn, New York. Tells about her stay at the seminary; about how she began with a lot of prejudices and how two years later found that becoming a Lubavitcher was the best thing that had happened in her life.

130. Cohen, Shaye J.D. "Women in the Synagogues of Antiquity." *Conservative Judaism* 34 (November/December 1980): 23-29.

Based on literary and archaeological evidence he tries to find answers to the following questions: 1) Did women take an interest in the building and maintenance of ancient synagogues? 2) Did men and women sit together during services? 3) Did women assume leadership roles in the congregation? The answer to 1) is an unqualified yes; to 2) the answer is unclear. Five possibilities are mentioned. To 3) the answer is a qualified yes.

131. Cohen, Steven Martin. "American Jewish Feminism: A Study in Conflicts and Compromises." *American Behavioral Scientist* 23 (1980): 519-58.

An investigation of the contradictions between Judaism and feminism through an examination of feminists' complaints against contemporary Jewry, conventional Jewry's reaction to modern feminism, and Jewish feminism. Asserts that bridgebuilding is the essence of Jewish feminism. Ideologically it stands between women's liberation and conventional Judaism.

132. Cohen, Steven M., Susan Dessel, and Michael Pelavin. "The Changing (?) Role of Women in Jewish Communal Affairs: A Look into the UJA." In *The Jewish Woman: New Perspectives*, edited by Elizabeth Koltun, 193-201. New York: Schocken Books, 1976.

133. Cohen, Steven Martin, Susan C. Dessel, and Michael A. Pelavin. "Women's Power and Status in Jewish

Communal Life: A Look at the UJA." *Response*,
no. 28 (1975-76): 59-66.

134. Coll, Regina, ed. *Women and Religion: A Reader for
the Clergy.* New York: Paulist Press, 1982.
140 pp.

Addresses, essays, and lectures on women in
Christianity and Judaism.

135. Collins, Adela Yarbro. "An Inclusive Biblical
Anthropology." *Theology Today* 34 (1978): 358-69.

Mostly about the New Testament but often with
reference to the Old Testament. Refers to the motif
of redemption; Yahweh's redemption of the people of
Israel from Egypt is the image of freeing persons
from slavery. In feminist theology this image has
been used to interpret the experience of women in
the current feminist movement. Thinks that the
image of redemption from slavery might be
meaningfully applied to any present situation which
involves the arbitrary curtailment of human beings
as they seek to discover, develop, and exercise their
gifts in a responsible way. One such situation is
certainly the discrimination against women so
prevalent today.

136. Collins, Sheila. "Religion and the Sexual Learning
of Children." In *Childhood Sexual Learning: The
Unwritten Curriculum*, edited by Elizabeth J.
Roberts, 213-42. Cambridge, Mass.: Ballinger
Publishing Company, 1980.

A discussion of the role of the religious
traditions of Judaism, Roman Catholicism, and
Protestantism in shaping the sexual learning of
American children. Four major subject areas are
examined: 1) authority and responsibility, 2) general
messages about human sexuality, 3) gender-role
patterns conveyed by Judaism, Roman Catholicism, and
Protestantism, and 4) the effect of worship and
religious architecture on sexual development.
Asserts that each of the religions discussed began as

a creative revolution against the dead weight of the
past. "Buried in each of the traditions are the
seeds of that creative fervor. Many people who have
grown up within these three traditions are now
beginning--with women, who for so long have been
denied the chance to define the parameters of
religious and social reality, at the forefront--to
recover those seeds and to reform those traditions
in ways that, it is hoped, will enable religion to
become once again a vital source of life and growth."

137. Conzelmann, Hans. "The Mother of Wisdom." In *The
      Future of Our Religious Past*, edited by James M.
      Robinson, 230-43. New York: Harper and Row, 1971.

138. Corne, Sharon. "The *Bat Mitzvah* Problem." *Response*,
      no. 18 (Summer 1973): 114-16.

      Bat Mitzvah was initiated in the nineteenth century
      in Italy and France for girls as *Bar Mitzvah* is for
      boys. Asserts that *Bat Mitzvah* has never been really
      integrated in Jewish society and finds it hard to
      believe that both ceremonies have equal status. *Bat
      Mitzvah* imitates the basic *Bar Mitzvah* form but lacks
      its weight and richness. One important difference
      is that the *Torah* reading is left out of the young
      women's service.

139. Cosby, Michael R. *Sex in the Bible: An Introduction
      to What the Scriptures Teach Us About Sexuality.*
      Englewood Cliffs, N.J.: Prentice-Hall, 1984.
      182 pp.

      An analysis of a limited number of texts from the
      Old Testament; the sexual laws of Deuteronomy, the
      Proverbs and the Song of Songs.

140. Costa, Margaret. "Effects of Sex and Social
      Affiliation on Self-Attitudes and Attitudes towards
      Peers of an Aging Jewish Population." Ed.D. diss.,
      Rutgers University. The State University of
      New Jersey, 1979. 97 pp.

141. Cowen, Ida, and Irene Gunther. *A Spy for Freedom:*
      The Story of Sarah Aaronsohn. Jewish Biography
      Series. New York: Lodestar Books, 1984. 156 pp.

142. Craghan, John P. "Esther, Judith, and Ruth:
      Paradigms for Human Liberation." *Biblical Theology*
      Bulletin 12 (1982): 11-19.

      Emphasizes the fact that the Books of Esther,
      Judith, and Ruth are the only books in the canon
      which bear the name of a woman as their title. Wants
      to examine the question of human liberation with
      these three women as paradigms. This is done by
      focusing on six points: 1) the setting of liberation,
      2) lamentation, 3) the emergence of the leader, 4)
      banqueting and empowering/disempowering, 5) the
      sexual element, and 6) communal concern. Concludes
      with discussing three different paradigms for human
      liberation, each in connection with each of the
      three women who gave name to the three books of
      Esther, Judith, and Ruth.

143. Cromer, Gerald. "Intermarriage and Communal Survival
      in a London Suburb." *Jewish Journal of Sociology*
      16 (1974): 155-69.

      A demographic research on the Anglo-Jewish
      community based on a comparative study of Jewish and
      non-Jewish family life in Wembley, a London suburb.
      The fieldwork consisted of two series of interviews,
      forty Jewish and forty non-Jewish families. Tries
      to find friendship patterns. The findings indicate
      that parents were more comfortable with Jews, while
      children were equally comfortable with Jews and
      non-Jews. Attitudes toward intermarriage were found
      to be closely related to the level of religious
      observance. Also many Jews were against inter-
      marriage because they were concerned with the future
      of the Jewish community.

144. Daniel, Rebecca. *Women of the Old Testament.*
      Carthage, Ill.: Good Apple, 1983. 32 pp.

145. Danto, Bruce, and Joan M. Danto. "Jewish and
     Non-Jewish Suicide in Oakland County, Michigan."
     Crisis 4, no. 1 (1983): 33-60.

     A demographic investigation of the suicide rate
     among Jewish and non-Jewish population in Oakland
     County, Michigan, for the period from 1969 to 1979.
     The findings show that among Jews as a whole, the
     rate of male suicides are higher than of female
     suicides. Most Jewish suicides were married. Most
     of the female suicides died from drug overdose.

146. Datan, Nancy. "Your Daughter Shall Prophesy.
     Ancient and Contemporary Perspectives on the Women
     of Israel." In *Israel: Social Structure and
     Change*, edited by Michael Curtis and Mordecai S.
     Chertoff, 379-88. New Brunswick, N.J.: Transaction
     Books, 1973.

147. Daum, Annette. "A Jewish Feminist View." *Theology
     Today* 41 (1981): 294-300.

148. Daum, Annette. "'Sisterhood' is Powerful." In
     *Spinning a Sacred Yarn: Women Speak from the
     Pulpit*, 45-54. New York: Pilgrim Press, 1982.

149. Davies, Peter. "No Nameless Heroes: An American
     Whose Devotion to Her Husband Kept Her in Germany
     and a Woman Who Openly Advocated the Overthrow of
     the Nazis." *Christian Century* 92 (1975): 377-83.

     About the courageous efforts of two Jewish women,
     Mildred Fish Harnack (1902-43) and Sophie Scholl
     (1922-43) in Germany during the Second World War.

150. Davies, Steve. "The Canaanite-Hebrew Goddess." In
     *The Book of the Goddess Past and Present. An
     Introduction to Her Religion*, edited by Carl Olson,
     68-79. New York: Crossroad, 1983.

     A discussion on the question whether there was any
     such thing as a Hebrew or Jewish Goddess. In

contrast to Raphael Patai who in his book *The Hebrew Goddess* asserts that there was such a thing, Davies thinks that we cannot meaningfully speak of a Hebrew or a Jewish Goddess. He admits that Hebrew-speaking people knew a goddess or goddesses, but this was only a way of speaking, not a way of worshipping. Their god was exclusively male. He had feminine attributes, but that does not mean that there has ever been a Hebrew or Jewish Goddess.

151. Davis, Moshe. "Mixed Marriage in Western Jewry: Historical Background to the Jewish Response." *Jewish Journal of Sociology* 19 (1968): 177-220.

Makes a distinction between mixed marriage and intermarriage. Mixed marriage means marriage between a Jew and a non-Jew in which neither part renounces religious faith. In intermarriage one of the partners adopts the faith of the other. Examines the attitude to mixed marriages in the early Jewish settlements of the United States, Great Britain, Canada, Australia, Argentina, and France. In all these societies the number of mixed marriages has increased. Opposition to mixed marriages was mainly based on concern for Jewish group survival. Today it is almost a daily event, and the opposition seems to be small.

152. Davis, Nira Yuval. *Israeli Women and Men: Divisions behind the Unity.* CHANGE Report, no. 6. London, 1982. 21 pp.

A presentation of data demonstrating the major facets of the sexual division of labor in Israeli society. The conclusion is that women participate less than men in the labor market, have less education, earn less money, and have fewer positions of authority.

153. Davis-Kram, Harriet. "The Story of the Sisters of the Bund." *Contemporary Jewry* 5, no. 2 (1980): 27-43.

A study of the role played by Russian Jewish women in the workers' movement of late nineteenth-century

Russia. Due to economic pressures many women had to work outside the home. This had a strong influence on their radicalization, and their support for and participation in the workers' movement. The Jewish Bund was developed in 1897.

154. Dawidowicz, Lucy S. "On Being a Woman in Shul."
     Commentary 46, no. 1 (1968): 71-74.

     About women in the synagogue (shul: Yiddish for synagogue). Tells about her own shul in Queens but discusses also the status of women in the shul generally. In Judaism women are assigned primacy at home, not in shul. They are not exempt from praying, but for the most part they go to shul only on Sabbaths and festivals.

155. Dawidowicz, Lucy S. "On Being a Woman in Shul." In *The Jewish Presence. Essays on Identity and History*, 46-57. New York: Holt, Rinehart and Winston, 1977.

     Speaks forthrightly against women invading the synagogue. Tells about her attending a Reconstructionist service one *Simchat Torah* morning and watching the women embrace the *Torah*, found herself seized by wicked and perverse thoughts. "Wicked; how insensible was this movement to the festival's symbolism, to its music and poetry. Perverse; only here could transvestitism appear as innocent farce." Fears that if ever men abdicate their synagogual responsibilities to women, the synagogue will succumb either to Italianization or to Hassadahrization.

156. Decter, Midge. "Liberating Women: Who Benefits?"
     Commentary 77, no. 3 (1984): 31-36.

     About cohabitation vs. marriage. Thinks that women gain nothing from cohabitation instead of getting married. Claims that they are not happy in such a relationship and that what they think is liberation for women rather is liberation for men since "coupledom" frees them from responsibility.

157. DeJong, Meindert. *Mighty Ones: Great Men and Women
      of Early Bible Days*. New York: Harper and Row,
      1959. 282 pp.

158. Delaney, Carol. "The Legacy of Abraham." In *Beyond
      Androcentrism: New Essays on Women and Religion*,
      edited by Rita M. Gross, 217-36. Missoula, Mont.:
      Scholars Press, 1977.

      About the story of the "sacrifice of Isaac." Asks
      why the theme of child sacrifice is *the* theme chosen
      by Biblical writers to express devotion to God and
      why Sarah's point of view is absent. Does the story
      have the same meaning for women, or is it a symptom
      of masculine culture? Tries to find other
      possibilities of meaning latent in the story than the
      willingness to kill a child as a test of piety. To
      do this, she compares the story with stories from
      other cultures and concludes that the meaning of the
      story is to be found in the establishment of father-
      right. The story functions to establish the
      authority of the father, and the idea of paternity
      forms the basis of father-right, the foundation of
      patriarchy.

159. Delaney, Janice, Mary Jane Lupton, and Emily Toth.
      "Woman Unclean: Menstrual Taboos in Judaism and
      Christianity." Chap. 4 in *The Curse: A Cultural
      History of Menstruation*. New York: New American
      Library, 1977.

      According to several texts in the Old Testament,
      the menstruating woman is unclean. She is kept out
      of the temples and out of the political and economic
      life. Asserts that the practices of the ancient
      Hebrews parallel the taboos and practices of many
      early societies. The difference is that even today
      an Orthodox Jewish woman is required to abstain from
      sex until seven days after the period has ended and
      she has taken *mikveh*, the ritual bath.

160. Della Pergola, Sergio. "A Note on Marriage Trends
      Among Jews in Italy." *Jewish Journal of Sociology*
      14 (1972): 197-205.

A study on demographic data relating to marriage
among Italian Jews. The rate of mixed marriages, age
of marriage, marital status, and choice of partners
are examined. The findings indicate that there have
been radical changes in the structure of Italian
Jewry in this century. A change in geographical
distribution has taken place and there has been an
upward mobility socially and economically. It seems
as if Italian Jews have a rather weak Jewish
identity. There is a low reproduction rate, and the
number of mixed marriages is increasing.

161. Della Pergola, Sergio. "Patterns of American Jewish
     Fertility." *Demography* 17 (1980): 261-73.

     Findings indicate a decrease in fertility among
     American Jews. Jewish couples marry later, have
     their first child later in the marriage, and have
     fewer children.

162. Denes, Magda. "Performing Abortions." *Commentary*
     62, no. 4 (1976): 33-37.

     A personal account on the feelings of persons
     involved in the performing of legal abortions. Has
     spent some time in an abortion hospital and talked
     with many of the aborting women. Describes also how
     she inspected the fetuses in the buckets where they
     were placed.

163. Deshen, Shlomo. "Women in the Jewish Family in
     Pre-Colonial Morocco." *Anthropological Quarterly*
     56, no. 3 (1983): 134-44.

     A study on the nature of the traditional extended
     family in Morocco and the position of married women.
     The study is based on Rabbinical court case materials
     from the eighteenth and nineteenth centuries, and the
     data are evaluated in conjunction with recent
     findings in anthropology. The marriages were
     patrilocal. Women were confined largely within the
     family compound. Scope for female assertion was
     limited to domestic roles.

164. Döller, Johannes. *Das Weib im Alten Testament.*
      Biblische Zeitfragen, Neunte Folge, Heft 7-9.
      Münster in Westfalen: Aschendorffsche
      Verlagsbuchhandlung, 1920. 83 pp.

      About the status of women in the Old Testament.

165. Donaldson, Mara E. "Kinship theory in the
      Patriarchal Narratives: The Case of the Barren
      Wife." *Journal of the American Academy of Religion*
      49 (1981): 77-87.

      An anthropological study on the patrilineal
      genealogies in the narratives of the patriarchs in
      Genesis.

166. Donat, Doris. "Emancipation of the Jewish Woman in
      Morocco." *In The Dispersion* 2 (1963): 127-36.

167. Dorkam, Joël. "La femme dans la société du
      kibboutz." In *L'autre dans la conscience Juive.*
      Le sacré et le couple. Données et débats, edited
      by Jean Halpérin and Georges Lévitte, 225-30.
      Paris: Presses Universitaires de France, 1973.

      A discussion of how women function in the kibbutz
      system and how kibbutzim influence the women. The
      article is followed by a debate, 230-31.

168. Dowty, Nancy. "To Be a Woman in Israel." *School
      Review* 80 (1972): 319-32.

      A sociological research study on how the
      transformation in women's lives, brought about by
      modernization, affects the typical cultural response
      of a woman to various aspects of middle age. Five
      Israeli subcultures were surveyed: Muslim Arab
      villagers, and Jewish immigrants from North Africa,
      Persia, Turkey, and Central Europe. The research was
      started because it had been suggested that middle age
      was a more difficult time of life among Western
      women than among Eastern women. Dowty presents a

contradictory theory. Proposes that among normal
samples it would be found that the modern Western
woman, who has actively planned her own life, would
be best able to cope with the variety of role
changes at middle age.

169. Dresner, Ruth Rapp. "The Work of Bertha Pappenheim."
     Judaism 30 (1981): 204-11.

170. Duncan, Erika. "The Hungry Jewish Mother." In *On
     Being a Jewish Feminist. A Reader*, edited by
     Susannah Heschel, 27-39. New York: Schocken Books,
     1983 (Reprinted from *The Lost Tradition: Mothers
     and Daughters in Literature*, edited by Cathy N.
     Davidson and E.M. Broner, 231-41. New York:
     Ungar, 1980).

     A survey of the literature treating the subject of
     the hungry Jewish mother.

171. Dworkin, Susan. "Henrietta Szold--Liberated Woman."
     In *The Jewish Woman: New Perspectives*, edited by
     Elizabeth Koltun, 164-70. New York: Schocken
     Books, 1976 (Reprinted from *Hadassah Magazine*
     February 1972).

     A biographical description of Henrietta Szold, born
     in 1860 in Baltimore. She was an extremely gifted
     woman, but even if she was blessed with an
     intellectual and professional freedom which was very
     unusual for women at her time, she had to fight her
     way in an extremely male-dominated society. All her
     life she worked for greater freedom for women but was
     also a loyal Jew.

172. Eaton, Joseph W. "Women and Israel. A Book Review
     Essay." *Kidma* 7, no. 2 (1975): 37-41.

     A review essay on English-language literature on
     the subject of women in Israel, published after the
     establishment of the state of Israel. Treats novels,
     biographies, and scientific works.

173.   Edelman, Lily. "Berye Power." *Keeping Posted* 17,
       no. 7 (1972): 20.

       About the *berye*. According to the *Modern English-
       Yiddish, Yiddish-English Dictionary* by Uriel
       Weinreich, 1968, the word *berye* means efficient,
       skillful person; efficient housewife. Looks at the
       berye and her place in the life of our own day.

174.   Edinger, Dora. "Bertha Pappenheim (1859-1936).
       A German-Jewish Feminist." *Jewish Social Studies*
       20, no. 3 (1958): 180-86.

       A biography of the woman who in 1904 founded the
       national organization of Jewish women (Jüdischer
       Frauenbund) in Germany. It was dissolved by the
       Nazis in 1938.

175.   Edwin, Samuel. "The Family." In *The Structure of
       Society in Israel*, 140-46. New York: Random House,
       1969.

       An analysis of the family in Israel. Compares some
       of his findings related to Arab/Muslim and Jewish
       families. Arabs have proportionately larger families
       and lower life expectancy than Jews. A Muslim man
       may have up to four wives. Polygamy is prohibited by
       Jewish religious law. Civil marriage and divorce do
       not exist in Israel but are the responsibility of the
       religious authorities of each community.

176.   Edwin, Samuel. "Men and Women--Age and Youth." In
       The Structure of Society in Israel, 147-54.
       New York: Random House, 1969.

       Asserts that Israeli society is still dominated by
       an adult male structure. The emancipation of women
       has been quickened by the egalitarian ideology of
       kibbutzim.

177.   Eisenpreis, Bettijane. "Majority Discrimination."
       European Judaism 15 (1981): 32-33.

Finds that the situation of the American Jewish
woman is worse than that of her non-Jewish sister
and that there is discrimination against Jewish
women by their fellow Jews everywhere. Is troubled
by the fact that what she holds to be the essential
goodness and justice of Judaism is not applied to
women as a general rule in any sphere of American
Jewish life. Wants a change and thinks that it is
necessary to start with women themselves.

178. Eisenstein, Ira. "A New Approach to Jewish Divorce."
     Journal of Divorce 6, no. 4 (1983): 85-90.

     Describes an initiative by Rabbis of the
     Reconstructionist Movement to innovate the
     traditional Jewish law of divorce. By means of
     this new type of divorce, the Jewish woman has the
     right to initiate a divorce and avoid becoming an
     agunot, an abandoned wife.

179. Elazar, Daniel J., and Rela Geffen Monson. "Women in
     the Synagogue Today." *Midstream* 27, no. 4 (1981):
     25-30.

     A study of attitudes toward granting Rabbinical
     ordination to women and their place in the synagogue.
     Describes different investigations on women's ritual
     participation among Reform, Conservative, and
     Orthodox Jews. Within Reform Judaism, equal
     participation is the norm, within the Orthodox
     movement sex-role segregation is dominant, while
     there are great differences within the Conservative
     movement.

180. Elazar, Daniel J., ed. "Working Conditions in
     Chicago in the Early Twentieth Century--Testimony
     before the Illinois Senatorial Vice Committee,
     1913." *American Jewish Archives* 21, no. 2 (1969):
     149-71.

     Presents part of the testimony of Jewish female
     employees and Jewish factory owners in Chicago's
     garment industry before a special committee

investigating the connections between prostitution
and poor working conditions.

181.   Eliach, Yaffa. *Hasidic Tales of the Holocaust*.
       New York: Oxford University Press, 1982. 266 pp.

       This collection, which is based on interviews and
       oral stories, is the first anthology of Hasidic
       stories about the Holocaust and the first ever, in
       which women play a large role--not merely as
       daughters, sisters, or wives, but because of their
       own faith, conviction, and moral courage.

182.   Elizur, Judith Neulander. "Women in Israel."
       Judaism 22, no. 2 (1973): 237-47.

183.   Elliman, Wendy. "Women's Conference in Jerusalem."
       Israel Digest 22, no. 16 (1979): 18-19.

       From a World Conference of Women Leaders in
       Jerusalem in June, 1979. There were women from many
       different countries as dissimilar as Togo and the
       United States, Thailand and New Zealand, Singapore
       and Finland. Even if they were different in many
       things, they agreed that women should have equal
       opportunity with men in all fields of life; politics,
       education, and employment.

184.   Ellman, Israel. "Jewish Intermarriage in the United
       States of America." In *The Jewish Family. A
       Survey and Annotated Bibliography*, edited by
       Benjamin Schlesinger, 25-62. Toronto:
       University of Toronto Press, 1971.

       Speculates on the high male rate of intermarriage
       among Jews in the United States. Suggests as one
       explanation that Jewish men are unable to relate
       sexually to Jewish women because of their experiences
       with their Jewish mothers.

185.   Elwell, Ellen Sue Levi. "The Founding and Early
       Programs of the National council of Jewish Women:

Study and Practices as Jewish Women's Religious
Expression." Ph.D. diss., Indiana University,
1982. 215 pp.

A study on one of the first Jewish women's
organizations in the United States. Concentrates on
the shift from trying to engage women in a program
of Jewish education that would naturally lead to
service, to being a philanthropic organization.
This happened during its formative period and there
were a variety of factors that led to this
development. Among them were rabbinical resistance
to the Council's efforts for religious expression and
education for women but also controversies between
women with different views on several issues
concerning their religion.

186. Elwell, Ellen Sue Levi, and Edward R. Levenson, eds.
The Jewish Women's Studies Guide. Fresh Meadows,
N.Y.: Biblio Press, 1982. 108 pp.

187. Elwess, Brewster. *The Most Beautiful Jewish Woman
in the History of Mankind.* Albuquerque:
Gloucester Art Press, 1978.

188. Engert, Thaddeus. *Ehe- und Familien Recht der
Hebräer.* München: J.J. Lentner, 1905. 108 pp.

189. Epstein, I. "The Jewish Woman in the Responsa:
900 C.E. - 1500 C.E." *Response*, no. 18
(Summer 1973): 23-31.

About women in feudalism, one of the darkest
periods of history. Asserts, however, that "the
darkness that covered the earth" did not penetrate
far into the Jewish home. Discusses part of the
Responsa literature which describes the position of
the Jewish woman. She is said to enjoy a larger
measure of freedom, influence, authority, and respect
than was the case with her Gentile sisters.

190.   Epstein, Joseph.   "Cynthia Ozick, Jewish Writer."
       Commentary 77, no. 3 (1984): 64-69.

       A review essay on Cynthia Ozick, a Jewish female
       writer of stories, novels, and essays.

191.   Epstein, Louis M.   *The Jewish Marriage Contract: A*
       Study on the Status of the Woman in Jewish Law.
       New York: Arno Press, 1973.   316 pp.   (Reprint of
       the 1927 edition, originally published in New York
       by the Theological Seminary of America).

       Traces the development of the Jewish marriage
       contract and its effect on marriage, divorce, family
       life, and woman's status.

192.   Epstein, Louis M.   *Marriage Laws in the Bible and*
       the Talmud.   Cambridge, Mass.: Harvard University
       Press, 1968   (Reprint of 1942 edition).

       Discusses Jewish marriage laws concerning polygamy,
       concubinage, Levirate marriage, intermarriage,
       incest, and other marriage prohibitions.

193.   Epstein, Louis M.   *Sex Laws and Customs in Judaism.*
       New York: Bloch Publ. Co., 1948.   251 pp.

       A companion to his earlier work, *Marriage Laws in*
       the Bible and the Talmud.   While the first deals with
       sex morality within marriage, this volume endeavors
       to present the Jewish standard of sex conduct outside
       marriage.   Traces the development of homosexuality
       and points out that love between women is not
       prohibited in the Bible even if the rabbis call it
       a "heathen practice."

194.   Epstein, Perle.   "Women in a War-Torn Society: In
       Israel: How Are They Holding up?"   *Present Tense* 2,
       no. 4 (1975): 68-73.

About problems when the husband goes out to fight
and his wife has to wait passively. Mentions
different examples of how women react in situations
of war. Seems to be negative about women's liberation
in Israel. Thinks that most Israeli feminists are
American-born and that Israeli-born women have not
had "the breathing space" between wars to think of
anything but keeping their families intact.

195. Erez, Esther. "The Sari and the Turban in Haifa."
      In *Women in Israel*, published by Israel Information
      Centre, 69-71. Tel Aviv: Israel Information
      Centre, 1975.

      About the Carmel International Center for
      Community Training in Haifa. The goal of this center
      is to make women capable of contributing to the
      advancement of society, especially women from
      developing countries.

196. Eslinger, Lyle. "The Case of an Immodest Lady
      Wrestler in Deuteronomy 25, 11-12." *Vetus
      Testamentum* 31 (1981): 269-81.

      The two verses in the Old Testament read: "When men
      fight with one another, and the wife of the one draws
      near to rescue her husband from the hand of him who
      is beating him, and puts out her hand and seizes him
      by the private parts, 12 then you shall cut off her
      hand; your eye shall have no pity" (RSV). States
      that this case provides the only explicit example of
      mutilative punishment in Israelite law. Wants to
      demonstrate that v. 12 is a perfect example of *lex
      talionis*, talionic punishment. Discusses different
      exegesis of this passage and compares it to similar
      passages of the Old Testament (Gen. 32:26, 33 and
      Song of Songs 5:5).

197. Falk, Ze'ev W. "Jewish Private Law." In The *Jewish
      People in the First Century. Historical Geography,
      Political History, Social, Cultural and Religious
      Life and Institutions*, vol. 1, edited by S. Safrai
      and M. Stern in cooperation with D. Flusser and

W.C. van Unnik, 504-34. Assen: Van Gorcum and
Comp., 1974.

About different aspects of Jewish private law.
Asserts that Jewish law did not divide the legal
norms into two spheres of private and public law.
Matters of public concern have been dealt with by
private law. Discusses family law, contract, and
criminal laws.

198. Falk, Ze'ev W. "The New Abortion Law of Israel."
      Israel Law Review 13 (1978): 103-8.

      In 1977 Israel got a new abortion law. The
      criminality of abortion is retained, but exemption
      is granted to a doctor performing the operation in a
      recognized hospital upon the approval of a committee.
      The committee may approve if they find justification
      in accordance with certain strict rules. Suggests
      that feminist ideology underlies the law since no
      mention is made of the father. The law sees the
      pregnancy and its termination as the personal
      private affair of the woman.

199. Falk, Ze'ev W. "Religious Law and the Modern Family
      in Israel." In *Family Law in Asia and Africa*,
      edited by J.N.D. Anderson, 235-54. London:
      Allen and Unwin, 1968.

200. Falk, Ze'ev. "Women's Equal Rights." *Israel Law
      Review* 7 (1972): 313-15.

      About a divorce case. Asserts that divorce cases
      have been problematic after the Women's Equal Rights
      Law came into force in 1951.

201. Farber, Gerald Mark. "Marital Satisfaction and the
      Topics of Self-Disclosure for Jewish Men and Women:
      A Correlation Study." Ed.D. diss., Boston
      University School of Education, 1979. 97 pp.

      Six variables of self-disclosure: attitudes and
      opinions, tastes and interests, work and study,

money, personality, and body, were correlated to
marital satisfaction. The results of the study
indicated a high correlation between individuals who
self-disclose to their spouse and marital
satisfaction. The relationship was significantly
greater for women than for men. The most significant
topic areas for women were body and personality. For
men the most relevant topics were attitudes and
opinions and money.

202. Farley, Frank H., Arie Cohen, Joel Goldberg, and Yoel
     Yinon. "Fears in American and Israeli Women."
     Journal of Social Psychology 106, no. 1 (1978):
     17-24.

     An investigation of fears in American and Israeli
     female college students. It comprises a study of the
     intensity and extremity of fear ratings, and the
     generality of fearfulness across a wide range of
     stimuli. The results have shown significantly
     greater generalized fear in the Israeli in comparison
     with the American sample, but no significant
     difference in extreme fear.

203. Fein, Helen. "Abused Women of Valor." *Midstream* 29,
     no. 9 (1983): 19-21.

     A 1975 U.S. survey indicates that American Jewish
     husbands are responsible for only 1 percent of wife-
     abuse and that Jewish wives are much more likely to
     abuse their husbands than vice-versa. In Israel,
     however, wife-beating is widespread. A Knesset
     subcommittee in 1976 estimated that 5 to 10 percent
     of married Israeli women were beaten by their
     husbands. It is reported to take place among all
     classes. Tries to find causes for the frequent wife-
     beating in Israel and reports about shelters for
     abused women.

204. Feldman, David Michael. *Marital Relations, Birth
     Control, and Abortion in Jewish Law.* New York:
     Schocken Books, 1974. 332 pp.

Attitudes towards sexual matters, birth control,
and abortion in the Biblical, Talmud and Responsa
literature are examined from an Orthodox point of
view.

205.   Feldman, David M. "Some Problems Ahead." *Judaism*
        33 (1984): 21-22.

        About the "problem" of ordination of women in
        Conservative Judaism.

206.   Feldman, David M. "Woman's Role and Jewish Law."
        In *Conservative Judaism and Jewish Law*, edited by
        S. Siegel, 293-305. New York: The Rabbinical
        Assembly, 1977 (Reprint from *Conservative Judaism*
        26, no. 4 [1972]: 29-39).

        Thinks that women should not be included in the
        prayer quorum, the *minyan*, because the ten people who
        make up the *minyan* share the obligation of public
        prayer. Admits, however, that if there is a *minyan*
        for purposes other than public prayer, it can be
        argued that women are to be equally included. There
        is no question of sex discrimination or inequality;
        rather it is a question of differing roles of men
        and women in the religious life of Judaism. Defends
        these differences.

207.   Feldman, Louis Jordan. "The Prohibition Against
        Idolatry, Sexual Trespass and Bloodshed as a Moral
        Absolute in Rabbinic Judaism." Ph.D. diss.,
        University of Southern California, 1978.

208.   Ferkiss, Barbara. "Family Life in the Israeli
        Kibbutz." *Berkeley Publications in Society and
        Institutions* 2, no. 1 (1956): 15-27.

        This paper is focused on the ways in which "family
        life in the kibbutz is integrated with, and
        reinforces the larger social structure of the
        kibbutz, and particularly with the way it conflicts
        with the needs and aims of the kibbutz, and thus
        opens the door to structural changes." Discusses

most aspects of family life in the kibbutz: the relation between husband and wife, the relationship of parents to their children, sex and reproduction, and women's activities.

209. Feuillet, André. "La dignité et le rôle de la femme d'après quelques textes Pauliniens: Comparison avec l'Ancien Testament." *New Testament Studies* 21 (1975): 157-91.

Asserts that Paul has often been accused of being negative towards the feminine world, that he is more Jewish than Christian in this respect, and that he regards women as inferior to men: an image of an image. Tries to refute these accusations.

210. Fine, Irene Ann. "Developing a Jewish Studies Program for Women: A Springboard to History." Ph.D. diss., The Union for Experimenting Colleges and Universities, 1980. 229 pp.

Shows that the Jewish history of educational literature is a male-dominated history. Tells about a new learning institute, Woman's Institute for Continuing Jewish Education, with classes, seminars, and special programs to help change the traditional focus of Jewish women and open up new roles and opportunities for women within the community.

211. Fine, Irene Ann. *Educating the New Jewish Woman: A Dynamic Approach*. San Diego, Calif.: Woman's Institute for Continuing Jewish Education, 1985. 80 pp.

212. Finestein, Israel. "An Aspect of the Jews and English Marriage Law during the Emancipation: The Prohibited Degrees." *Jewish Journal of Sociology* 7 (1965): 3-21.

Discusses the status of Jewish marriages in England in the nineteenth century.

213.   Fink, Greta. *Great Jewish Women: Profiles of
       Courageous Women from the Maccabean Period to the
       Present.* New York: Menorah Publ., 1978. 197 pp.

       Biography on Jewish women.

214.   Finkelstein, Eleanor. "A Study of Female Role
       Definitions in a Yeshivah High School (A Jewish
       Day School)." Ph.D. diss., New York University,
       1980. 274 pp.

       An examination on the impact of the woman's
       movement and outside cultural trends on women's roles
       and status in an Orthodox Jewish high school.

215.   Fiorenza, Elisabeth Schüssler. "The Jesus Movement
       as Renewal Movement within Judaism." In *Memory of '
       Her. A Feminist Theological Reconstruction of
       Christian Origins*, 105-59. New York: Crossroad,
       1983.

       An attempt to find out what it was like for women
       in Palestine to be involved with Jesus and his
       movement. Insists on seeing these women as Jewish
       women. Places the Jesus stories about women within
       the overall story of Jesus and his movement in
       Palestine, in order to find their subversive
       character. "In the discipleship of equals the role
       of women is not peripheral or trivial, but at the
       center, and thus of utmost importance to the praxis
       of solidarity from below."

216.   Fisch, Linda Yellin. "Patterns of Religious and
       Feminist Socialization among Jewish College Women."
       Ed.D. diss., Columbia University Teachers College,
       1983. 195 pp.

       A case study on female Jewish undergraduates who
       attended Barnard College in 1977-79. The patterns of
       their socialization experiences are examined,
       religious and feminist, and the tensions between the
       two. Factors that affected the patterns of feminist
       and religious socialization were analyzed.

217. Fishman, Leora, and Aviva Zuckoff. "A Guide to
     Jewish Women's Activities." In *The First Jewish
     Catalog. A Do-It-Yourself Kit*, edited by Richard
     Siegel, Michael Strassfeld and Sharon Strassfeld,
     252-61. Philadelphia: The Jewish Publication
     Society of America, 1973.

     Goes through different aspects of Jewish women's
     lives: women's movements, the question of
     consciousness-raising groups, women and *Halakhah*, and
     women in Jewish institutions, religious and secular.
     Suggests activities to encourage education and higher
     Jewish learning among women.

218. Fox, Karen L. "Whither Women Rabbis?" *Religious
     Education* 76 (1981): 361-68.

     Discusses different opinions concerning the
     question of women rabbis. Liberal branches of
     Judaism recognize women rabbis because they see
     reforms as part of changes in the modern world. The
     view of congregants is discussed; do they accept
     women rabbis or not? Concludes that they will and
     is anxious to see what women will contribute to the
     rabbinate.

219. Frager, Robert. "Jewish Mothering in Japan."
     Sociological Inquiry 42 (1972): 11-17.

220. Frank, Blanche Beverly. "The American Orthodox
     Jewish Housewife: A Generational Study in Ethnic
     Survival." Ph.D. diss., City University of New
     York, 1975. 319 pp.

     A study on the process of Americanizing among
     American Jewish Orthodox housewives over a period of
     three generations. Using generations as links in a
     culture chain, Frank puts forward the following
     hypotheses: The first generation of Orthodox Jews in
     America retained the traditional Judaic commitment
     and the Eastern European cultural ways (most of them
     came from Eastern Europe). The second generation
     acquired American ways but departed from traditional
     Judaism and East European ways, and the third

generation managed a cultural resolution that
includes a commitment to traditional Judaism
alongside American cultural ways. The results of
the research showed that this hypothesis on the
whole was correct.

221. Freedman, M. "Israel: What's a Radical Feminist
     Doing in a Place Like This?" *Psychology of Women
     Quarterly* 2 (1978): 354-62.

     Asserts that Israel needs feminism. From the 1950s
     women have been sent back home after years of
     pioneer work. In 1978 only 30 percent of Israeli
     women worked outside their homes, almost all of them
     in jobs and professions recognized as feminine or
     "suitable" for women. Concludes that masculinism has
     failed. Israel needs social justice, individual
     freedom, and egalitarianism between men and women.

222. Freedman, Marcia. "A Lesbian in the Promised Land."
     In *Nice Jewish Girls. A Lesbian Anthology*, edited
     by Evelyn Torton Beck, 211-21. Trumansburg, N.Y.:
     Crossing Press, 1982.

     About the life of a lesbian in Israel.

223. Freedman, Marcia. "The Woman on the Tractor. Where
     Is She Now?" *Israel Magazine* 5, no. 9 (1973):
     79-84.

     Examines women's status in different professions in
     Israel. Finds that most women work in areas which
     are traditionally women's jobs: kitchens, nurseries,
     and laundries. In jobs where they are supposed to
     work side by side with men, in the kibbutz, in the
     army, and in politics, they do the typical female
     jobs. Married women with a job outside the home have
     double work. Thinks there will be no equality of
     women in Israel until a redefinition of equality is
     made.

224. Freund, Miriam. "'Make My Eyes Look to the Future':
     Henrietta Szold Centennial Address." *Publications*

of the *American Jewish Historical Society* 49, no. 3 (1960): 159-72.

About Henrietta Szold (1860-1945), a teacher who did a lot to improve education for women. She was the first woman student at the Jewish Theological Seminary of New York. During World War II she organized Youth Aliyah, an organization which saved one hundred thousand Jewish children from the Nazis.

225. Friedlander, Dov. "Family Planning in Israel: Irrationality and Ignorance." *Journal of Marriage and the Family* 35 (1973): 117-24.

In Israel attempts to activate fast population growth have been made for several decades, mainly for political ends. As a result family planning programs have been neglected by the government. Nevertheless, family size is generally small or in the process of decline.

226. Friedlander, Judith. "The Jewish Feminist Question." *Dialectical Anthropology* 8 (1983): 113-20.

Thinks it is important to examine the historical bases of related minority groups in order to find strategies for improving the status of Jewish women and for the work of Jewish feminist groups. The Jews of Eastern Europe as a group are analyzed. The similarity between this group and Jewish feminists is their wish to free themselves from aspects of traditional Judaism for political reasons and at the same time maintain a Jewish identity.

227. Friedman, Milton Kenneth. "Jewish Marriage Contracts in the Palestinian Tradition: Documents from the Cairo Geniza." Ph.D. diss., University of Pennsylvania, 1969. 498 pp.

The Cairo Geniza, which were discovered in the late nineteenth century, are documents deposited in the store room of the synagogue of the Palestinians in Old Cairo. Many of these documents are old marriage contracts (*ketubba*). For this dissertation about

700 of these contracts, mostly from the tenth to
thirteenth centuries, were examined. A general
pattern which emerged through the analysis was that
of a contract between two equal parties. Marriage
is called a "partnership," and a clause therein gave
the wife the right to initiate divorce proceedings on
her own.

228. Friedman, Mordechai Akiva. *Jewish Marriage in
      Palestine. A Cairo Geniza Study.* 2 vols. Tel
      Aviv: The Cham Rosenberg School of Jewish Studies,
      1980-81.

      The first of these two volumes treats the tradition
      of marriage contracts (*ketubba*) of Eretz Israel, and
      the second contains the *ketubba* texts.

229. Friedman, Shamma. "The Case of the Woman with Two
      Husbands in Talmudic and Ancient Near Eastern Law."
      Israel Law Review 15 (1980): 530-58.

      About women who remarry only to have the first
      husband return. There are two operative rules in
      Mesopotamian law: 1) when the husband disappears for
      a specified period and leaves his wife without
      adequate maintenance, she is permitted to remarry;
      and 2) when her first husband was compelled to leave
      by force, his wife is restored to him upon his
      return, whereas if he fled willingly, he has no such
      right to his wife. The wife is supposed to conduct
      a thorough investigation into her husband's fate
      before she remarries. If not, she might be punished.
      According to the Mishna she may return to the first
      husband if she has married the second man without
      the authorization of the *Beth Din*, whereas if she
      remarries with such authorization, she has no option
      but to leave both men on the return of the first
      husband.

230. Friedmann, Meir. "Mitwirkung von Frauen beim
      Gottesdienste." *Hebrew Union College Annual* 8-9
      (1931-32): 511-23.

A responsum to the President of the Israeli
Community in Vienna on the question of the
participation of women in the religious service of
the synagogue, written in 1893.

231. Frymer-Blumfield, Hanita. "The Maintenance of Ethnic
Identity among Jewish Women in an Urban Setting."
Ph.D. diss., The American University, 1977. 141 pp.

232. Fuchs-Kreimer, Nancy. "Feminism and Scriptural
Interpretation: A Contemporary Jewish Critique."
Journal of Ecumenical Studies 20 (1983): 534-48.

About the change in attitudes toward women in
Judaism since 1970 and the development of a Jewish
feminist movement. Mentions the increasing number of
women in leadership positions in Jewish life and
clergy, the new birth ceremonies for baby girls, the
publishing of a new prayer-book for women, and
several books and articles discussing women's status
in Judaism. Discusses the problem of being a
feminist and a Jew and warns against making religion
a separate part of life. "All life is to be holy;
all life is to be whole." Asserts that Judaism
must recognize a world in which women live with men
as equals.

233. Furstenberg, Rochelle. "A Unique Feminism."
Midstream 28, no. 8 (1982): 35-39.

Compares the current wave of feminism with the
young women pioneers of the second and third *aliyot,*
the *chalutzot.* The *chaluzot's* feminism was a
uniquely Zionist feminism. They were young pioneers
who had to face hard work, sickness, and loneliness,
but they were inspired by a wish to transform Jewish
people from different parts of the world into a
nation living and working on its own land. Claims
that their feminism was born to the needs of the
Jewish people. Calls today's feminists "leisure
liberationists" and finds it unlikely that Western
feminism can take root. Thinks it undermines the
family.

234. Gabriel, K.R. "Nuptiality and Fertility of Origin
     Groups in Israel." *Jewish Journal of Sociology* 2
     (1960): 74-97.

     A study of nuptiality and fertility in Israel
     starting with a description of these phenomena in the
     Jewish population as a whole. Goes on to deal in
     detail with individual origin groups and finally
     reviews some data on trends on nuptiality and
     fertility which are connected with length of stay in
     the country. Is specially concerned with the
     differences between origin groups and their
     assimilation.

235. Gantz, Paula. "Our Golden Years--You Should Live So
     Long!" *Lilith* no. 10 (Winter 1982-83): 6-10.

     Tells about the fates of some elderly Jewish women
     in New York. Close to a quarter of a million Jews
     over the age of sixty-five live within the five
     boroughs of New York City, according to the Jewish
     Association for Services of the Aged. Most of them
     are women and poor.

236. Garfinkel, P. "The Best Jewish Mother in the World."
     Psychology Today 17, no. 9 (1983): 56-60.

237. Garson, Catherine. "Femmes en Israel et politique."
     *Revue francaise d'études politiques
     méditerranéennes*, no. 27 (1977): 59-66.

     Describes the role of women in Israeli politics.
     Thinks that Israel has not yet the infrastructure to
     allow women any role of importance in the politics of
     the country. Kibbutzim have not answered to
     expectations as far as the status of women are
     concerned.

238. Gebhard, Paul H., et al. *Pregnancy, Birth and
     Abortion*. New York: Harper and Bros., 1958.
     282 pp.

A study based on interviews conducted by Kinsey Institute researchers between 1938 and 1949.

239. Geller, Laura. "Reactions to a Woman Rabbi." In *On Being a Jewish Feminist. A Reader*, edited by Susannah Heschel, 210-13. New York: Schocken Books, 1983.

Has met different reactions. Feels that there is less social distance between the congregant and the clergy when women function as clergy. People do not attribute to women the power and prestige that they often attribute to men. The ordination of women will lead to change in the way Jews think about God. A female rabbi will force people to think about God as more than male or female.

240. Geller, Laura, and Elizabeth Koltun. "Single and Jewish: Toward a New Definition of Completeness." In *The Jewish Woman: New Perspectives*, edited by Elizabeth Koltun, 43-49. New York: Schocken Books, 1976.

Marriage is viewed by Judaism as the paradigm of completeness. Suggests a new definition of completeness.

241. Geller, Ruth. "A Morning for Memories." In *Nice Jewish Girls. A Lesbian Anthology*, edited by Evelyn Torton Beck, 133-45. Trumansburg, N.Y.: Crossing Press, 1982.

A short story.

242. Geller, Ruth. *Triangles*. Trumansburg, N.Y.: Crossing Press, 1984. 192 pp.

A Jewish lesbian novel.

243. Gellis, Audrey. "The View from the Back of the Shul." *Ms. Magazine* 3, no. 1 (1974): 79-82.

Tells about why she gave up her Jewish identity
finding that she could not accept the way in which
women were expected to behave and their social and
religious role.

244. Gendler, Mary. "The Restoration of Vashti." In
      The Jewish Woman: New Perspectives, edited by
      Elizabeth Koltun, 241-47. New York: Schocken
      Books, 1976.

      Vashti was King Ahasuaru's first wife. Because she
      refused to display her beauty in front of the king
      and other drunken princes, she lost her royal
      position and most probably her life (The Book of
      Esther).

245. Gendler, Mary. "The Vindication of Vashti."
      Response, no. 18 (Summer 1973): 145-60.

246. Gendler, Mary. "Mary Gendler Replies." *Response*,
      no. 26 (1975): 117-19.

      A reply to Melvin Granatstein on the discussion of
      new rituals for women. (See 247 and 295).

247. Gendler, Mary. "Sarah's Seed. A New Ritual for
      Women." *Response*, no. 24 (1974-75): 65-75.

      Proposes new rituals as an equivalent to the
      circumcision ceremony for boys. 1) A ritual
      rupturing of the hymen soon after birth. The
      operation should be performed by a woman. 2)
      A special blessing and perhaps celebration (if the
      girl wishes it) upon the occasion of her first
      menstruation.

248. Gerson, Menachem. *Family, Women, and Socialization
      in the Kibbutz*. Lexington, Mass.: Lexington
      Books, 1978. 142 pp.

249. Gerson, Menachem. "Lesson from the Kibbutz: A
     Cautionary Tale." In *The Future of the Family*,
     edited by Louise Kapp Howe, 326-38. New York:
     Simon and Schuster, 1972.

     Asserts that the kibbutz has achieved fundamental
     changes in the social status of women: 1) women are
     no longer economically dependent on men, 2) the
     conflict created in women by dual roles has been
     resolved, 3) official kibbutz philosophy demands that
     women take full part in all spheres of social
     activity, 4) the sexual double standard has been
     eliminated, 5) women have gained equal education, and
     6) both sexes share household tasks.

250. Gerson, Menachem. "Women in the Kibbutz." *American
     Journal of Orthopsychiatry* 41 (1971): 566-73.

251. Gerson, Menachem. "Women in the Kibbutz." In
     Family, Women, and Socialization in the Kibbutz,
     27-44. Lexington, Mass.: Lexington Books, 1978.

     Points to the positive achievements that have been
     attained by women in the kibbutz but finds that
     traditional sex typing has developed in the wake of
     increasing sex role differentiation. Educators
     should find ways to overcome this development. "What
     is needed now is a new concept of woman, one which
     takes for granted the value of marriage and mother-
     hood but also acknowledges woman's need for
     creativity, independence, and achievement."

252. Gertel, Elliot B. "Confessions of a Rabbinical
     Student." *Midstream* 27, no. 1 (1981): 43-47.

     An adherent of Conservative Judaism describes his
     changing attitudes to the equality between men and
     women in Judaism.

253. Gilad, L. "Contrasting Notions of Proper Conduct--
     Yemeni Jewish Mothers and Daughters in an Israeli
     Town." *Jewish Social Studies* 45 (1983): 73-86.

254. Ginat, Joseph. "A Rural Arab Community in Israel:
      Marriage Patterns and Woman's Status." Ph.D.
      diss., University of Utah, 1975. 421 pp.

      An investigation of a rural Arab society in the
      Samarian mountains of Israel. The subjects of
      marriage patterns and the status of women are dealt
      with and analyzed through individual case studies.
      Included are discussions of employment, education,
      housing, changing agricultural techniques, and the
      physical and historical setting.

255. Ginsberg, Yona. "Joint Leisure Activities and Social
      Networks in Two Neighborhoods in Tel Aviv."
      Journal of Marriage and the Family 37 (1975):
      668-76.

      About differences in the degree of joint leisure
      activities of two neighborhoods in Tel Aviv.
      Married men in the one area seem to share their
      leisure activities with their wives to a much lesser
      degree than married men of the other.

256. Ginsburg, Ruth Bader. "The Status of Women."
      American Journal of Comparative Law 20 (1972):
      585-723.

      Report from a symposium on the status of women in
      different countries. Subjects such as property
      rights, abortion, child care, and employment are
      discussed. There are also discussions on differences
      in women's status between capitalist, socialist, and
      developing countries.

257. Gittlesohn, Roland Bertram. *The Extra Dimension: A
      Jewish View of Marriage.* New York: Union of
      American Hebrew Congregations, 1983. 228 pp.

      This book is a supplement to his basic sex
      education text, *Love, Sex and Marriage* (see 258). It
      is primarily intended for newly married couples or
      couples considering marriage.

258. Gittelsohn, Roland Bertram. *Love, Sex and Marriage: A Jewish View.* New York: Union of American Hebrew Congregations, 1976. 134 pp.

259. Gittelsohn, Roland B. "Women's Lib. and Judaism." *Midstream* 17, no. 8 (1971): 51-58.

Thinks that Judaism has expressed far more understanding and acceptance of women as persons than other civilizations. Asserts that most outrageous attitudes toward women are represented by individual men. Incident after incident in the *Torah* gives high praise to women. Gittelsohn tries to diminish the blessing pronounced each morning by traditionally observant Jewish males: "Praised be the Eternal our God, Ruling Spirit of the Universe, who did not make me a woman," by mentioning that commentators throughout the time have made it "unmistakably clear that the man who thanked God daily for making him male was no more downgrading woman than the *cohayn* who, in parallel blessing, voiced gratitude for having been made a priest, meant to disparage others." Seems to think that there is almost full equality between the sexes today and warns against judging the past by conditions prevailing now.

260. Glanz, David. "An Interpretation of the Jewish Counterculture." *Jewish Social Studies* 39, no. 1-2 (1977): 117-28.

The ideology of the Jewish counterculture movement is dispersed into several different and overlapping spheres. The impact on the broad spectrum of American Jewry has been considerable. Their representatives, mostly young people, are sympathetic to the feminist movement and usually concentrated on finding a Jewish identity.

261. Glanz, Rudolf. *The Jewish Woman in America: Two Female Immigrant Generations, 1820-1929*, 2 vols. New York: Ktav Publishing House, 1976.

A historical study of Jewish immigrant women in America based on a wealth of primary sources,

newspapers, journals, memoirs, institutional and
governmental records and publications. The role of
Jewish women in the economy, the labor movement, the
home, and the community is discussed. Volume 1
treats the Eastern European Jewish woman and Volume
2 the German Jewish woman.

262. Glazer, Mark. "The Dowry as Capital Accumulation
     among the Sephardic Jews of Istanbul, Turkey."
     International Journal of Middle East Studies 10
     (1979): 373-80.

     The giving of a dowry in this society has three
     main goals: 1) the assurance of a woman's livelihood
     through marriage, 2) the enhancing of the prestige of
     the giver of the dowry (the father) and 3) the
     providing of capital to the groom.

263. Glenn, Susan Anita. "The Working Life of Immigrants:
     Women in the America Garment Industry, 1880-1920."
     Ph.D. diss., University of California, Berkeley,
     1983. 364 pp.

     A study of the social, cultural, and industrial
     adjustment of Jewish immigrant women who entered
     America's garment industry between 1880 and the close
     of World War I. Describes some of the problems that
     these women met both as women and as Jews.

264. Goitein, Shelemo Dov. "A Maghrebi Living in Cairo
     Implores His Karaite Wife to Return to Him."
     Jewish Quarterly Review 73 (1982): 138-45.

265. Golan, Naomi. "Wife to Widow to Woman." *Social Work*
     20 (1975): 369-73.

     From 1948 to 1975, 2130 women in Israel lost their
     husbands in war. Examines the particular problems of
     the war widow. Describes the bereavement process as
     consisting of three stages: protest and denial;
     despair and disorganization; and reorganization.
     Tries to relate these stages to the role of the war

widow and suggests how she can adjust to her new role in society.

266. Goldberg, Harriet. "Two Parallel Medieval Commonplaces: Antifeminism and Antisemitism in the Hispanic Literary Tradition." In *Aspects of Jewish Culture in the Middle Ages*, edited by Paul E. Szarmach, 85-119. New York: State University of New York Press, 1979.

267. Goldenberg, Judith Plaskow. "Epilogue: The Coming of Lilith." In *Religion and Sexism. Images of Woman in the Jewish and Christian Traditions*, edited by Rosemary Radford Ruether, 341-43. New York: Simon and Schuster, 1974.

This is a parable of the story of Lilith; the first woman created. According to the sources, God in the beginning created Adam and Lilith from dust--to be equal in all ways. Lilith left Adam because he tried to compel her obedience by force, and God created a second companion for Adam. He created Eve out of one of Adam's ribs. Eve and Lilith met and talked, and a bond of sisterhood grew between them which made both God and Adam afraid.

268. Goldenberg, Judith Plaskow. "The Jewish Feminist: Conflict in Identities." *Response*, no. 18 (Summer 1973): 11-18.

Sees a conflict between being a woman and being a Jew. Discusses the conflict in three of its aspects: The first level on which the conflict is experienced is between communities, between the women's movement and the religious traditions. The second problem is that the Jewish community will not let feminists feel at home in it. The third aspect of the conflict is that Jewish feminists have no way to express their experiences in the women's movement.

269. Goldenberg, Naomi. R. *Changing of the Gods. Feminism and the End of Traditional Religions*. Boston: Beacon Press, 1979. 152 pp.

About Judaism, Christianity, and feminism. Asserts
that women are totally excluded from the Patriarchal
religions and describes different feminist attitudes
toward this dilemma through time. Some have
advocated the complete abandonment of Judaism and
Christianity while others have tried to save the
religions by reform of the sexist practices in their
traditions. The book contains a description of the
"rebels of the Bible" and a theology, "the logic of
the Goddess religion."

270. Goldenberg, Naomi Ruth. "Important Directions for a
      Feminist Critique of Religion in Works of Sigmund
      Freud and Carl Jung." Ph.D. diss., Yale
      University, 1976. 239 pp.

      Suggest how the psychological theories of Freud and
      Jung can be used for a feminist critique of Judaism
      and Christianity and in building new concepts for
      spirituality. Both Judaic and Christian traditions
      are found to be incapable of providing imagistic
      models for the sort of religion that feminists want.
      Freud can be useful in challenging a father-god.
      Jung can be especially useful in the endeavor to use
      "experience" as a source for building new spiritual
      concepts.

271. Goldfeld, Anne. "Women as Sources of Torah in the
      Rabbinic Tradition." In *The Jewish Woman: New
      Perspectives*, edited by Elizabeth Koltun, 257-71.
      New York: Schocken Books, 1976 (Reprint from
      Judaism 24, no. 2 [1975]: 245-56).

272. Goldin, Hyman E. *The Jewish Woman and Her Home*.
      New York: Hebrew Publishing Co., 1941. 354 pp.

      A historical and social story of the Jewish woman
      in family and religious life.

273. Goldman, Aviva Dayan. "American Feminism, an Alien
      Philosophy." *Response*, no. 34 (1977): 106-8.

A comment on Barbara Rubin's interview with Marcia
Freedman (see 654).

274. Goldscheider, Calvin, and Sidney Goldstein.
"Generational Changes in Jewish Family Structure."
Journal of Marriage and the Family 29 (1967):
267-76.

This paper examines family structure differences of
Jews and non-Jews, generational changes in the Jewish
family, and differential family structure within the
Jewish population.

275. Goldscheider, Calvin. "Ideological Factors in Jewish
Fertility Differentials." *Jewish Journal of
Sociology* 7 (1965): 92-104.

Tries to find a relationship between religion and
fertility. The findings show that Orthodox Jews of
the first generation had higher fertility, i.e.,
larger families, earlier marriages, and shorter birth
intervals, than Conservative or Reform Jews of that
generation. In later generations the difference
between Orthodox Jews and other Jews was smaller.
Found also that religious divisional identification
reflects social class differences. Concludes that
ideology has little relationship to Jewish fertility.
Most differences can be explained by social class
difference.

276. Goldscheider, Calvin. "Out-of-Wedlock Births in
Israel." *Social Problems* 21 (1974): 550-67.

An examination of Jewish out-of-wedlock births in
Israel during the period from 1966 to 1968. Looked
for variations in birth by selected socio-demographic
variables associated with immigration patterns and
origin groups. The findings indicate that the
relationship between the variables and out-of-wedlock
births are complicated by various factors.

277. Goldscheider, Calvin. "Socio-Economic Status and
     Jewish Fertility." *Jewish Journal of Sociology*
     7 (1965): 221-37.

     A sociological study of the relationship between
     socio-economic status and fertility among Jews in the
     United States. Among first-generation Jews it was
     hypothesized that people with most education and the
     highest status occupations had lowest fertility and
     the data collected confirm this hypothesis. This
     inverse relationship does not characterize more
     recent generations. It is difficult to prove a
     direct relationship between socio-economic status
     and Jewish fertility in the next generations. An
     alternative framework for the explanation of Jewish
     fertility may be an analysis of the social-
     psychological implications of minority status of
     Jews; their cultural values, and more broadly the
     changing nature of social structure in the process
     of acculturation.

278. Goldstein, Elyse M. "Take Back the Waters. A
     Feminist Reappropriation of Mikvah." *Lilith*,
     no. 15 (Summer 1986): 15-16.

     The author, being a Reform rabbi, describes her own
     mikvah experiences. Thinks that the institution of
     mikvah by sexist interpretations has been used to
     debase women. *Mikvah* is primarily tied to
     menstruation, one type of "impurities," only for
     married women and linked to making oneself ready
     to return to sexual intercourse with the husband.
     Proposes that this ritual of immersion be redefined
     and revived.

279. Goldstein, Sidney. "Completed and Expected
     Fertility in an American Jewish Community." *Jewish
     Social Studies* 33, no. 2-3 (1971): 212-27.

280. Goldstein, Sidney, and Calvin Goldscheider. "Social
     and Demographic Aspects of Jewish Intermarriages."
     Social Problems 13, (1965): 386-99.

Asserts that the survival of a minority group is
threatened when losses to the majority through
assimilation are heavy. Intermarriage between
members of the majority and members of the minority
may contribute to the assimilation process.
Investigations in the United States have shown that
the assimilation of the Jewish group has been minor
compared to other groups. This study is based on a
random sample of 1603 households in the greater
Providence area and suggests that the extent of
intermarriages is relatively low.

281. Golomb, Deborah Grand. "The 1893 Congress of Jewish
Women: Evolution or Revolution in American Jewish
Women's History." *American Jewish History* 70
(1980): 52-67.

About the Congress of Jewish Women held in
conjunction with the World Parliament of Religions at
the World's Columbian Exposition in Chicago, 1893.
The women were predominantly Reform Jews. Many of
them had their background in social and philanthropic
activities. The congress led to the organization of
a permanent congress, the National Congress of Jewish
Women.

282. Golub, Ellen. "Honey from the Rock: The Function of
Food, the Female, and Fusion in Jewish Literature."
Ph.D. diss., State University of New York at
Buffalo, 1978. 258 pp.

The conclusion of this dissertation is that the
ambivalent desire to be both apart and a part is one
of the most important themes in the Hebrew
imagination. The people of the book are given a land
flowing with milk and honey as a reward for setting
themselves apart from others. But they are
discontented. The theme of cleavage as it recurs in
the Bible, modern American Jewish writers, and a
Yiddish play is analyzed.

283. Gordis, Robert. "Be Fruitful and Multiply--
Biography of a Mitzvah." *Midstream* 28, no. 7
(1982): 21-29.

Reviews the history of attitudes towards
procreation in Jewish culture. In the Biblical
period, polygamy was practiced, which served to
increase the number of children in the family. This
was, however, the prerogative of the royal household.
In later times the rule has been that the "blessings"
of procreation has been a *mitzvah*, an obligation
incumbent upon the Jew. Today different strategies
are proposed for increasing the Jewish birthrate.

284. Gordis, Robert. "The Jewish Concept of Marriage."
     Judaism 2 (1953): 225-38.

285. Gordis, Robert. *Love and Sex. A Modern Jewish
     Perspective.* New York: Farrar Straus Giroux,
     1978. 290 pp.

     Treats Jewish moral concepts past and present. The
     old order was the patriarchal family as the basic
     social unit. In contemporary society far-reaching
     changes are taking place. Individual freedom and the
     fulfillment of personal desires are important
     aspects. Tries to see the cultural connections
     between old and new morality. Discusses such issues
     as marriage/divorce, birth control, abortion,
     homosexuality, pre- and extramarital sexual
     relationships, and adultery. As far as women's
     status is concerned, there are many problems.
     Apologists for the tradition on the whole deny that
     women are discriminated against in the *Halakhah* or in
     life. They do not see difference in status as any
     form of discrimination. Modern feminists disagree
     with this view. They have called attention to many
     disabilities under which women labor in civil, family
     and ritual law as well as in custom. Thinks that the
     key to the contradiction lies in the gap between law
     and life.

286. Gordis, Robert. "The Ordination of Women."
     Midstream 26, no. 7 (1980): 25-32.

     The most common argument against the ordination of
     women for the rabbinate is that it is forbidden by
     the *Halakhah*. Other arguments are homiletic rather

than *Halakhic*. The strongest *Halakhic* argument is
the contention that the traditional *Halakhah*
exempted women from prayer together with the Talmudic
principle that "women are free from commandments that
must traditionally be performed at specific times."
Thinks that the objections based on the *Halakhah* are
indirect at best and farfetched at worst. The
Halakhah neither sanctions nor forbids the ordination
of women. Finds no other valid argument against
ordination and concludes that their ordination is
highly desirable and a necessary element in any
program designed to advance the health of Judaism
and strengthen the survival of the Jewish community.

287. Gordis, Robert. "The Ordination of Women: A History
      of the Question." *Judaism* 33 (1984): 6-12.

288. Gordis, Robert, ed. "Women as Rabbis: A Many-Sided
      Examination of All Aspects--Halakhic, Ethical,
      Pragmatic." *Judaism* 33 (1984): 6-90.

289. Gordis, Robert. *Sex and the Family in the Jewish
      Tradition*. Jeffersonville, Pa.: The Burning Bush
      Press, 1967. 64 pp.

290. Goshen-Gottstein, Esther R. "Treatment of Young
      Children among Nonwestern Jewish Mothers in Israel:
      Sociocultural Variables." *American Journal of
      Orthopsychiatry* 50 (1980): 323-40.

      A comparison between foreign-born mothers of
      Oriental origin and foreign-born mothers of Western
      origin showing that the first group engaged in fewer
      of the childrearing practices accepted as normal by
      Western social scientists than the second group. The
      first group was found to be more "compulsive" and
      "disorganized." Differences in cultural and
      educational background are used as an explanation for
      this.

291. Gottlieb, Freema. "Three Mothers." *Judaism* 30
      (1981): 194-203.

An analytical interpretation of the conflict in the
consciousness of Deborah, the prophetess, in her role
as national "Mother."

292. Gottlieb, Lynn. "The Secret Jew. An Oral Tradition
      of Women." In *On Being a Jewish Feminist. A
      Reader*, edited by Susannah Heschel, 273-77.
      New York: Schocken Books, 1983 (Reprint from
      Conservative Judaism 30, no. 3 [1976]: 59-62).

      About the Marrano communities during the
      Inquisition. The women of the Marrano communities
      thought of themselves as Queen Esther, living a
      secret existence very different from the reality
      perceived by the outside world. *The Secret Jew*,
      a prayer to Esther, was written to let a voice of
      the past speak to the present.

293. Gottlieb, Lynn. "Spring Cleaning Ritual on the Eve
      of Full Moon Nisan." In *On Being a Jewish
      Feminist. A Reader*, edited by Susannah Heschel,
      278-80. New York: Schocken Books, 1983 (Reprint
      from *Response*, no. 41-42 [1982]: 29-31).

      About a ritual used in the ceremony which unites
      the spring celebration of Passover and the removing
      of the *hametz* (winter) from one's physical and
      spiritual house.

294. Gradwohl, Rebecca J. "The Jewess in San Francisco--
      1896." *Western States Jewish Historical Quarterly*
      6 (1974): 273-76.

      About some of the outstanding Jewish women of San
      Francisco engaged in charities and other societies.

295. Granatstein, Melvin. "Why I Won't Rupture My
      Daughter's Hymen. Reflections on Mary Gendler's
      'New Ritual for Women.'" *Response*, no. 26 (1975):
      107-17.

      (See 246 and 247).

296. Green, Arthur. "Bride, Spouse, Daughter. Images of
     the Feminine in Classical Jewish Sources." In *On*
     Being a Jewish Feminist. A Reader, edited by
     Susannah Heschel, 248-60. New York: Schocken
     Books, 1983.

     Tries to look for sources for images of the
     feminine in Jewish religious literature. Puts the
     question if it is only women who are in need of
     feminine imagery and if images of the divine feminine
     belong only to women. Points to the Kabbalah where a
     female component of divinity is given place, often
     named *shekhinah*, which symbolizes the feminine
     principle of God immanent in the world. Maintains
     that the establishment of a truly feminine and truly
     Jewish spirituality is one of the urgent tasks of
     our age.

297. Green, Kathy. "One Woman's Religious Concerns within
     Heterodoxy." *Response*, no. 18 (1973): 19-23.

     An attempt to formulate a "Jewish-feminist
     theology."

298. Greenberg, Blu. "Abortion: A Challenge to Halakhah."
     Judaism 25 (1976): 201-8.

299. Greenberg, Blu. "Feminism: Is It Good for the Jews?"
     In *A Coat of Many Colors. Jewish Subcommunities in*
     the United States, edited by Abraham D. Lavender,
     263-71. Westport: Greenwood Press, 1977.

     Finds feminism extremely important, with a positive
     relationship between the Women's Movement and
     traditional Jewish values. They need each other.
     On the whole Jewish tradition has been and is
     suspicious of feminist ideology. Asserts that what
     is needed today is a dialectical tension between
     Jewish values and "the mores of modern society in
     light of the far-reaching implications of Women's
     Liberation." Mentions four areas in Jewish life
     where the goals of feminism can be applied in a
     dialectical fashion: in the synagogue; in Jewish
     education; in the religious courts; and in communal
     leadership.

300. Greenberg, Blu. "Jewish Women: Coming of Age."
      Tradition 16, no. 4 (1977): 79-94.

301. Greenberg, Blu. "Judaism and Feminism." In *The
      Jewish Woman: New Perspectives*, edited by Elizabeth
      Koltun, 179-92. New York: Schocken Books, 1976.

302. Greenberg, Blu. "Marriage in the Jewish Tradition."
      Journal of Ecumenical Studies 22 (1985): 3-20.

      A description of different aspects of marriage in
      Jewish tradition. "Judaism teaches that marriage is
      good, very good; that it is the Jewish way." Starts
      with the written sources and describes the
      obligations of marriage, the wedding ceremony and
      the functions of marriage in society. Also discusses
      intermarriage, divorce, and how to deal with sexism.
      Tradition has much of value to teach, including
      something important about role distinctiveness in
      male/female relationships but Jewish divorce law is
      unequivocally sexist. Jewish law must undergo
      reinterpretation in order to eliminate potential
      abuse and to incorporate the principle of equity in
      Jewish divorce proceedings.

303. Greenberg, Blu. *On Women and Judaism: A View from
      Tradition*. Philadelphia: Jewish Publication
      Society of America, 1981. 178 pp.

      Finds many problems in being a feminist and an
      Orthodox Jew. It is difficult to reconcile the
      values of Jewish tradition and modern feminism.

304. Greenberg, Blu. "Will There be Orthodox Women
      Rabbis?" *Judaism* 33 (1984): 23-33.

305. Greenberg, C. "Textbook Treatments of the Roles of
      Ritual and Women in Judaism." *Jewish Social
      Studies* 46 (1984): 73-82.

306. Greenburg, Dan. *How to be a Jewish Mother*. Los Angeles: Price, Stern, Sloan Pubs., Inc., 1965.

307. Greenfield, Gloria Z. "Shedding." In *Nice Jewish Girls. A Lesbian Anthology*, edited by Evelyn Torton Beck, 5-27. Trumansburg, N.Y.: The Crossing Press, 1982.

A diary from a journey to Europe. The purpose of the journey was to research the escalation of anti-Semitism throughout history and in our time.

308. Greengus, Samuel. "Sisterhood Adoption at Nuzi and the 'Wife-Sister' in Genesis." *Hebrew Union College Annual* 46 (1975): 5-31.

A discussion of similarities between Biblical and Nuzi cultural traditions, particularly with respect to marriages augmented by sisterhood adoption.

309. Gronau, Reuben. "The Allocation of Time of Israeli Women." *Journal of Political Economy* 84 (1976): 201-20.

This paper is based on the author's study "Israeli Married Women: An Economist's Point of View," conducted at the Falk Institute, Jerusalem, and the National Bureau of Economic Research, New York. It discusses the factors affecting the family's allocation of time. This is followed by a brief reexamination of married women's pattern of labor force participation and a discussion of their allocation of time in the home sector. The study ends with a comparison of the Israeli and the U.S. experience.

310. Gross, David C. *Pride of Our People: The Stories of One Hundred Outstanding Jewish Men and Women*. New York: Doubleday, 1979. 448 pp.

311. Gross, Rita M., ed. *Beyond Androcentrism. New Essays on Women and Religion*. American Academy of

Religion's Aids for the Study of Religions, no. 6.
Missoula, Mont.: Scholars Press, 1977. 345 pp.

312.   Gross, Rita. "On Being a Religious Jewish Woman."
       Anima 1, no. 1 (1974): 22-32.

       The starting point is being a female human being,
       scholar of religions, religious, and Jewish. Tries
       on this background to understand woman's role in
       Judaism and her own frustration with that role.
       Makes a distinction between two modes of self-concept
       for a person: a relational and an essential one.
       The relational mode emphasizes one's existence in
       relation to other people: one exists because of and
       for the sake of others. In the essential mode the
       stress is much more on what one is in one's own
       right. In the practice of Judaism only the
       relational mode is fully available to women. Asserts
       that women in Judaism are defined primarily as wives
       and mothers, and the synagogues are not available to
       them. One mode is not enough for a meaningful human
       life. And women are not able to live out their
       Jewishness in the essential mode as well as in the
       relational mode.

313.   Gross, Rita M. "Steps toward Feminine Imagery of
       Deity in Jewish Theology." In *On Being a Jewish
       Feminist. A Reader*, edited by Susannah Heschel,
       234-47. New York: Schocken Books, 1983 (Reprint
       from *Judaism* 30 [1981]: 183-93).

       Asserts that we need a Goddess to break stereotypes
       of the feminine and thus free women from the
       limitations of that stereotype. Besides, a Goddess
       completes the image of God and brings wholeness.
       Dimensions of deity have been lost or attenuated
       during the centuries when God was only male: such
       dimensions as acceptance and immanence in contrast
       to intervention and transcendence; nature and cyclic
       round in contrast to history and linear time.
       Indicates that God, as well as women, has been
       imprisoned in patriarchal imagery.

314. Grossman, Edward. "An Interview with Shulamit
     Aloni." *Response*, no. 21 (1974): 21-31.

315. Grossman, Lawrence. *The Pornography Issue: A Jewish
     View*. New York: American Jewish Committee.
     Institute of Human Relations, 1984. 21 pp.

     A discussion of the Jewish view on pornography.
     Pornography and the Jewish tradition are
     incompatible. The key issue in pornography is not
     sexuality but objectification, dehumanization, and
     exploitation of others. Judaism is not hostile to
     sexuality.

316. Gutmann, David. "Men, Women, and the Parental
     Imperative." *Commentary* 56, no. 6 (1973):
     59-64.

     Discusses two books, written by Steven Goldberg and
     George Gilder. Both books attack Women's Liberation.
     Sees them as a sample of the potential masculinist
     counterattack to Women's Lib. and the sentiments in
     the silent male majority. Asserts that most men who
     have written on the women's movement in the recent
     years (the early seventies) have praised it.

317. Hackett, Jo Ann. "In the Days of Jael: Reclaiming
     the History of Women in Ancient Israel." In
     *Immaculate and Powerful: The Female in Sacred Image
     and Social Reality*, edited by Clarissa W. Atkinson,
     Constance H. Buchanan, and Margaret R. Miles,
     15-38. Boston: Beacon Press, 1985.

318. Halpérin, Jean, and Georges Lévitte, eds. *L'autre
     dans la conscience Juive. Le sacré et le couple.
     Données et débats*. Paris: Presses Universitaires
     de France, 1973. 336 pp.

     Essays from a congress by La Section Française du
     Congrès Juif Mondial. Mostly about the question of
     desacralization and much about women.

319. Hanna. "The Independent Woman." *Response*, no. 18
      (Summer 1973): 176-77.

      Some reflections on how difficult it is to be both
      a housewife and a working woman. "Crumbling under
      the double yoke--her job and her family."

320. Hanson, Paul D. "Masculine Metaphors for God and
      Sex-discrimination in the Old Testament."
      Ecumenical Review 27 (1975): 316-24.

      Asserts that the dominance of the male metaphor in
      designations of the deity is no historical accident
      of indifference in the discussion of sex-
      discrimination in Biblical religion. It is a product
      of a patriarchal society. These metaphors have been
      taken up by contemporary males in a systematic
      discrimination of women. To some women, he says, it
      is inevitable that the masculine metaphors are a
      tremendous obstacle to worship and appreciation of
      Biblical tradition.

321. Hapgood, Hutchins. "The Old and the New Woman."
      Chap. 3 in *The Spirit of the Ghetto: Studies of the
      Jewish Quarter of New York*. New York: Funk and
      Wagnalls, 1965. 300 pp.

      A study of Lower East Side Jewish women immigrants
      in New York.

322. Harman, Zena. "Israel." In *Women in the Modern
      World*, edited by Raphael Patai, 267-89. New York:
      The Free Press, 1967.

      Stresses the fact that most Israeli women are
      immigrants and members of a society which is in
      constant development. Asserts that they are greatly
      influenced by the societies from which they have come
      and discusses how this affects their accommodation to
      the new society.

323. Harris, Monford. "Marriage as Metaphysics. A Study
of the *'Iggereth Hakodesh.*" *Hebrew Union College
Annual* 33 (1962): 197-220.

    'Iggereth Hakodesh is a work from the thirteenth
    century Spanish community. It is a treatise devoted
    completely to the mystical understanding of marriage
    usually attributed to Moses Maimonides. It purports
    to be a personal letter written for the education and
    edification of a young man. The letter is written on
    two levels, exoteric and esoteric, and treats marital
    intercourse and reproduction as a vehicle for
    metaphysical teaching.

324. Hartman, Moshe, and William F. Stinner. "International Migration and Labor Force Participation
of Married Women." *Population and Environment* 5
(1982): 123-36.

    An analysis of native-born and immigrant Jewish,
    urban, married females in the Israeli labor force.
    The impact of education, socioeconomic status, ethnic
    origin, and childcare burdens on women's labor force
    participation is investigated.

325. Hartman, Moshe. "The Role of Ethnicity in Married
Women's Economic Activity in Israel." *Ethnicity* 7
(1980): 225-55.

    An analysis of the effect of ethnicity on labor
    force participation by Israeli married women.
    Factors such as ethnic origin, length of residence in
    Israel, education, number of children, the age of the
    children, and husband's occupation were examined.

326. Harvey, Warren Z. "The Obligation of Talmud on Women
According to Maimonides." *Tradition* 19 (1981):
122-30.

327. Hauptman, Judith. "Images of Women in the Talmud."
In *Religion and Sexism. Images of Woman in the
Jewish and Christian Traditions,* edited by Rosemary

Radford Ruether, 184-212. New York: Simon and
Schuster, 1974.

An attempt to elicit from the Talmud material the
rabbinic attitudes toward women; their legal and
social status, their role in life, and their most
common characteristics. Analyzes the different
aspects of women's life as it is regulated by
rabbinic legislation: betrothal, marriage, divorce
laws, women and commandments, civil and criminal law,
laws of inheritance etc. Concludes that the rabbis
view women's foremost tasks as caring for husband,
children, and home; always dependent on a man, be it
the father, husband, or son. Given this framework,
the rabbis endeavor to evolve specific ethical
guidelines for the treatment of women. Careful not
to erode man's dominant position, they attempt to
secure the greatest possible good for women. Their
most intense concern is for the least fortunate
woman, the orphan, the divorcée, and the widow.

328. Hauptman, Judith. "Women in the Talmud." *Response*,
     no. 18 (Summer 1973): 161-65.

     According to Talmud, women are light-headed,
     emotional, prone to gossip, and incapable of serious
     study. Asserts that they were taught to accept a
     nurturing role in life, to be soft, compassionate,
     supportive, self-sacrificing, and docile. In spite
     of this there are several stories of women who
     bucked the tradition and asserted themselves,
     speaking out, using their minds to solve life's
     problems and contradict their male leaders.

329. Haut, Irwin H. *Divorce in Jewish Law and Life*.
     Studies in Jewish Jurisprudence, vol. 5. New York:
     Sepher-Hermon Pr., 1983. 146 pp.

330. Hazleton, Lesley. Israeli Women. *The Reality behind
     the Myths*. New York: Simon and Schuster, 1977.
     235 pp.

     Asserts that the majority of Israeli women live by
     myths and tries to find out how these myths were born

and how they endure and persist. The myths give the image of the liberated Israeli woman. In reality Israeli women have chosen femininity instead of feminism and liberation. They are more interested in security than independence. The stereotypes in sexual relationships and the persistence of the myth of women's liberation are obstacles to true equality between the sexes.

331. Hazleton, Lesley. "Israeli Women. Three Myths." In *On Being a Jewish Feminist. A Reader*, edited by Susannah Heschel, 65-87. New York: Schocken Books, 1983.

An attack on the myth of the liberation of Israeli women. The ideology of sexual equality was stated in 1948 in Israel's Declaration of Independence, but the contradiction between ideology and reality is great. Women's participation in public life is minimal and their average annual income is 60 percent of men's. In academic and government service, women's representation is pyramidal, with many women at the bottom of the ladder and few or none at the top.

332. Hecht, Dina, and Nira Yuval-Davis. "Ideology without Revolution: Jewish Women in Israel." *Khamsin* 6 (1978): 97-117.

About the contradiction between the export image of Israel: women conscripts, women in the Kibbutz, a woman prime minister, i.e., the myth of the equal, liberated, and emancipated Israeli woman, and the actual situation. Describes women's status in Israel from the early colonization period to the present time, with reference to Zionist ideology.

333. Heinemann, Marlene Eve. "Women Prose Writers of the Nazi Holocaust." Ph.D. diss., Indiana University, 1982. 325 pp.

A study on themes, modes of characterization, and authenticating strategies in two novels and four fictionalized memoirs about the Nazi Holocaust.

334. Henry, Sondra, and Emily Taitz. *Written out of*
      History: A Hidden Legacy of Jewish Women Revealed
      Through Their Writings and Letters. New York:
      Bloch Pub. Co., 1978. 293 pp.

335. Hertz, Deborah. "Salonieres and Literary Women in
      Late Eighteenth-Century Berlin." *New German*
      Critique 14 (1978): 97-108.

      Describes the relationship between sex, cultural
      sphere, and social/religious origin and inclusion in
      the *salonieres* in eighteenth-century Berlin where the
      participation of Jewish women was very high.

336. Heschel, Susannah, ed. *On Being a Jewish Feminist.*
      A Reader. New York: Schocken Books, 1983. 288 pp.

      An anthology consisting of twenty-four articles by
      different authors. It represents current thinking of
      Jewish feminists on problems they face as women and
      Jews.

337. Higgins, Jean M. "Anastasius Sinaita and the
      Superiority of the Woman." *Journal of Biblical*
      Literature 97 (1978): 253-56.

      About different interpretations of the temptation
      scene in Gen. 3:1-6. Most interpreters understand it
      as an instance of woman's weakness. The text shows
      that woman is the stronger of the two partners. New
      interpretations influenced by feminism have argued
      this, but we also find this interpretation in the
      Irenaeus fragment XIV, appended to the standard
      editions of Irenaeus and excerpted in the
      Anagogicarum Contemplationum of Anastasius Sinaita.
      Here the woman is described as the stronger. "For
      she alone stood up to the serpent. She ate from the
      tree, but with resistance and dissent, and after
      being dealt with perfidiously. But Adam partook of
      the fruit given by the woman, without even beginning
      to make a fight, without a word of contradiction--a
      perfect demonstration of consummate weakness and a
      cowardly soul."

338. Higgins, Jean M. "The Myth of Eve: The Temptress."
     Journal of the American Academy of Religion 44
     (1976): 639-47.

     Tries to refute the exegeses of Gen. 3:6 which make
     Eve the temptress, who tempted Adam to commit the
     first sin. Asserts that Gen. 3:6 says nothing about
     any temptation of Adam by Eve. Thinks that the myth
     of Eve the temptress reflects each commentator's own
     presuppositions and cultural expectations, not the
     actual Biblical text.

339. "Highlights of a Round-Table Discussion on Women's
     Role in Israel's Development." *Kidma*, no. 7
     (2, no. 3) (1975): 35-37.

     Report from a "mini"-symposium on women's role in
     the development of Israel held by the Working Women's
     Council of the *Histadrut*, Israel's General Federation
     of Labour. The participants discussed such subjects
     as: women in the Kibbutzim, women and economy, women
     in public life and in Israel society, and women and
     the defense forces. The work for better
     opportunities should primarily be women's own
     struggle.

340. Hoch-Smith, Judith, and Anita Spring, eds. *Women in
     Ritual and Symbolic Roles.* New York and London:
     Plenum Press, 1978. 289 pp.

     This volume of essays grew out of a symposium for
     the 1974 American Anthropological Meeting.

341. Hochman, Judith Whitman. "An Exploratory
     Investigation into the Nature of the Adult Years
     in the Life Cycle of a Selected Group of Married
     Jewish Women." Ed.D. diss., Temple University,
     1984. 421 pp.

     In this study the adult life cycles of nine married
     Jewish women were compared to the life cycles of men
     in a study conducted by Yale psychologist, Daniel
     Levinson. The focus of the study was on the role of
     religion and ethnicity in the subjects' lives during

their preadulthood and adulthood. Concludes that the
underlying universal patterns of the lives of men and
women are similar but details are different.

342. Holladay, William L. "Jeremiah and Women's
     Liberation." *Andover Newton Quarterly* 12 (1972):
     213-23.

     Points out that the title of the article is no
     joke. Proposes to direct attention to Jer. 31:21-22,
     which has been object of misunderstanding and
     puzzlement almost from the days of Jeremiah. The
     exegesis offered in this article hopes to throw some
     light on contemporary debate concerning the relation
     between the sexes. The last words of v. 22 have
     caused most puzzlement. Here the following
     translation is used: "For the Lord has created a new
     thing on the earth: a woman protects a man."
     Discusses different exegesis. His own lays stress
     on the use of "femaleness" in v. 22.

343. Horner, Thomas Marland. "Ruth and Naomi." In
     *Jonathan Loved David: Homosexuality in Biblical
     Times*, 40-46. Philadelphia: Westminster Press,
     1978.

     A discussion of the love between Ruth and Naomi.
     Suggests that it might be more than just spiritual.

344. Hornik, Edith Lynn. "The Jewish Drinking Woman."
     In *The Drinking Woman*, 105-11. New York:
     Association Press, 1977.

345. Horowitz, Maryanne Cline. "The Image of God in Man:
     Is Woman Included?" *Harvard Theological Review* 72
     (1979): 175-206.

     A discussion of Gen. 1:26-27 and some of the
     interpretations. The term *adam* here obviously is a
     generic term for men and women. Asserts that the
     translation of *adam* as "man" and the question "is
     woman included in the image of God as man?" proceeds
     from androcentrism, the masculine perspective of

viewing the male human being as generic and
normative. Throughout the ages different exegesis
have given different interpretations as to whether
woman is created in God's image or not. Focuses on
literature from ancient and early medieval period of
Western thought because this period provided the
major texts for later exegesis of the Bible and
because she wants to show that there is a usable
tradition for women within the Judao-Christian
heritage.

346. Horvitz, Eleanor F. "The Jewish Woman Liberated:
     A History of the Ladies' Hebrew Free Loan
     Association." *Rhode Island Jewish Historical
     Notes*, no. 7 (1978): 501-12.

     The Ladies' Hebrew Free Loan Association (LHFLA)
     was established in 1931 to provide a loan fund for
     Jewish women. There already existed such an
     association for men. LHFLA was disbanded in 1965.

347. Horvitz, Eleanor F. "Marion L. Misch: An
     Extraordinary Woman." *Rhode Island Jewish
     Historical Notes*, no. 8 (1980): 7-65.

     About Marion L. Misch (1869-1914), an outstanding
     Jewish businesswoman, suffragette, educator, and
     world traveler.

348. Horvitz, Eleanor F. "The Years of the Jewish Woman."
     Rhode Island Jewish Historical Notes, no. 7
     (1975): 152-70.

     About various benevolent organizations established
     by Jewish women in Rhode Island from ca. 1877 to
     1975.

349. Horwitz, Shelley. "Letter from Jerusalem." In *Nice
     Jewish Girls. A Lesbian Anthology*, edited by
     Evelyn Torton Beck, 196-200. Trumansburg, N.Y.:
     The Crossing Press, 1982.

A letter to a friend from an American-born lesbian
feminist activist in Israel. Much about how she is
looked upon by feminists from America and Europe,
especially because she defines herself as a Zionist.

350. Hoz, Ron, and Mordecai Nisan. "The Effects of the
     Yom Kippur War on Values of Israeli Female
     Students." *Journal of Youth and Adolescence* 8
     (1979): 161-69.

     Research on value changes. The effects of the Yom
     Kippur war have been likened by the mass media to the
     impact of an "earthquake."

351. Hunter, Jean E. "Images of Women." *Journal of
     Social Issues* 32, no. 3 (1976): 7-17.

     An analysis of social attitudes toward women in
     several cultures, including the Jewish culture.
     Three dominant images were found: 1) women as
     inferior to men, 2) women as evil (leading men into
     sin), and 3) women as love objects.

352. Hyman, Frieda Clark. "Women of the Bible." *Judaism*
     5 (1956): 338-47.

353. Hyman, Paula E. "Immigrant Women and Consumer
     Protest: The New York City Kosher Meat Boycott of
     1902." *American Jewish History* 70 (1980): 91-105.

     A study of boycott activists during the May 1902
     kosher meat riots in New York City. These women
     displayed a sharp understanding of consumer power,
     political rhetoric, and had a clear political
     strategy for their actions.

354. Hyman, Paula. "Is It Kosher To Be a Feminist?"
     Ms. Magazine 3, no. 1 (1974): 76-79.

     Considers the status of Jewish women in marriage
     and family life. Asserts that in many respects the
     situation has not changed much since the days when

Talmud was written in the first centuries A.D. Jewish women still suffer from the consequences of the patriarchal worldview of the rabbinic tradition whenever they come into contact with traditional law and customs. Tells about the first steps of the Jewish feminist movement, which works for legal and ritual changes within Judaism and to redress the ceremonial imbalance and age-old sexism by developing meaningful rituals celebrating the birth and maturation of girls and by drawing up non-sexist curricula for all levels of Jewish education.

355. Hyman, Paula. "The Jewish Family. Looking for a Usable Past." In *On Being a Jewish Feminist. A Reader*, edited by Susannah Heschel, 19-26. New York: Schocken Books, 1983 (Reprint from *Congress Monthly* 42, no. 8 [1975]: 10-15).

Asserts that myth-making about the Jewish family, especially the woman, has become a preoccupation of the contemporary society. One myth is that the Jewish family has preserved the Jews and Judaism. Another is the suggestion that the Jewish woman has always played the central role in transmitting Judaism to her children, i.e., Jewish woman is supposed to have been the culture bearer within Judaism as mother and teacher for her children. Warns against the assumption that the transmission of Jewish culture lies in cleaning the house, baking *hallah*, lighting candles, and raising children. The Jewish working mother has a long and noble history which modern women should emulate.

356. Hyman, Paula E. "The Other Half: Women in the Jewish Tradition." *Response*, no. 18 (Summer 1973): 67-75.

Account of Jewish women trying to enforce the ideals of the women's movement within Judaism. Jewish feminists do not seek apologetics but change based on acknowledgement of the ways in which the Jewish tradition has excluded women from entire spheres of Jewish experience and has considered them intellectually and spiritually inferior to men.

357. Hyman, Paula. "The Other Half: Women in the Jewish
      Tradition." In *The Jewish Woman: New Perspectives*,
      edited by Elizabeth Koltun, 105-13. New York:
      Schocken Books, 1976 (Reprint from *Conservative
      Judaism* [Summer 1972]).

358. Ichilov, Orit, and Shmuel Bar. "Extended Family Ties
      and the Allocation of Social Rewards in Veteran
      Kibbutzim in Israel." *Journal of Marriage and the
      Family* 42 (1980): 421-26.

      Data for this examination were collected from four
      veteran kibbutzim for the period 1969-74 and show
      that in two of the kibbutzim members of extended
      families are in an advantageous position, while in
      the other two, they are not.

359. Ichilov, Orit, and Bracha Rubineck. "The Relation-
      ship between Girls' Attitudes Concerning the Family
      and Their Perception of the Patterns Existing in
      the Family of Origin." *Journal of Marriage and
      the Family* 39 (1977): 417-22.

      The attitudes of sixteen- to eighteen-year-old pupils
      at a training center of the Woman's Labor Council and
      the Ministry of Labor are examined in this study.
      The study examines the relationship between lower-
      class Israeli girls' perceptions of various patterns
      in their families of origin and their attitudes
      concerning desirable patterns in their future
      families. All the girls came from families of Asian
      and African origin.

360. Ide, Arthur Frederick. *Jews, Jesus and Woman in the
      Apostolic Age.* Women in History Series, vol. 8 B.
      Mesquite, Tex.: Ide House, 1984. 115 pp.

361. Ide, Arthur Frederick. *Woman in Ancient Israel
      under the Torah and Talmud with a Translation and
      Critical Commentary on Genesis 1-3.* Women in
      History Series, vol. 5 B. Mesquite, Tex.: Ide
      House, 1982. 84 pp.

A description of woman as viewed by Genesis 1-3 and
the Talmud, containing chapters on the status of
women without children, women and work, adultery, and
Rosh Hadesh, the woman's holiday.

362. Israel Information Centre, publ. *Women in Israel.*
      Special Edition of *Features of Israel*, no. 24.
      Tel Aviv, 1975. 74 pp.

363. Israeli, Dafna N. "Sex Structure of Occupations: The
      Israeli Experience." *Sociology of Work and
      Occupations* 6 (1979): 404-29.

      A comparison between female participation in
      occupational life in Israel and the United States
      which indicates that in both countries females tend
      to be concentrated in a small number of occupations--
      the traditional occupations for women.

364. Israeli, Dafna N. "The Zionist Women's Movement in
      Palestine, 1911-1927. A Sociological Analysis."
      Signs 7 (1981): 87-114.

      The Zionist women's movement was started because
      women felt they had a too limited role in the
      movement. Their aim was to work for women's rights
      and secure full participation in building the state
      of Israel. Describes and analyses the movement from
      its beginning in 1911 up to 1927--how it became a
      separate part of the socialist movement. Asserts
      that this movement "helped to perpetuate the myth
      of equality and to discourage the emergence of
      alternative definitions around which women could
      organize."

365. Jacob, Edmond. "Féminisme ou Messianisme? A propos
      de Jérémie 31:22." In *Beiträge zur
      Alttestamentlichen Theologie. Festschrift für
      Walther Zimmerli zum 70. Geburtstag*, edited by
      H. Donner, 179-84. Göttingen: Vandenhoeck und
      Ruprecht, 1977.

Jeremiah 31:22 is one of the verses in the Old
Testament which says something about the female-male
relationship, and there has been much disagreement
about the translation and interpretation. Against
this background, Jacob discusses this verse asking
"feminism or Messianism?"

366. Jacobs, Louis. *A Tree of Life. Diversity,*
      Flexibility, and Creativity in Jewish Law.
      New York: Oxford University Press, 1984. 310 pp.

      Discusses many of the laws relating to sexuality
      and finds much injustice regarding women. Looks at
      the history of these laws and finds that they have
      undergone many changes as sexual mores have changed
      in particular times and places.

367. Jacobs, Louis. "Woman." In *Encyclopedia Judaica*,
      vol. 16, 623-27. Jerusalem: Keter Publishing
      House, 1971.

      Describes the status of women and the attitudes
      toward women in the classical writings of Judaism.

368. Jacoby, Susan. "World of Our Mothers: Immigrant
      Women, Immigrant Daughters." *Present Tense* 6,
      no. 3 (1979): 48-51.

      Thinks that the immigrant women of past generations
      have been uniformly neglected in literature. Finds
      the autobiographical novels of Anzia Yezierska,
      published between 1920 and 1932, to be probably the
      most significant primary source of information about
      the conflict between American-educated Jewish
      immigrant daughters and their parent. Mentions other
      writers who have written on the role of immigrant
      Jewish women in the United States. These books have
      enjoyed a modest revival as a result of the current
      feminist interest in the hidden history of immigrant
      women.

369. Jakobovits, Immanuel. "Jewish Views on Abortion."
      Child and Family 7 (1968): 142-56.

A discussion of the Jewish view on abortion based
on Biblical writings, Talmud, and contemporary
scholars. Concludes that only the safety of the
mother is a valid reason for an abortion.

370. Jakobovits, Immanuel. *Order of the Jewish Marriage
Service.* New York: Bloch, 1959. 23 pp.

371. James, Janet Wilson. "Women and Religion: An
Introduction." *American Quarterly* 30 (1978):
579-81.

An investigation of the status of women in
Protestantism, Catholicism, and Judaism. Stresses
the following paradox: women outnumber men, but men
have the authority.

372. Janait, Rachel. "Stages." In *The Jewish Woman: New
Perspectives,* edited by Elizabeth Koltun, 171-75.
New York: Schocken Books, 1976 (Reprinted and
slightly abridged from *The Plough Woman: Records
of the Pioneer Women of Palestine,* edited by Rachel
Katznelson-Rubashow. New York: Herzl Press, 1975).

About women workers.

373. Jankélévitch, Vladimir. "Prochaine et lointaine, la
femme...." In *L'autre dans la conscience Juive.
Le sacré et le couple. Données et débats,* edited
by Jean Halpérin and Georges Lévitte, 159-63.
Paris: Presses Universitaires de France, 1973.

Asserts that woman is no appendix to man; neither
is she a complement to nor a duplicate of him. The
feminine is not an extract of masculinity. Woman is
like man, though different.

374. Jochnowitz, George. " ... Who Made Me a Woman."
Commentary 71, no. 4 (1981): 63-64.

One of the best well-known blessings in Judaism is
the following: "Blessed Thou, O Lord Our God, King of

the Universe, who did not make me a woman." Women
have another type of blessing. They bless God "who
made me according to His will." The author has
discovered one exception: Roth manuscript 32, a
fourteenth- or fifteenth-century translation of the
daily prayers into *Shuadit*, which was the language of
the Jews of Southern France until the early
nineteenth century. This blessing ends with the
words: "Blessed art Thou ... who made me a woman."
Has tried to find parallels in other prayerbooks but
has found none.

375. Johnson, George E. "Halakha and Women's Liberation."
      Midstream 20, no. 1 (1974): 58-61.

      Young Jewish feminist women have focused on the
      Halakha. They reject traditional role models and
      traditional relationships such as marriage and family
      life. They demand change in the *Halakha*, challenging
      the position of women in Jewish law. Emphasizes that
      the feminists' protest against traditional
      conceptions of legal and social relationships affords
      an excellent opportunity for American Jews to engage
      each other in a redefinition of the significance of
      the Jewish tradition.

376. Jones, Bruce William. "Two Misconceptions About the
      Book of Esther." *Catholic Biblical Quarterly* 39
      (1977): 171-81.

      Asserts that the Book of Esther has been regarded
      with hostility by Christians because of its apparent
      cruelty and Jewish nationalism and also by liberated
      women because of the chauvinistic attitude toward
      women which they perceive. Tries to show that these
      attitudes are misguided. The objections stem from
      the fact that they have not given sufficient
      attention to the humorous nature of the book.

377. Jordan, William Chester. "Jews on Top: Women and the
      Availability of Consumption Loans in Northern
      France in the Mid-Thirteenth Century." *Journal of
      Jewish Studies* 29 (1978): 39-56.

378. Jospe, Raphael. "Status of Women in Judaism: From Exemption to Exclusion." *Iliff Review* 35 (1978): 29-39.

Examines some passages of the Bible which treat women as the equals of men and some which imply that women are men's inferiors. Thinks that in rabbinic *Halakhah* this ambiguity was preserved. Is optimistic regarding possibilities for an improvement of women's status within the existing *Halakhah*.

379. Jung, Leo. *Love and Life*. New York: Philosophical Library, 1979. 24 pp.

Essays on women in Judaism.

380. Kahan, Hazel. "Women's Liberation--An Israeli Perspective." *New Outlook* 16 (June 1973): 21-26, continued on page 19.

Discusses the question of whether there is any need for a women's liberation movement in Israel. Do women in the army, a female Prime Minister, and a theory of sexual equality in the kibbutzim mean that there is complete equality between the sexes? Thinks that there is a need for women's liberation groups in Israel and that they should originate in the special needs of the country, its history and institutions. Many changes can be achieved by legislation, but it is also important to change women's consciousness, for example, through consciousness-raising groups.

381. Kahana, Kalman. *Daughter of Israel. Laws of Family Purity*. Jerusalem and New York: Feldheim Publ., 1970. 136 pp.

About ceremonial purity in Jewish law. Hebrew and English on opposite pages.

382. Kahana, Kalman. *The Theory of Marriage in Jewish Law*. Leiden: Brill, 1966. 99 pp.

A discussion of women's status in marriage based on
the old Jewish law. According to the author, Jewish
marriage law is not a matter of doctrine but embodies
social and moral concepts of the highest order.

383. Kahanoff, Jacqueline. "Independence." In *Women in
     Israel*, published by Israel Information Centre,
     32-36. Tel Aviv, 1975 (Previously published in
     Dvar Hapoelet).

Claims that women's liberation is only beginning to
affect Israel. In vocational training, for example,
Israel is conservative if not reactionary. For years
vocational schools have trained girls in home
economics, secretarial work, sewing, and hair
dressing. "Masculine" professions like electronics
and technology were inaccessible to women. Women
often feel ashamed at being attracted to "masculine"
professions. States the importance of women's
participation in all parts of life but emphasizes
that equal rights also mean equal burdens.

384. Kapelovitz, Abbey Poze. "Mother Images in American-
     Jewish Fiction." Ph.D. diss., University of
     Denver, 1985. 300 pp.

A study of twentieth-century American fiction by
Jewish authors. The aim of the dissertation is to
see if the image of the mother in American-Jewish
fiction varies according to the generation and the
gender of the writer. The findings show that the
mother image has changed over the century and that
she is viewed differently by male and female writers.

385. Kaplan, Marion. "Bertha Pappenheim: Founder of
     German-Jewish Feminism." In *The Jewish Woman: New
     Perspectives*, edited by Elizabeth Koltun, 149-63.
     New York: Schocken Books, 1976.

Bertha Pappenheim (1859-1936) founded the Jewish
feminist movement in Germany and led it for twenty
years (1904-24).

386. Kaplan, Marion A. "German-Jewish Feminism: The
     Jüdischer Frauenbund, 1904-1938." Ph.D. diss.,
     Columbia University, 1977. 648 pp.

     This study on the Jüdischer Frauenbund focuses upon
     the organization's aim to combine feminist goals and
     Jewish identity. The efforts of the Frauenbund were
     mainly directed toward such specifically feminist
     issues as women's suffrage and jobs for women. The
     dissertation also examines the organization's role in
     the German-Jewish community and the extent to which
     women shaped their own destinies and the extent to
     which they were constrained by circumstances.

387. Kaplan, Marion A. "German-Jewish Feminism in the
     Twentieth Century." *Jewish Social Studies* 38
     (1976): 39-53.

     One of many writings by the author on the Jüdischer
     Frauenbund (The League of Jewish Women). At the
     most, 20 percent of Germany's Jewish women were
     members of the League, mostly middle-class women.

388. Kaplan, Marion A. *The Jewish Feminist Movement in
     Germany. The Campaigns of the Jüdischer
     Frauenbund, 1904-1938.* Contributions in Women's
     Studies, no. 8. Westport, Conn.: Greenwood Press,
     1979. 229 pp.

389. Kaplan, Marion A. "Prostitution, Morality Crusades
     and Feminism: German-Jewish Feminists and the
     Campaign against White Slavery." *Women's Studies
     International Forum* 5 (1982): 619-27.

     The Jüdischer Frauenbund engaged in the struggle
     against white slavery after Bertha Pappenheim learned
     about it at a conference sponsored by the Jewish
     committee in 1902. They worked against all abuse of
     women, also sexual abuse, and tried to promote a
     higher social status for women through education,
     jobs, and legal reforms. The white slavery issue
     attracted a wide and dedicated following from the
     Jewish community, and moral outrage against white

slavery and prostitution led many religious
housewives to join the Jüdischer Frauenbund.

390. Kaplan, Marion A. "Religious Continuity and Family
      Traditions in the German Jewish Communities,
      1871-1918" ("Continuita religiosa e tradizioni
      familiari nelle communita ebraiche tedesche
      1871-1918." *Memoria* 5 (1982): 108-14.

      This Italian article treats the loss of religious
      faith and assimilation tendencies among Jews in
      Germany. Refutes the opinion that women were
      responsible for these tendencies. Asserts that even
      if Jewish women had to adapt themselves to the new
      industrial society, they were always loyal to their
      faith and family traditions.

391. Kaplan, Marion A. "Tradition and Transition: The
      Acculturation, Assimilation and Integration of
      Jews in Imperial Germany: A Gender Analysis."
      Leo Baeck Institute Year Book 27 (1982): 3-35.

      Discusses the relationship between assimilation,
      acculturation, and integration of Jews in Germany.
      Assimilation implies submersion into a majority
      culture and the loss of ethnic and religious identity
      while acculturation does not imply such a loss even
      if the person accepts many of the cultural patterns
      and customs of the majority. Jewish women avoided
      integration into German society because of
      anti-female and anti-Semitic attitudes.

392. Kaplan, Rosa Felsenburg. "The Noah Syndrome." In
      On Being a Jewish Feminist. A Reader, edited by
      Susannah Heschel, 167-70. New York: Schocken
      Books, 1983.

      A discussion of the single woman's status within
      Judaism. Her situation is difficult and has always
      been whether she is unmarried, divorced, or a widow.
      Asserts that if women are to be truly equal to men,
      they have to be included in communal activity on a
      par with men.

393. Kartagener, Manes. "Uber Spuren und Reste des Matriarchats im Judentum." *Zeitschrift für Religions- und Geistesgeschichte* 29 (1977): 134-51.

Searches for any traces of matriarchy in Judaism. Uses Bachofen as a source to look for matriarchal traits in the Old Testament. Concludes that Judaism is a strictly patriarchal culture, but there are still matriarchal traits even if they lack force.

394. Karti, Zohar. "Women in Israel's Labour Force." *Kidma* 2, no. 3 (1975): 30.

Describes the demographic structure of women in the labor force: 38 percent government and public service, 19 percent industries, 10 percent personal services, 6 percent agriculture and 27 percent miscellaneous (commerce, transport, banking).

395. Katz, Esther, and Joan M. Ringelheim. *Women Surviving: The Holocaust--Proceedings of the Conference.* Occasional Papers, no. 1. New York: The Institute for Research in History, 1983. 100 pp.

396. Katz, Jacob. "Family, Kinship, and Marriage among *Ashkenazim* in the Sixteenth to Eighteenth Centuries." *Jewish Journal of Sociology* 1 (1959): 4-22.

The term *Ashkenaz* in the Bible refers to Armenia (Gen. 10:3), but the term came to be associated with Germany in medieval rabbinic literature. However, *Ashkenazic* distinctiveness is seen to be cultural rather than geographic.

397. Katz, Raye T. "Exploring the Link Between Womanhood and the Rabbinate: Lilith Interviews the First Woman Ordained in the Conservative Movement." *Lilith*, no. 14 (Fall/Winter 1985-86): 19-24.

An interview with Rabbi Amy Eilberg, ordained by the Jewish Theological Seminary in May 1985. She is the 110th woman ordained as a rabbi by the Reform,

Reconstructionist, and now Conservative movements.
She is asked a lot of questions: why she wanted to
become a rabbi, about being a woman and a Jew, about
women and *Halakhah*, etc.

398. Katz, Ruth. "The Loneliness of Old Age." In *Jewish
      Grandmothers*, edited by Sydelle Kramer and Jenny
      Masur, 138-51. Boston: Beacon Press, 1976.

      Arrived from Poland to America in 1913. Describes
      many of the hardships of being an immigrant. Is
      also very concerned about the fear and depression of
      many old people.

399. Katzir, Yael. "Yemenite Jewish Women in Israeli
      Rural Development: Female Power versus Male
      Authority." *Economic Development and Cultural
      Change* 32 (1983): 45-61.

      An examination of women's roles in an Israeli
      cooperative *moshav* community. Previous examinations
      on rural development programs have indicated that
      they have a negative effect on females in economic
      power and social status. The present examination,
      however, shows that women achieved power and status
      through private sales of produce. The study focuses
      on fifty-nine married couples, four widows and one
      widower, all Yemeni Jews who had migrated to Israel
      in 1950.

400. Katznelson, Rivka. "Women in the Creative Arts."
      In *Women in Israel*, published by Israel Information
      Centre, 37-48. Tel Aviv, 1975 (Previously
      published in *Dvar Hapoelet*).

      Treats the role of women in literature, journalism,
      theater and film, the art of dance, painting and
      sculpture, and music.

401. Kaufman, Alan. "Rabbanit Bracha Kapach.
      Personification of *Tzedaka*." *Israel Digest* 22,
      no. 16 (1979): 9-11.

About Bracha Kapach, who came to Israel from Yemen in 1943. She spends all her time and money helping the underprivileged of Jerusalem.

402. Kaufman, Debra Renee. "Women Who Return to Orthodox Judaism. A Feminist Analysis." *Journal of Marriage and the Family* 47 (1985): 543-51.

Has the growing interest in the New Right and fundamentalist religions led to a change in women's gender roles? In this study the author tries to explore the meaning of gender-role differences by comparing and contrasting the attitudes, practices, and beliefs of fifty *baalot teshuva* women who have "returned" to Orthodoxy with some of the current theoretical perspectives in feminist scholarship. Preliminary findings of in-depth interviews with the women suggest that while the affirmation of gender difference clearly leads to a focus on femininity, mothering, and domesticity, it does not necessarily result in a reaffirmation of patriarchal values and practices.

403. Kaye-Kantrowitz, Melanie. "Some Notes on Jewish Lesbian Identity." In *Nice Jewish Girls. A Lesbian Anthology*, edited by Evelyn Torton Beck, 28-44. Trumansburg, N.Y.: The Crossing Press, 1982.

Starts with proclaiming that she does not go to *shul* and never did; does not pray, does not even know the prayers; thinks "Israel is a boiling contradiction." Describes how she experiences being a lesbian and a Jew. As a Jewish lesbian, she finds homophobia in Israel especially heartbreaking "when I consider the Nazis would have killed me for being gay as well as Jewish."

404. Kegler, Jürgen. "Debora--Erwägungen zur politischen Funktion einer Frau in einer patriarchalischen Gesellschaft." In *Frauen in der Bibel*. Vol. 2 of *Traditionen der Befreiung. Sozialgeschichtliche Bibelauslegungen*, edited by Willy Schottroff and

Wolfgang Stegemann, 37-59. München: Kaiser/
Burckhardthaus-Laetare, 1980.

What do we know about Debora? Was she a female
alibi for a patriarchal society? Was she a woman who
had adapted herself so well to male values and the
interests of men that she could fill the male role
better than man himself? These and similar questions
are asked by the author. He tries to apply a socio-
historical interpretation. Supplies a translation
and an interpretation of Judges 5.

405. Kendall, Thena. "Memories of an Orthodox Youth."
      In *On Being a Jewish Feminist. A Reader*, edited
      by Susannah Heschel, 96-104. New York: Schocken
      Books, 1983.

      A personal account of a child's and a young woman's
      experience of the discrepancies between Orthodox
      practice and Orthodox teachings as well as the
      author's inability to confront the problems of life
      in twentieth-century Britain.

406. Kenner, Zipora. "Women in the Knesset." *Israel
      Magazine* 3 (July/August 1971): 74-78.

407. Kessler, Hannah. "The Problems of Jewish Women."
      In *Deliver Us from Eve*, edited by Barbara Elizabeth
      Thiering, 63-70. Sydney: Australian Council of
      Churches. Commission on the Status of Women, 1978.

408. Kessler-Harris, Alice. "Organizing the
      Unorganizable: Three Jewish Women and Their Union."
      Labor History 17 (1976): 5-23.

      About three Jewish women organized in the Inter-
      national Ladies' Garment Workers' Union in the first
      half of the twentieth century. Claims that their
      lives reveal a persistent conflict between their
      experiences as women and their tasks as union
      officers. They were class conscious. They were not
      feminists, but they drew strength and support from
      the solidarity of women inside and outside unions.

"When their class consciousness and their
identification as women conflicted, they bowed to
tradition and threw in their lot with the working
class."

409. Kessner, Thomas, and Betty Boyd Caroli. "New
Immigrant Women at Work: Italians and Jews in
New York City, 1880-1905." *Journal of Ethnic
Studies* 5, no. 4 (1978): 19-31.

A comparison between Italian and Jewish female
immigrants in New York City. The analysis indicates
that Italian women (more than Jewish women) tended to
work more often outside of the home and did such
income-earning homework as sewing and artificial
flower-making. The next generation moved into
different occupational categories. The Italian
daughters moved upward from unskilled blue-collar to
skilled blue-collar jobs. Jewish girls started at
higher-status levels and continued to move up
rapidly in white-collar positions.

410. Key, Ellen S. *Rahel Varnagen.* Pioneers of the
Woman's Movement: An International Perspective
Series. Westport, Conn.: Hyperion Press, 1976.
312 pp. (Reprint of 1913 edition).

Biography of Rahel Varnagen (1771-1833).

411. Kidwai of Gadia, Shaikh M.H. "Woman under Judaism."
In *Women under Different Social and Religious Laws
(Buddhism, Judaism, Christianity, Islam)*, 13-16.
New Delhi: Light and Life Publ., 1978.

A short survey by a Muslim of what he regards as
the "low status" of women under Judaism.

412. Kipust, Philip Joseph. "Moral Development and Self-
Concept of Hasidic Adolescent Boys and Girls."
Ed.D. diss., Yeshiva University, 1983. 215 pp.

A comparison of Hasidically educated boys and
girls, in grades 9 and 11, as to moral development

and self-concept. One of the issues dealt with was
women's status in Orthodox Jewish education and
tradition. The findings, among other things,
supported the contention of the Orthodox Jewish
leaders that the status of women in their community,
as reflected by their self-concept and moral
development scores, is on par with that of men.

413. Klagsbrun, Francine. "Love, Sex, and Marriage."
     In *Voices of Wisdom. Jewish Ideals and Ethics for
     Everyday Living*, 87-154. New York: Pantheon Books,
     1980.

     This chapter of the book treats such subjects as
     the question of sex without marriage; the time to
     marry; a husband's obligations to his wife; what is
     to be done if a husband beats his wife; the ideal
     wife, adultery, and grounds for divorce.

414. Klein, Isaac. *"Teshuvah* on Abortion." In
     Conservative Judaism and Jewish Law, edited by
     Seymour Siegel, 257-63. New York: The Rabbinical
     Assembly, 1977.

     The author, one of the leading authorities in the
     Conservative Jewish movement, presents the
     Conservative view on abortion. Abortion is only
     permitted for therapeutic reasons.

415. Klepfisz, Irena, and Melanie Kaye-Kantrowitz, eds.
     The Tribe of Dinah: A Jewish Women's Anthology.
     Rockland, Maine: Sinister Wisdom Books, 1985.
     288 pp.

416. Knierim, Rolf. "The Role of Sexes in the Old
     Testament." *Lexington Theological Quarterly* 10,
     no. 4 (1975): 1-10.

     Emphasizes that the sexual distinctiveness has been
     laid down by God in the creation of the world as
     expressed in the two creation reports in Genesis 1
     and 2. The relation between sexes was experienced in
     three dimensions by the ancient Israelites: in the

sphere of what we call marriage (the Hebrew language
had no special word for marriage); in the sphere of
physical sexual encounter; and in the emotional and
voluntary dimension of love. Discusses these three
dimensions and where they are to be found in the Old
Testament.

417. Kobler, Franz. *Her Children Call Her Blessed: A
      Portrait of the Jewish Mother.* New York: Stephen
      Daye Press, 1955. 392 pp.

418. Kohut, Rebekah. *My Portion (An Autobiography).*
      New York: Albert and Charles Boni, 1927. 301 pp.
      (First published in 1925).

      The memoirs of Mrs. Kohut, founder of the National
      Council for Jewish Women. The autobiography presents
      a picture of Jewish life in San Francisco in the last
      part of the nineteenth century.

419. Koller-Fox, Cherie. "Women and Jewish Education."
      In *The Jewish Woman: New Perspectives*, edited by
      Elizabeth Koltun, 31-42. New York: Schocken Books,
      1976.

      In order to educate a young woman to take her place
      in society, it is necessary to find where questions
      of Jewishness and womanhood intersect. Asserts that
      the life-cycle rituals are the obvious place to look
      for such peak moments: birth, the ritual of naming,
      puberty, *bat mitzvah*, marriage, and the wedding
      ritual. Among these rituals, however, the *bat
      mitzvah* is unique, because it is the one occasion in
      Jewish life in which the girl is asked to confirm her
      personal membership in the Jewish people and to link
      her fate with theirs.

420. Kolodziej, Joyce Story. "Eliza Orzeszkowa's Feminist
      and Jewish Works in Polish and Russian Criticism."
      Ph.D. diss., Indiana University, 1975. 535 pp.

      Eliza Orzeszkowa's (1841-1910) feminist works met
      with qualified success in Poland and Russia. Works

that discussed the need for women to be trained for
gainful employment won support, but only female
critics recognized as valuable her writings in which
she treated questions of woman's rights from a
broader point of view. Her Jewish works met with
enthusiasm in both Poland and Russia.

421. Koltun, Elizabeth, ed. *The Jewish Woman: New
      Perspectives.* New York: Schocken Books, 1976.
      289 pp.

      A collection of essays written by Jewish feminists.

422. Kraemer, Ross. "Women in the Religions of the Greco-
      Roman World." *Religious Studies Review* 9 (1983):
      127-39.

      A short review of research on women in Judaism,
      pages 130-31.

423. Kramer, Sydelle, and Jenny Masur, eds. *Jewish
      Grandmothers.* Boston: Beacon Press, 1976. 256 pp.

      Personal accounts of ten Jewish women who have
      emigrated from countries in Eastern Europe to America
      between the turn of the century and the 1920s.

424. Kranzler, Gershon. "The Changing Orthodox Jewish
      Family." In *Dimensions of Orthodox Judaism*, edited
      by R. Bulka, 359-72. Hoboken, N.J.: Ktav Publ.,
      1983.

425. Krause, Corinne. *Grandmothers, Mothers and Daughters
      in Ethnic America.* New York: American Jewish
      Committee, 1978. 176 pp.

426. Krause, Corinne Azen. "Italian, Jewish, and Slavic
      Grandmothers in Pittsburgh: Their Economic Roles."
      Frontiers 2, no. 2 (1977): 18-28.

An investigation of occupation and the motivation
to work outside of the home in three generations of
Italian, Jewish, and Slavic women in Pittsburgh. It
indicates that ethnic culture influenced the
occupation of the oldest generation. However, the
motivation of all women, regardless of ethnic group,
was their own survival and the welfare of their
families.

427. Krause, Corinne Azen. "Urbanization Without
     Breakdown: Italian, Jewish, and Slavic Immigrant
     Women in Pittsburgh--1900-1945." *Journal of Urban
     History* 4 (1978): 291-306.

     This investigation, based on interviews with
     immigrant women in Pittsburgh, suggests that most of
     them adjusted remarkably well to the "cultural shock"
     of immigration.

428. Krausz, Judith. "The Role of Women in Israel's
     Development." *Kidma*, no. 7 (1975): 20-23.

     About the status of women in the beginning of the
     kibbutz movement and the early goals of the women's
     organizations and their role after the establishment
     of the state of Israel: women in the defense force;
     women at work; labor laws and social legislation; and
     the new feminist movement.

429. Krebs, Walter. "Lilith--Adams erste Frau."
     Zeitschrift für Religions- und Geistesgeschichte
     27 (1975): 141-52.

     About the queen of demons, Lilith, who in rabbinic
     literature is described as Adam's wife before God
     created Eve. Discusses literary and figurative
     representations of Lilith in different cultures
     throughout the time.

430. Kriger, Sara F., and William H. Kroes. "Child-
     rearing Attitudes of Chinese, Jewish, and
     Protestant Mothers." *Journal of Social Psychology*
     86 (1972): 205-10.

Asserts that the socio-cultural process of the
child-rearing extends beyond the nuclear family.
There is a great potential for diversity in child-
rearing attitudes of mothers who belong to different
subcultures in the United States. This study is
focused on the attitudes of Chinese, Jewish, and
Protestant mothers. No significant differences were
found.

431. Kruger, Mollee. *Daughters of Chutzpah: Humorous
      Verse on the Jewish Woman*. New York: Biblio Press,
      1983. 112 pp.

432. Kuzmack, Linda. "Aggadic Approaches to Biblical
      Women." In *The Jewish Woman: New Perspectives*,
      edited by Elizabeth Koltun, 248-56. New York:
      Schocken Books, 1976.

      Aggadah is nonlegal Jewish literature which tries
      to complement the teaching of *Halakhah*, folk stories
      and legends, and comments on and interpretations of
      the Bible.

433. Lacks, Roslyn. *Women and Judaism: Myth, History, and
      Struggle*. Garden City: Doubleday and Co., 1980.
      218 pp.

      A survey of the Jewish history of women from the
      goddesses of pre-Old Testament time up to
      contemporary female rabbis.

434. Lahav, Pnina. "Raising the Status of Women through
      Law: The Case of Israel." In *Women and National
      Development: The Complexities of Change*, edited by
      the Wellesley Editorial Committee, 193-209. *Signs*
      3, no. 1 (1977). Chicago and London: The
      University of Chicago Press, 1977.

      Article considers law as an instrument for altering
      traditional sex roles within family and society. The
      Women's Equal Right Law of 1951 is analyzed to find
      why so few changes have been obtained. Concludes
      that equality between sexes cannot be obtained by

altering the law. Attention should be directed more to social actualities and less to formal standards.

435. Lahav, Pnina. "The Status of Women in Israel--Myth and Reality." *The American Journal of Comparative Law* 22 (1974): 107-29.

Attacks the "myth" that there is equality between the sexes in Israeli law. States that the myth is rooted in ideological principles and beliefs around kibbutzim and the defense forces. In actuality equality has not been achieved, neither in practice nor in law. Women are still subject to discrimination. They play traditional roles within the whole society.

436. Lamm, Maurice. *The Jewish Way in Love and Marriage.* San Francisco: Harper and Row, 1980. 288 pp.

Jewish marriage customs and rites considered from an Orthodox perspective.

437. Lamm, Norman. *A Hedge of Roses: Jewish Insights into Marriage and Married Life.* New York: Philipp Feldheim, 1966. 92 pp.

Marriage and married life from an Orthodox point of view.

438. Lamm, Norman. "The Role of the Synagogue in Sex Education." In *The Jewish Family in a Changing World*, edited by Gilbert S. Rosenthal, 156-76. New York: Thomas Yoseloff, 1970.

Points to the lack of sex education in Jewish schools. Thinks that the schools are the place where sex education should be given and it should not be "qualitatively different" from other topics taught. Thinks also ethics should be an important part of the sex curriculum.

439. Lamm, Norman. "Separate Pews in the Synagogue: A
      Social and Psychological Approach." *Tradition* 1,
      no. 2 (1958-59): 141-64.

440. Landsberger, Michael. "Children's Age as a Factor
      Affecting the Simultaneous Determination of
      Consumption and Labor Supply." *Southern Economic
      Journal* 40 (1973): 279-88.

      A sociological investigation that maintains men's
      and women's labor supply is related to consumption
      and children's age.

441. Lankin, Doris. "In Modern Erez Israel." In
      Encyclopaedia Judaica, vol. 16, 623-30. Jerusalem:
      Keter Publishing House, 1971.

      About Jewish women in the twentieth century.
      Mostly about the legal status. Refers to the new
      laws of equality: The Nationality Law of 1952, and
      the Equal Pay for Equal Work Law of 1964.

442. Laska, Vera, ed. *Women in the Resistance and in the
      Holocaust: The Voices of Eyewitnesses.*
      Contributions in Women Studies, no. 37. Westport,
      Conn.: Greenwood, 1983. 330 pp.

      Personal narratives by twenty-seven eyewitnesses
      from various phases of the Holocaust: from the
      resistance work; from concentration camps; and from
      life in hiding.

443. Laurentin, René. "Jesus und die Frauen: Eine
      verkannte Revolution?" In *Frauen in der
      Männerkirche*, edited by Bernadette Brooten and
      Norbert Greinacher, 94-111. München: Kaiser, 1982.

      Emphasizes that women's status was much improved at
      the time of Jesus and early Christianity compared to
      women's status in an earlier time, i.e., during
      Judaism.

444. Laut, Renate. *Weibliche Züge im Gottesbild Israelitisch-Jüdischer Religiosität.* Arbeitsmaterialen zur Religions-geschichte, no. 9. Köln: Brill, 1983. 96 pp.

About goddesses in Jewish religion, especially the Great Mother.

445. Lavender, Abraham D., ed. *A Coat of Many Colors. Jewish Subcommunities in the United States.* Contributions in Family Studies, no. 1. Westport, Conn.: Greenwood Press, 1977. 324 pp.

This collection of essays on Jewish subcommunities in the United States contains four essays on Jewish women.

446. Lavender, Abraham D. "Jewish College Females: Future Leaders of the Jewish Community?" In *A Coat of Many Colors. Jewish Subcommunities in the United States,* edited by Abraham D. Lavender, 252-62. Westport, Conn.: Greenwood Press, 1977.

A study of why Jewish women obtain college degrees. Is it because of the status conferred, in preparation for continuation of the mother/housewife roles, or do they plan a career outside the home? Asks also if higher education for women will mean that they lose their level of Jewish identity, which is supposed to be higher than that of Jewish men. The sample of the study consisted of 488 Jewish undergraduate students, 264 females and 224 males, at the University of Maryland. Concludes that the American Jewish community deprives itself of much-needed talent to the extent that it does not encourage all individuals, regardless of sex, to participate in its leadership positions.

447. Lazar, Morty M. "The Role of Women in Synagogue Ritual in Canadian Conservative Congregations." *Jewish Journal of Sociology* 20 (1978): 165-71.

Asserts that Reform Judaism formally abolished inequalities in religious practices long ago. In

Orthodox Judaism men and women have their separate,
but "equal" obligations which are spelled out in the
Halakhah. In Conservative Judaism it is different.
Thinks that one reason is that it lacks a clearly
understood and exact ideological position, both
internally and vis-à-vis the two other major branches
of Judaism. Changes must be decided by the Committee
on Jewish Law and Standards of the Rabbinical
Assembly. Results from a survey among Canadian
synagogues show that Conservative congregations in
Canada are not providing full equality for women in
public ritual participation. Concludes that the
Rabbinical Assembly has made significant advances in
the religious enfranchisement of women, but the
congregations have lagged behind.

448. Lazerwitz, Bernard. "Fertility Trends in Israel and
      Its Administered Territories." *Jewish Social
      Studies* 33 (1971): 172-86.

A demographic analysis of Israel and its
administered territories with the 1,416,000 Christian
and Moslem Arabs and Druze within Israel's territory.
The findings show the Christian Arabs have a
considerably lower fertility rate than the Moslem
Arabs. If birth rates alone were to determine the
future population of Israel, the country would become
increasingly Moslem. It is estimated, however, that
the immigration of Jews and a high Jewish fertility
should maintain a 2/3-1/3 ratio of Jews to Arabs
throughout Israel and its administered territories.

449. Lazerwitz, Bernard. "Intermarriage and Conversion:
      A Guide for Future Research." *Jewish Journal of
      Sociology* 13 (1971): 41-63.

A large number of studies on the characteristics
and consequences of intermarriage have been published
recently. All researchers agree that intermarriage
is increasing. The present study is based on data
gathered as part of a survey of religio-ethnic
identification in the Chicago, Illinois, metropolitan
area. 572 Jews, 464 white Protestants, and 257 white
Catholics were interviewed. Intermarriages were

analyzed in relation to components and consequences
of religio-ethnic identification.

450. Lazerwitz, Bernard. "Jewish-Christian Marriages and
     Conversions." *Jewish Social Studies* 43 (1981):
     31-46.

     Jewish women are no more likely to convert to
     another religion than are Jewish men. There are more
     Jewish women in the terminated intermarriage
     sub-groups than one would expect on the basis of the
     substantially greater number of Jewish men who
     intermarry, i.e., there is a higher divorce rate for
     women than for men.

451. Leaphart, Susan. "Frieda and Belle Fliegelman: A
     Frontier-City Girlhood in the 1890s." *Montana*
     32, no. 3 (1982): 85-92.

     Biographical essay on two Jewish sisters describing
     their girlhood and Jewish background.

452. Lebeson, Anita. *Recall to Life: The Jewish Woman in
     America*. South Brunswick, N.J.: T. Yoseloff,
     1970. 351 pp.

     An account of Jewish women from the seventeenth
     century.

453. Leibler, Dulcy. "During War of Independence, Women
     in the Underground." *Israel Digest* 22, no. 16
     (1979): 6-7.

     About Doris Lankin, a former member of *Irgun Zvai
     Leumi*, an underground organization. She was active
     for many years, in whatever capacity possible, in
     field kitchens, as a nurse, in an Irgun hospital, as
     a driver, and she was also a good shot.

454. Leifer, Daniel I., and Myra Leifer. "On the Birth of
     a Daughter." In *The Jewish Woman: New
     Perspectives*, edited by Elizabeth Koltun, 21-30.

New York: Schocken Books, 1976 (Reprinted from
Response, no. 18 [Summer 1973]: 91-100).

About Jewish rituals and ceremonies marking the
birth of a daughter. Describes how they tried to
celebrate the birth of their daughter with the same
equality and dignity that the birth of a son
traditionally receives. Ceremonies for women's life,
from birth to death, are traditionally absent.

455. Leifer, Daniel I. "On Writing New *Ketubot*." In
      The Jewish Woman: New Perspectives, edited by
      Elizabeth Koltun, 50-61. New York: Schocken Books,
      1973.

      About the marriage contract.

456. Leonard, Jeanne Marie. "La femme de Teqoa et le fils
      de David: Etude de 2 Samuel 14:1-20." *Communio
      Viatorum* 23 (1980): 135-48.

      A discussion of 2 Samuel 14:1-20.

457. Lerner, Anne Lapidus. "In God's Image was Humanity
      Created." *Judaism* 33 (1984): 34-38.

      About the question of ordination of women in
      Conservative Judaism.

458. Lerner, Diana. "Preparing for the High Holidays."
      Israel Digest 22, no. 16 (1979): 8.

      Tells about women's role in the preparing for the
      High Holidays. In Israel the different festivals are
      given individual interpretations by different ethnic
      groups. A common trait is that women are the
      dominant force behind the preparations.

459. Lerner, Elinor. "Jewish Involvement in the New York
      City Woman Suffrage Movement." *American Jewish
      History* 70 (1981): 442-61.

Discusses the role of three Jewish women in the
suffrage movement in New York and asserts that the
efforts of these women never were recognized after
the victory was finally attained.

460. Levav, Itzhak, and Hiroko Minami. "Mothers and
Daughters and the Psychogeriatric Patient."
Gerontologist 14 (1974): 197-200.

An investigation based on interviews with forty-
eight Jewish mothers of Western and Eastern origin
and one of their daughters regarding their attitudes
to a psychogeriatric patient. The findings indicate
that when a person is both aged and mentally ill, the
majority of the respondents answered that the family
is responsible for treatment situations.

461. Levenberg, Diane Esther. "*Yom Tov* Twilight."
Response, no. 18 (Summer 1973): 143-52.

A story of memories of a *Rosh Hashonah* (The Jewish
New Year).

462. Levi, Shonie B., and Sylvia R. Kaplan. *A Guide for
the Jewish Homemaker.* New York: Schocken Books,
1964. 256 pp. (2nd rev. edition of *Across the
Threshold: A Guide for the Jewish Homemaker.*
New York: Farrar, Straus and Cudahy, 1959).

463. Levin Schneir. "Breast Feeding: Religious
Influences." *Journal of Psychology and Judaism* 3
(1979): 195-200.

A comparison of the breast-feeding of fifty
Orthodox and fifty secular Jewish mothers. The
findings indicate that there was a very small
difference. The Orthodox mothers were slightly more
successful.

464. Levinas, Emmanuel. "Judaism and the Feminine
Element." *Judaism* 18, no. 1 (1969): 30-38.

A discussion of women and the feminine element in
the Bible and the Talmud.

465.   Levine, Jacqueline. "The Changing Role of Women in
       the Jewish Community." *Response*, no. 18
       (Summer 1973): 59-65.

       Wants women as well as men to have a chance to
       share in communal responsibility. Finds it important
       that women's talents for maintaining Jewish life
       through the centuries should not be set aside on the
       grounds of prefabricated sexual roles.

466.   Levine, Renée C. "Women in Spanish Crypto-Judaism,
       1492-1520." Ph.D. diss., Brandeis University,
       1983. 425 pp.

       Concerns the Inquisition. The Spanish Inquisition
       was established in order to extirpate heresy. Jews
       who converted to Christianity but continued to
       observe their former faith, the Crypto-Jews, were
       regarded as heretics and brought to trial. Several
       women were charged with the "crime" of Judaizing
       during the years 1492-1520. Dossiers from this
       period, including accusations, confessions, and
       witness testimonies, illustrate the attempts to
       preserve and transmit Jewish tradition despite the
       surveillance of the Inquisition.

467.   Levine, Shlomo D. "A Study of the Effects of Group
       Counseling on Religious Attitudes and Verbal
       Behaviors of Members of a Conservative Synagogue."
       Ed.D. diss., The College of William and Mary in
       Virginia, 1974. 143 pp.

       An examination of the effects of small group
       counseling on the religious attitudes and verbal
       behaviors of a group of women affiliated with a
       Conservative synagogue.

468.   Lewy, Immanuel. "The Feminine Element in Biblical
       Judaism." *Judaism* 2, no. 4 (1953): 399-44.

469. Lichtenstein, Diane Marilyn. "On Whose Native
      Ground?" Nineteenth-Century Myths of American
      Womanhood and Jewish Women Writers." Ph.D. diss.,
      University of Pennsylvania, 1985. 377 pp.

      A study of Jewish women writers of Sephardic and
      German descent and how they tried to reconcile the
      conflicting demands of their Jewish and American
      identities. In order to ease the tensions between
      the different expectations from the two cultures,
      some of the writers published essays to educate
      Americans about Jews, while others wrote fiction.
      This dissertation analyzes some of this literature.

470. Lindheim, Irma L. *Parallel Quest. A Search of a
      Person and a People.* New York: Thomas Yoseloff,
      1962. 458 pp.

      A personal account of the author's life in Israel
      from the time when the state of Israel was founded.

471. Linker, Mollie. "The Mother in the Community." In
      Jewish Grandmothers, edited by Sydelle Kramer and
      Jenny Masur, 90-102. Boston: Beacon Press, 1976.

      Speaks about the meaning of motherhood, based on
      the experiences of her own relationship to her mother
      and to her children. As an immigrant to the United
      States, she speaks with nostalgia of ghetto life in
      Russia. Thinks of it as a place where Jewish
      traditions remained unquestioned and where motherhood
      was the "backbone" of family life.

472. Linzer, Norman. *The Jewish Family: Authority and
      Tradition in Modern Perspective.* New York: Human
      Sciences Press, 1984. 217 pp.

473. Lipman, Eugene J. "Woman's Lib and Jewish
      Tradition." In *A Coat of Many Colors. Jewish
      Subcommunities in the United States*, edited by
      Abraham D. Lavender, 239-42. Westport, Conn.:
      Greenwood Press, 1977.

Lists some of the demands that have been expressed
by the modern feminist movement. Asserts that the
status and role of women have been the concern of
Halakhah since the Biblical era. Mentions some
examples from the Mishnah to prove that the Jewish
woman was far ahead of her time in the amount of
freedom and equality she enjoyed.

474. Lipscomb, W. Lowndes. "Wives of the Patriarchs in
      the Ekloge Historian." *Journal of Jewish Studies*
      30 (1979): 91.

475. Lipstadt, Deborah E. "And Deborah Made Ten." In
      On Being a Jewish Feminist. A Reader, edited by
      Susannah Heschel, 207-9. New York: Schocken Books,
      1983.

An account of how the author, a woman, was allowed
to be the tenth member of a *minyan*, a quorum of ten
(usually men), required for communal prayer service,
at the *yahrzeit*, memorial anniversary of the death of
her father.

476. Lipstadt, Deborah E. "Women and Power in the
      Federation." In *On Being a Jewish Feminist. A
      Reader*, edited by Susannah Heschel, 152-66.
      New York: Schocken Books, 1983.

Analyzes the changes within the Council of Jewish
Federations (CJF), with the increasing influence of
the feminist movement. Thinks that there have been
changes but these have been slow, sporadic, and
hesitant. However, there is an increasing number of
women in leadership positions or on the way to them.

477. Litman, Jane. "Is Judaism a Matriarchal Religion?"
      Lilith, no. 10 (Winter 1982-83): 32.

A personal account of her ties to Judaism. States
that she is primarily attached to Judaism because of
its elevation of family and community, and the
holidays, and not the law.

478. Litwin-Grinberg, Ruth R. "Lives in Retrospect: A
Qualitative Analysis of Oral Reminiscence as
Applied to Elderly Jewish Women." D.S.W. diss.,
University of California, Berkeley, 1982. 204 pp.

About the phenomena of reminiscence and
retrospection in old age. The life histories of
eight Eastern Europe-born Jewish women, aged seventy-
six to ninety-six, were analyzed. The findings
showed that the participants tended to reevaluate
their lives through "a conscious search for the
meaning of important events and experiences." Most
of these experiences were concerned with losses:
losses of persons, losses of dreams and aspirations,
and also losses due to aging.

479. Livneh, Ernst. "On Rape and the Sanctity of
Matrimony." *Israel Law Review* 2 (1967): 415-22.

"Unlawful sexual intercourse" in Israeli law
obviously means extramarital intercourse. However,
"rape" of a married woman by her husband has been
referred to on some occasions by judges.

480. Lockett, Darby Richardson. "Feminist Footholds in
Religion." *Foundations* 19, no. 1 (1976): 33-39.

A review of the feminist movements in American
Judaism, Catholicism, and Protestantism. Emphasizes
the anti-feminism in many religious organizations.

481. Löhr, Max. *Die Stellung des Weibes zu Jahwe-Religion
und- Kult.* Beiträge zur Wissenschaft vom alten
Testament, Heft 4. Leipzig: J.C. Hinrichs'sche
Buchhandlung, 1908. 54 pp.

In the first part of this study the author lists
all female names in the Old Testament and explains
what they mean. Discusses the social status of women
in Israel. Asserts that even if *Vaterrecht*
(patriarchate) is the dominating practice, there are
traces of *Mutterrecht* (matriarchate). Woman as wife
and mother has a much higher position than the formal
jurisprudence indicates. In the Jahwe-cult women

play a minor part; it is mainly a religion for men.
Women's tasks in religion, as in other parts of life,
was to serve the men.

482. Loewe, Raphael. *The Position of Women in Judaism.*
      London: SPCK, 1966. 63 pp.

      An evaluation of negative and positive attitudes
      toward womanhood, especially with reference to the
      post-Biblical material: *Halakhah* and *'Aggada*.

483. Loewenstein, Andrea. "Excerpts from an Israeli
      Journal." In *Nice Jewish Girls. A Lesbian
      Anthology*, edited by Evelyn Torton Beck, 201-10.
      Trumansburg, N.Y.: The Crossing Press, 1982.

      A diary from some August days in 1979 on a visit to
      Israel. Presents some of her impressions. Stresses
      that she has a strong sense of her identity as a
      lesbian-feminist but little sense of herself as a
      Jewish woman.

484. Longstaff, Thomas R.W. "The Women at the Tomb:
      Matthew 28:1 Re-Examined." *New Testament Studies*
      27 (1981): 277-82.

      An answer to Michael D. Goulder's comments on the
      resurrection story. Goulder finds this story
      incoherent, especially the part on the women's visit
      to the tomb of Jesus. Longstaff asserts that this
      part makes good sense if you take Jewish burial and
      mourning practices into account.

485. Lowenstein, Ariela. "Coping with Stress: The Case of
      Prisoners' Wives." *Journal of Marriage and the
      Family* 46 (1984): 699-708.

      An investigation based on data collected through
      structured personal interviews with 143 Jewish
      prisoners' wives whose husbands were first-timers
      serving terms of thirteen months to life
      imprisonment.

486. Lowenthal, Marvin. *Henrietta Szold: Life and Letters.* Westport, Conn.: Greenwood Press, 1975. 350 pp.

487. Lowin, Robin G. "Cross-Generational Transmission of Pathology in Jewish Families of Holocaust Survivors." Ph.D. diss., California School of Professional Psychology, San Diego, 1983. 205 pp.

    A psychological study of concentration camp survivors. Examines whether the syndrome which has been documented as specific to concentration camp survivors with such symptoms as anxiety, paranoia, guilt, somatization and personality changes, has been passed on from parents to offspring. The findings indicate that the symptom picture was not replicated in the children of the survivors.

488. Lowry, Charles B. "'The City on a Hill' and Kibbutzim: Seventeenth Century Utopias as Ideal Types." *American Jewish Historical Quarterly* 64 (1974): 24-41.

    A sociological comparison of seventeenth-century Puritan New England towns and twentieth-century Israeli kibbutz societies. Their agricultural character, the position of women, and intellectual bent are compared.

489. Maccoby, Hyam. "Sex According to the Song of Songs." *Commentary* 67, no. 6 (1979): 53-59.

    Asks why the emphasis falls on female rather than male desire in this love poem, which is a product of a patriarchal society. Discusses different interpretations and polemicizes against the many allegorical interpretations. Even if Judaism is a patriarchal religion, it still contains many anti-patriarchal elements.

490. Macdonald, Elizabeth Mary. "Women in the Hebrew Codes." In *The Position of Women as Reflected in Semitic Codes of Law*, 50-69. University of Toronto

Studies Oriental Series, no. 1. Toronto: The
University of Toronto Press, 1931.

491.   Magen, Zipora. "Re-Forming the Boundaries: A Trans-
       Cultural Comparison of Positive Experiences Among
       Adolescent Males and Females." *Adolescence* 18
       (1983): 851-58.

       A cross-cultural study of positive experiences
       among 357 Israeli-Jewish, 351 Israeli-Arab, and 386
       American fourteen- to fifteen-year-old adolescents.
       The findings indicate that the differences between
       the sexes go in the same direction across the three
       cultures.

492.   Maggid, Aliza. "Lesbians in the International
       Movement of Gay/Lesbian Jews." In *Nice Jewish
       Girls*. *A Lesbian Anthology*, edited by Evelyn
       Torton Beck, 114-19. Trumansburg, N.Y.: The
       Crossing Press, 1982.

       Discusses the role of lesbians in the International
       Movement of Gay/Lesbian Jews. This movement was
       started in 1976, and has groups in many countries.
       The aim of the movement is to work against the many
       "-isms" that oppress all lesbians and gays, all Jews,
       all people of color, and all minorities. The
       lesbians have been very active in the movement from
       the start.

493.   Maier, Johann. "Die Stellung der Frau im jüdischen
       Recht." In *Die Braut. Geliebt, verkauft,
       getauscht. Zur Rolle der Frau im Kulturvergleich*,
       edited by Gisela Völger and Karin V. Welck, vol. 1,
       164-71. Köln: Rautenstrauch-Joest Museum für
       Völkerkunde, 1985.

       Asserts that Jewish woman has a low status as far
       as ritual-cultic conditions are concerned. On the
       other hand the contractual character of marriage and
       the high valuation of family life allow for
       considerable rise in status as compared to other
       patriarchal societies.

494. Maimon, Ada. *Women Build a Land*. New York: Herzl
     Press, 1962. 294 pp.

     An autobiography of the struggles from the time the
     author came to Palestine as a young girl in 1912,
     joining other pioneers. She became one of the
     leaders in the Working Women's Council of Israel's
     General Federation of Labour. By the time this book
     was published, she had become a labor leader and a
     member of the Knesset.

495. Malinowitz, Harriet. "Coffee and Cake." In *Nice
     Jewish Girls. A Lesbian Anthology*, edited by
     Evelyn Torton Beck, 179-89. Trumansburg, N.Y.:
     The Crossing Press, 1982.

     A fictitious story from a coffee and cake meeting
     between the story's "I" and her brother, where "I"
     admits that she is a lesbian, and her brother's
     reaction to this.

496. Maller, Allen S. *God, Sex, and Kabbalah (Messianic
     Speculations)*. Los Angeles: Ridgefield Publishing
     Company, 1983. 186 pp.

     Chapters IV-VII of this book deal particularly with
     the role of the female in Jewish mystical thought.
     The holy significance of sexual intercourse; the role
     of woman in man's ascent from the Garden of Eden; the
     image of the female as God and as demon; all are
     dealt with. Chapter VII tells the story of Lilith
     from the manuscript by Alphabeth of Ben Sira.

497. Maller, Allen S. "Mixed Marriage and Reform Rabbis."
     Judaism 24, no. 1 (1975): 39-48.

498. Mann, Denese Berg. *The Woman in Judaism*. Hartford,
     Conn.: Jonathan Publ., 1979. 76 pp.

     This book treats attitudes toward women from the
     days of the Bible, the Talmud, the Renaissance, the
     Shtetl, through the 1940s up to the present day.
     There are chapters on marriage, abortion, divorce,

birth control, morality, and sex. The author is an
American Jewish woman, the mother of four children,
and presently engaged in private practice in
counseling and family therapy.

499. Mansbach, Ivonne K., Hava Palti, Bella Pevsner,
     Helen Pridan, and Zvi Palti. "Advice from the
     Obstetrician and Other Sources: Do They Affect
     Women's Breast Feeding Practices? A Study among
     Different Jewish Groups in Jerusalem." *Social
     Science and Medicine* 19 (1984): 157-62.

     This examination of the effects of advice from
     alternative sources on the breast-feeding practices
     of Jewish women shows that the obstetrician's advice
     particularly affects the duration of breast-feeding.
     The examination also shows that women of higher
     social classes and women of Western origin
     breast-feed more and for a longer period of time than
     others.

500. Marciano, Teresa Donati. "A Note on Phantom Triads:
     Family Coalitions and Religious Observance after
     Divorce." *Jewish Social Studies* 44 (1982): 315-22.

     A study on children of divorced Jewish mothers with
     minor children. It was found that under certain
     circumstances the children could argue against
     mothers by going into coalition with the "phantom"
     (absent) father. Other "phantom" coalitions were
     also found.

501. Marcus, Jacob R. *The American Jewish Woman,
     1654-1980.* New York: Ktav Publishing House.
     Cincinnati: American Jewish Archives, 1981.
     231 pp.

     Asserts that the Jewish woman has been ignored in
     the standard chronicles of American Jewry. This
     study intends to describe the American Jewish woman
     from 1654 to 1980 as she emerges from the documents,
     the letters, the memoirs, the congregational minutes,
     and a large assortment of memorabilia. Every

statement in this study has been based on data which
the author deems authentic.

502. Marcus, Jacob. R. *The American Jewish Woman. A
     Documentary History.* New York: Ktav Publishing
     House. Cincinnati: American Jewish Archives, 1981.
     1047 pp.

     This documentary history is intended as a
     supplement to Jacob R. Marcus: *The American Jewish
     Woman, 1654-1980.* It is a presentation of the
     documents which the author describes in the earlier
     book. It also contains many photographs. "In a
     larger sense these documents speak for themselves and
     permit every reader to be his/her own historian."
     Bibliographical note: 189-218.

503. Margolis, Jill Beth. "Mid-Life Jewish Families in
     Minneapolis: An Empirically Derived Profile."
     Ph.D. diss., University of Minnesota, 1985.
     173 pp.

     A comparison between mid-life Jewish families and
     mid-life Lutheran families. The object of the study
     was to delineate the profile of the sample of Jewish
     families using variables and measures from current
     family social science research and to investigate how
     Jewish families compare with non-Jewish families.
     Three hypotheses were developed for the Jewish
     families: the family stress would be higher, family
     cohesion levels would be higher, and family
     adaptability levels would be higher. The results of
     the data analysis showed that these hypotheses were
     not confirmed.

504. Mariampolski, Hyman. "Changes in Kibbutz Society:
     Their Implications for the Situation of the Sexes."
     International Review of Modern Sociology 6 (1976):
     201-16.

     An examination of two kibbutzim during a period of
     thirteen months in order to investigate current sex
     roles in terms of six changes in kibbutz society.
     These are: 1) the dissipation of the agricultural

ethic; 2) increasing emphasis upon professionalism
and careerism; 3) the decline of asceticism; 4) a
shift from an ideological to a pragmatic orientation;
5) a decline of a vanguard consciousness; and 6) the
resurgence of familism. The study shows that wide
disparities in sex-role performance are observed in
the Israeli kibbutz. Occupational roles of men and
women are different. The amount of power differs and
variations in household tasks are evident. Discusses
why this development has taken place. Does not see
the re-domestication of women as a problem. "By
orienting women to the familistic private life and
men to the communal public life, the society has
resolved the dilemma of competing commitments and can
function without strain."

505. Marmorstein, Emile. "The Veil in Judaism and Islam."
     Journal of Jewish Studies 5 (1954): 1-11.

506. Mayer, Egon. "Processes and Outcomes in Marriages
     between Jews and Non-Jews." *American Behavioral
     Scientist* 23 (1980): 487-518.

     A report on Jewish intermarriages in the United
     States, based on a study conducted between 1975 and
     1978, in which 446 couples were surveyed. One of the
     conclusions is that the assimilation of Jews does not
     follow intermarriage; rather it is a result of
     processes of interaction between Jews and non-Jews
     from early socialization on. States also that the
     spouses choose one another in a pattern that seems to
     enhance their respective statuses.

507. Mazow, Julia Wolf, ed. *The Woman Who Lost Her Names.
     Selected Writing by American Jewish Women.*
     San Francisco: Harper and Row, 1980. 222 pp.

     This anthology consists of short stories,
     autobiographical sketches, and excerpts from novels
     (some previously unpublished) written by American
     Jewish women. It is accompanied by the editor's
     commentary and biographical notes on each
     contributor.

508. McCauley, Deborah, and Annette Daum. "Jewish-Christian Feminist Dialogue: A Wholistic Vision." *Union Seminary Quarterly Review* 38, no. 2 (1983): 147-90.

509. McCracken, Samuel. "'Julia' and Other Fictions by Lillian Hellman." *Commentary* 77, no. 6 (1984): 35-43.

Mostly about *Pentimento*, a memoir containing a portrait of Julia, a childhood friend. Discusses Hellman's "honesty" after she had been accused of writing lies. Finds that many of the facts misrepresented by Hellman are not in themselves very important. What may be criticized is "that she has manipulated millions of readers and moviegoers into admiring her as an ethical example and as a ruthlessly honest writer."

510. McKeating, Henry. "Jesus Ben Sira's Attitude to Women." *Expository Times* 85 (1970): 85-87.

Jesus Ben Sira, the author of *Ecclesiasticus*, is the most explicit of the wisdom writers as far as woman is concerned. In the wisdom literature men are the innocent ones; women are the lustful sex. Ben Sira praises the good wife and mother, but says more about the "curse of a bad one." Women's biggest faults are unfaithfulness and nagging. About daughters, he asserts that they are always a terrible liability. McKeating suggests that any supporter of women's liberation might be excused for calling Ben Sira a male chauvinist pig number one.

511. McMurry, Martha. "Religion and Women's Sex Role Traditionalism." *Sociological Focus* 11 (1978): 81-95.

An analysis of the relationship between religion and sex-role orientations among white married women. A sample was drawn of women from five religious categories. The findings indicated big differences among religious groups. The most traditional sex-role attitudes were found among Baptists,

Catholics, and fundamentalist Protestants. Then
follow mainline Protestant, Jews, and non-believers.

512. Meir, Golda. "First Days in Kibbutz Merhavia. A
      Memoir." *Midstream* 16, no. 5 (1970): 24-29.

      Tells about her life and experiences with members
      of the kibbutz Revivim. Mentions problems and
      pleasures in the daily life of kibbutzim.

513. Meiselman, Moshe. *Jewish Woman in Jewish Law*.
      Library of Jewish Law and Ethics, vol. 6.
      New York: Ktav Publishing House, Yeshiva
      University Press, 1978. 218 pp.

      This book dealing with the whole issue of the study
      of Torah by women, is often called a classic of the
      apologist school. According to the author, the
      purpose of the work is to evaluate the issue of
      feminism from a Jewish perspective. The topics are
      said to have been selected with an eye to the current
      feminist critique of Judaism: family, marriage, Torah
      knowledge for women, women's obligations in *Mitzvot*,
      women as witnesses, women and contract, inheritance,
      women and prayer.

514. Menczer, J., M. Modan, and L. Katz. "Cervical-
      Carcinoma in Jewish Women." *Lancet*, no. 8329
      (1983): 875.

515. Mennis, Bernice. "Repeating History." In *Nice Jewish
      Girls. A Lesbian Anthology*, edited by Evelyn
      Torton Beck, 89-96. Trumansburg, N.Y.: The
      Crossing Press, 1982.

      Points to the fact that at certain historical
      moments individual prejudices have become transformed
      into societal and historical "solutions." Those in
      power validate certain channels of hatred. Asserts
      that historically the designated channels have been
      homophobia, anti-Semitism, racism, and sexism. "In
      different countries and at different times, the

targets shift, but there remains a universality to
these hatreds."

516. de Merode-de Croy, Marie. "Die Rolle der Frau im
     Alten Testament." In *Frauen in der Männerkirche*,
     edited by Bernadette Brooten and Norbert
     Greinacher, 93-93. München: Kaiser, 1982.

     Thinks that the Old Testament plays an important
     part concerning the modern Church's view on women.
     Mentions a recent document from the Church of Rome
     on women's accessibility to priesthood. The two
     arguments against are: 1) the example of Christ, as
     he did not have women as apostles, and 2) the fact
     that Christ was a man himself and the priest was the
     sacrament of Christ. A female priest would not
     fulfill the task of being a token (*Zeichen*).
     Examines some passages of the Old Testament which
     deal with women and finds that the attitudes on the
     whole are negative.

517. Meron, Ya'akov. "A Muslim Solution." *Israel Law
     Review* 7 (1972): 315-18.

     A discussion of the Women's Equal Rights Law of
     1951 compared to Muslim law concerning married
     women's legal capacity to deal with property.

518. Mettinger, Tryggve N.D. "Eva och revbenet: Manligt
     och kvinnligt i Exegetisk belysning." *Svensk
     Teologisk Kvartalskrift* 54 (1978): 55-64.

     About Genesis 2:18 ff, the creation of woman from
     a rib, and Genesis 1:26 ff, the creation of man in
     the image of God. Thinks that a main point in
     Gen. 2:18 ff. is the deep community between man and
     woman. Woman is the partner of man, equal and
     different. According to Gen. 3:16, however, man
     shall rule over woman. This subordination by woman
     is seen as a result of human disobedience to God.
     Tries to relate the role of woman in the creation
     account in Genesis to similar motives in other
     cultures and to motives in Paul.

519. Meyers, Carol. "Procreation, Production, and
      Protection: Male-Female Balance in Early Israel."
      Journal of the American Academy of Religion 51
      (1983): 569-93.

      Tries to see sex-roles and attitudes in Biblical
      Israel from a sociological and anthropological point
      of view. Finds it useful to utilize materials and
      paradigms from outside the Bible on Biblical texts
      because many of the sanctions regulating men's and
      women's behavior require reexamination and
      revaluation within the dynamics of the socio-economic
      situation.

520. Meyers, Carol. "The Roots of Restriction: Women in
      Early Israel." *Biblical Archaeologist* 41 (1978):
      91-103.

      Asserts that the late Bronze Age was characterized
      by famines, plagues, and burnings. The population
      was severely reduced. In this situation female
      creativity and labor were highly valued. In light of
      the demographic crisis, sanctions and laws
      regulating sexuality were made and eventually
      expressed in Biblical laws dealing with incest, rape,
      adultery, virginity, bestiality, exogamy,
      homosexuality, and prostitution. During the
      establishment of monarchy, the restriction of women
      to domestic circles was strengthened and their social
      importance diminished. During the monarchy the
      equal-participation momentum of the formative period
      was transformed into masculine domination and female
      subordination. This development continued into
      modern times.

521. Michel, Sonya. "Mothers and Daughters in American
      Jewish Literature: The Rotted Cord." In *The Jewish
      Woman: New Perspectives*, edited by Elizabeth
      Koltun, 272-82. New York: Schocken Books, 1976.

522. Mikaelsson, Lisbeth. "Sexual Polarity: An Aspect
      of the Ideological Structure in the Paradise
      Narrative, Genesis 2:4-3:24." *Temenos* 16 (1980):
      84-91.

Asserts that the Paradise narrative does not
evaluate man and woman in the same way. Three
narrative elements reveal evaluation of the sexes:
1) the creation of man and woman, 2) Adam's naming of
the animals and Eve, and 3) woman's part in the fall.
Concludes that the myth's pattern of interaction
constitutes a polar, hierarchal structure: the active
and dominant "worldbuilders" Yaweh and Adam on the
one side, and the passive and subjected figures of
Eve and the animals on the other.

523. Miller, Arlene Adrian. "An Exploration of Ethnicity
      in Marriages between White Anglo Saxon Protestants
      and Jewish Americans." Ed.D. diss., Boston
      University School of Education, 1983. 183 pp.

      A study of the experiences of the spouses in
      marriages between Jews and white Protestants. To
      what degree were they aware of cultural differences
      and how did they cope with these differences?
      Concludes that intermarriage made the spouses more
      aware of their ethnic identity. Intermarriage is a
      cultural awareness process. The chances of success
      depend on the degree of mutual understanding of each
      other's behavior.

524. Miller, Sally M. "From Sweatshop Worker to Labor
      Leader: Theresa Malkiel, A Case Study." *American
      Jewish History* 68 (1978): 189-205.

      Theresa Serber Malkiel (1874-1949) was a leader in
      the labor movement; she was particularly interested
      in women's questions and gave much attention to women
      and the labor party, unionizing of women workers,
      foreign-born women, woman suffrage, and the party
      commitment to sexual equality.

525. Mintz, Jacqueline A. "The Myth of the Jewish Mother
      in Three Jewish, American Female Writers."
      Centennial Review 22 (1978): 346-53.

      The works of three female Jewish American writers
      over three generations are examined in order to
      explore the effects that the "Jewish mother myth"

has had and still has on woman's psyche and her role
in family and society. These writers are Tillie
Olsen, Anzia Yezierska, and Susan Fromberg Schaeffer.
They have all dealt with the myth of the perfect
Jewish mother and the burdens it placed on women who
were expected to live up to its demands of total
involvement with family and endless, selfless giving
and nurturing.

526. Mischel, Harriet N. "Sex Bias in the Evaluation of
      Professional Achievements." *Journal of Educational
      Psychology* 66 (1974): 157-66.

      A description of three studies on sex bias in the
      evaluation of professional achievements in different
      fields comparing U.S. and Israeli samples. The
      Israeli subjects showed less prejudice than did the
      U.S. subjects. The Israeli subjects did not
      distinguish in their evaluations of professional
      articles according to the sex of the attributed
      author. Concludes by indicating that in a culture
      where women have no professional opportunities and
      are seen as more equal to men in their abilities,
      there would be little evaulative sex bias. That
      might be the case in Israel where women are found in
      a greater variety of fields.

527. Monson, Rela Geffen. "The Case of the Reluctant
      Exogamists: Jewish Women and Intermarriage." *Gratz
      College Annual of Jewish Studies* 5 (1976): 121-26.

      Possible explanations of why more Jewish men than
      Jewish women intermarry and an analysis of the
      potential impact of the women's movement in the
      United States on the rate of female Jewish inter-
      marriages. Discusses the reasons why Jewish women
      have been so reluctant to intermarry. Suggests that
      the sex-role definitions which are reinforced through
      familial and social structures limit both women's
      path to success and access to the outside social
      world. The impact of the woman's movement may be
      seen in the fact that women's role in Jewish communal
      structures, religious and secular, has broadened.
      Their identity is not so much dependent on parental

validation, and they are less susceptible to being pushed into "suitable" marriage.

528. Montley, Patricia. "Judith in the Fine Arts: The Appeal of the Archetypal Androgyne." *Anima* 4, no. 2 (1978): 37-42.

About the story of Judith, the rich and virtuous widow who saves her people from destruction by the Assyrians. The apocryphal story of Judith has been treated by visual artists, musicians, and writers of every age.

529. Morgan, Douglas N. "Love in the Hebrew Bible." *Judaism* 5 (1956): 31-45.

530. Morton, Leah. *I Am A Woman—and a Jew.* New York: J.H. Sears and Co., 1926. 362 pp.

Autobiography by a Jewish feminist writer of the 1930s; describes how it is to be a woman and a Jew.

531. Moscowitz, Pearl. "The Child Immigrant." In *Jewish Grandmothers*, edited by Sydelle Kramer and Jenny Masur, 48-59. Boston: Beacon Press, 1976.

An account of how she and her family emigrated from a rural farm in Russia to America. She was eleven when they left Russia.

532. Moskowitz, Moshe A. "Intermarriage and the Proselyte: A Jewish View." *Judaism* 28 (1979): 423-33.

533. Munkacsi, Naomi Winkler. "Jewish Religious Observance in Women's Death Camps in Germany." *Yad Vashem Bulletin* 20 (1967): 35-38.

On the observance of lighting Sabbath and holiday candles, the keeping of feastdays, and weekday

mourning customs in concentration camps in Germany
during the Nazi rule.

534. Myerhoff, Barbara G. "Bobbes and Zeydes: Old and New
Roles for Elderly Jews." In *Women in Ritual and
Symbolic Roles*, edited by Judith Hoch-Smith and
Anita Spring, 207-41. New York and London:
Plenum Press, 1978.

An anthropological study of elderly Eastern
European Jewish immigrants to the United States and
their previous life in the small Jewish villages
known as *shtetls*.

535. Navé, Pnina. "Die Frau im Judentum." In *Begegnungen
mit dem Judentum*, edited by Bernhard Rübenach,
189-97. Berlin: Kreuz Verlag Stuttgart, 1981.

Describes women's status in religious, social, and
family life. Starts by asking how it is that Jews
exist all over the world and answers that Jews have
been able to shape a social network where men and
women work together in family, in communities, in
religious and other organizations all of which work
for the continuation of a meaningful Jewish life.

536. Navé Levinson, Pnina. "Die Jüdische Frau."
Informationen für die Frau 26 (1977): 19-20.

537. Navé-Levinson, Pnina. "Women and Judaism."
European Judaism 15, no. 2 (1981): 25-28.

Asserts that Jewish women have always been partners
in education, social work, financial management in
family and congregation, as well as in reading,
writing, and publishing. Self-realization has been
considered important since Biblical times. Argues
that Judaism may be described as a powerful
matriarchate half hidden under apparent male
authority.

538. Nesvisky, Matthew. "Women's Liberation and the
     Kibbutz." *Jewish Spectator* 38 (October 1973):
     19-20.

     Points to the "myth" that women are equal to men in
     the kibbutz. Equality of the sexes was one of the
     main concerns of the kibbutz from the beginning.
     Communal child-raising was organized in order to give
     women the opportunity to participate in the kibbutz
     life on an equal footing with men. However, after so
     many years there is still the traditional division of
     labor: women do the service work, laundry, kitchen
     work, and child care. Men do the productive work
     which brings in money. Emphasizes the importance of
     woman's independence of man in financial matters.

539. Neu, Irene D. "The Jewish Businesswoman in America."
     American Jewish Historical Quarterly 66 (1976):
     137-54.

     About Jewish businesswomen in America from colonial
     days to the present. They were not many in the
     beginning; women's place was in the home. This
     situation has gradually changed.

540. Neuberger, Julia. "Woman in Judaism: The Fact and
     the Fiction." In *Women's Religious Experience:
     Cross-Cultural Perspectives*, edited by Pat Holden,
     132-42. London: Croom Helm, 1983.

     This essay by Rabbi Julia Neuberger, questions the
     view that Judaism subjugates women to their husbands
     and gives them a legal status inferior to that of
     men.

541. Neuberger, Julia. "Women and Judaism." *European
     Judaism* 15, no. 2 (1981): 29.

     A personal account by a female rabbi. Thinks that
     attitudes have changed during her four years in the
     rabbinate towards a greater degree of acceptance.

542. Neusner, Jacob. "From Scripture to Mishnah: The
      Origins of Mishnah's Division of Women." *Journal
      of Jewish Studies* 30 (1979): 138-53.

      A survey of the third of Mishnah's six divisions,
      The Order of Women, which consists of seven
      tractates. Concludes that the survey shows that the
      division of women is essentially distinct from
      Scripture at those points at which Mishnah treats the
      topics critical to Mishnah's definition of the
      distinctive problematic of its theme. The three
      tractates *Ketubot, Gittin*, and *Qiddushin*, which
      discuss the transfer of women and of property
      associated therewith, are totally independent of
      Scripture; and *Yebamot* is autonomous of Scripture,
      though using Scripture's facts. Number five, *Sotah*,
      adds some minor details and amplifications.

543. Neusner, Jacob. "From Scripture to Mishnah. The
      Origins of Tractate Niddah." *Journal of Jewish
      Studies* 29 (1978): 135-48.

      About the Mishnah-tractate, *Niddah*, which treats
      two subjects in the Scripture: 1) the rule that
      bodily excretions of women, in particular,
      menstruants, women after childbirth, and the *Zabah*
      (Lev. 15:1 ff.), are unclean; 2) the consideration
      of matters of doubt in connection with these same
      excretions. "Are excretions of intermediate order--
      between what is definitely unclean and definitely
      clean--deemed unclean or clean, for example, the
      bloodstain in respect to the menstrual and *Zibah*-
      blood and the abortion in respect to the women who
      give birth."

544. Neusner, Jacob. *A History of the Mishnaic Law of
      Women*. 5 vols. Studies in Judaism in Late
      Antiquity, vol. 33. Leiden: Brill, 1980.

      A translation and explanation of the division in
      History of the Mishnaic Law of Women.

545.   Newmark, Rosa. "A Letter from Mother to Daughter--
       Los Angeles to New York, 1867." *Western States
       Jewish Historical Quarterly* 5 (1973): 274-84.

       Describes the Jewish marriage celebration, and
       attendant social customs, of her daughter, Harriet,
       in Los Angeles.

546.   Niditch, Susan. "The Cosmic Adam: Man as Mediator in
       Rabbinic Literature." *Journal of Jewish Studies*
       34 (1983): 137-46.

       An exploration of one of the Golem texts, Gen.
       Rab. 8:1, from a structuralist perspective to find
       that the imagery of the Midrash mediates various
       dichotomies important elsewhere in rabbinic thought
       and literature: worthiness-unworthiness, male-female,
       man-cosmos, celestial-earthly.

547.   Niditch, Susan. "The Wronged Woman Righted: An
       Analysis of Genesis 38." *Harvard Theological
       Review* 72 (1979): 143-49.

       This analysis deals with the role of women in the
       Old Testament. The young woman is allowed only two
       proper roles. She is either an unmarried virgin in
       her father's home or she is a faithful child-
       producing wife in her husband's or husband's family
       home. Harlots are also allowed a place in the
       society. They seem to have an accepted outcast
       place.

548.   Noble, Shlomo. "The Jewish Woman in Medieval
       Martyrology." In *Studies in Jewish Bibliography,
       History, and Literature in Honor of I. Edward Kiev*,
       edited by Charles Berlin, 347-55. New York: Ktav
       Publishing House, 1971.

       Asserts that Jewish women showed devotion to their
       faith in the Middle Ages. Women took a leading part
       in the struggle against Christianity and were reputed
       to excel their men in contempt for Christian
       sanctities. Their share in apostasy was also most
       likely much smaller than that of the Jewish male.

549. Novak, David. "Annulment in Lieu of Divorce in
      Jewish Law." In *Halakhah in a Theological
      Dimension*, 29-44. Chico, Calif.: Scholars Press,
      1985.

      About an alternative to *get*, divorce, in cases
      where the husband refuses to give divorce to his
      wife. Asks how this can be done within the system
      of Halakhah. Refers to cases presented in the Talmud
      where marriages were annulled by rabbinic
      authorities. Finds that without the practical power
      to annul some marriages, the law is encouraging
      immoral blackmail and vengeance.

550. Novak, David. "Divorce and Conversion: Is a
      Traditional-Liberal Modus Vivendi Possible?" In
      Halakhah in a Theological Dimension, 45-60.
      Chico, Calif.: Scholars Press, 1985.

551. Novak, David. "Women in the Rabbinate?" In *Halakhah
      in a Theological Dimension*, 61-71. Chico, Calif.:
      Scholars Press, 1985.

      Discusses the problem of whether women may become
      rabbis. Refers to the important role of Jewish
      feminists in this question. Deals with the halakhic,
      historical, theological, and philosophical questions
      pertaining to the ordination of women and concludes
      that the basic demands of Jewish feminists have no
      adequate foundation in these aspects of traditional
      Judaism. Concludes with the suggestion that if women
      want to assume new roles in Judaism, they should
      create new religious institutions without essentially
      altering the ones already in existence.

552. Novak, David. "Women in the Rabbinate?" *Judaism* 33
      (1984): 39-49.

553. Nunnally-Cox, Janice. "Woman and Israel." In
      Foremothers. Women of the Bible, 1-96. New York:
      Seabury Press, 1981.

This chapter treats women in the Old Testament. The first part is about the matriarchs: Sarah and Hagar, Lot's daughters, Rebekah, Leah and Rachel. Part two treats women of the Exodus; part three is about women of the Promised Land; part four, about women of the Kingdom; and part five, about women of the Prophets' times.

554. Nyk, Miriam. "The 'Ingathered' Attire." In *Women in Israel*, published by Israel Information Centre, 65-86. Tel Aviv, 1975 (Previously published in *Dvar Hapoelet*).

About women and clothing.

555. Ochs, Carol. *Behind the Sex of God. Toward a New Consciousness--Transcending Matriarchy and Patriarchy*. Boston: Beacon Press, 1977. 177 pp.

About how the dichotomy of matriarchy and patriarchy has affected religious thought.

556. Oestereicher, John M. "Piety and Prayer in Jewish Home." *Worship* 27 (1953): 540-49.

557. Orbach, William. "Homosexuality and Jewish Law." *Journal of Family Law* 14 (1975/76): 353-81.

Traces references to homosexuality in the Old Testament through medieval and modern halachic codes and the Responsa literature, to modern time and the emergence of gay synagogues. States that there are very few references to female homosexuality.

558. Ostrov, Stewart. "Sex Therapy with Orthodox Jewish Couples." *Journal of Sex and Marital Therapy* 4 (Winter 1978): 266-78.

The sexual relationship of the Orthodox Jewish couple is strictly regulated by laws. Describes different kinds of treatment of sexual dysfunctions within this group.

559. Otwell, John H. *And Sarah Laughed. The Status of
      Women in the Old Testament.* Philadelphia: The
      Westminster Press, 1977. 222 pp.

      Describes the standing of woman in the Old
      Testament based upon more than 700 scriptural
      passages in which a woman or women are mentioned.
      The following subjects are treated: the creation of
      woman; sexual attraction; marriage; woman as mother;
      the subservience of women; widows, divorcées;
      freedom of action; women in the cult; and female
      personifications. Concludes that the status of
      woman in the Old Testament is high and that she
      exercised full participation in the life of the
      community.

560. Ozick, Cynthia. "Notes toward Finding the Right
      Question." In *On Being a Jewish Feminist. A
      Reader*, edited by Susannah Heschel, 120-51.
      New York: Schocken Books, 1983 (Reprint from
      Lilith, no. 6 [1979]).

      An attempt to formulate the right question
      concerning the status of Jewish women. Asserts that
      the subordination of women is not deeply rooted in
      Torah but is the result of historical customs and
      practices, which can be halakhically repaired. The
      right question is a sociological, not a theological
      one.

561. Ozick, Cynthia. "Torah as the Matrix for Feminism."
      Lilith, no. 12/13 (Winter/Spring 1985): 47-48.

      A defense of Torah as a source of feminism. "Torah
      as feminism, feminism as Torah."

562. Padan-Eisenstark, Dorit D. "Are Israeli Women Really
      Equal? Trends and Patterns of Israeli Women's
      Labor Force Participation: A Comparative Analysis."
      Journal of Marriage and the Family 35 (1973):
      538-45.

      Asserts that Israeli women have not achieved a
      higher degree of equality within the labor force than

women in other industrial countries. They are
predominantly occupied in teaching, nursing, clerical
work, and sales occupations. Except for medicine,
they are underrepresented in all managerial and high
status professional occupations.

563. Padan-Eisenstark, D. "Career Women in Israel: Their
Birth Order and Their Sibling Groups' Sex
Composition." *Journal of Marriage and the Family*
34 (1972): 552-56.

A study on career women in high status positions in
order to find the correlation between career status
on the one hand, and sibling groups' birth order and
sex composition on the other hand.

564. Padan-Eisenstark, Dorit D. "Girls' Education in the
Kibbutz." *International Review of Education* 19
(1973): 120-25.

An investigation into the success of the kibbutz
educational system in solving problems concerning
modern women's role in society. Examines whether
girls and boys are given equal chances of development
and whether girls are given the opportunity to choose
the role they wish to play. Concludes that the
kibbutz has not yet solved this problem completely
but this is a transitory situation and the kibbutz
system will be able to solve the problems of women's
role in the future.

565. Padan-Eisenstark, Dorit. "Image and Reality: Women's
Status in Israel." In *Women Cross-Culturally.
Change and Challenge*, edited by Ruby Rohrlich-
Leavitt, 491-505. World Anthropology, vol. 15.
The Hague: Mouton, 1975.

This study is a factual survey of the extent of
equality achieved by Israeli women in the areas of
work and political activity. Its conclusion is that
Israel has not achieved equality but has adopted it
as an ideal and as part of its central value system.

566. Padan-Eistenstark, Dorit. "The Uneven Pace of
      Equality: A Comparative Perspective of Women's
      Changing Status in Israel." *Kidma*, no. 7
      (1975): 24-29.

      Asserts that the "double role" ideology is
      prevalent in Israel. A woman's employment is
      regarded as only an addition to her central role as
      housewife and mother. As a result very few women
      enter high-ranking positions. The "double role"
      ideology shows itself also in the political sphere,
      in the defense forces, and even in the kibbutzim.
      Maintains that although the "double role" ideology
      creates a subjective feeling of equality between the
      sexes, it does not enable women to have full share
      in society's resources and rewards. However, there
      is hope for change in the future.

567. Paige, Karen Ericksen, and Jeffrey M. Paige. *The
      Politics of Reproductive Ritual*. Berkeley:
      University of California Press, 1981. 380 pp.

      This study in comparative social science started as
      an analysis of women's pollution beliefs and
      menstruation practices but evolved into an analysis
      of the mechanisms used by men to control
      reproduction. A vast range of societies are
      examined, among them the ancient Hebrew and modern
      Jewish societies.

568. Palgi, A. "Ethnic-Differences in Hemoglobin
      Distribution of Asian and European Jewish Women in
      Israel, Both Pregnant and Non-Pregnant." *American
      Journal of Public Health* 71 (1981): 847-51.

569. Parrinder, Geoffrey. "Hebrew Affirmations." In *Sex
      in the World's Religions*, 178-201. London: Sheldon
      Press, 1980.

      A description of the view on sexuality and women's
      position in Biblical and post-Biblical literature.
      Stresses the misogynic attitudes found in the Torah
      and the Talmud but emphasizes also the positive

aspects toward sexuality of Jewish teachings and traditions.

570. Patai, Raphael. *The Hebrew Goddess.* Jerusalem: Ktav Publ. House, 1967. 349 pp.

571. Patai, Raphael. *Sex and Family in the Bible and the Middle East.* New York: Doubleday, 1959. 282 pp.

572. Pearlmutter, Fishel A. "The Case of Women Rabbis." *Judaism* 33 (1984): 50-53.

    A discussion of women rabbis in Conservative Judaism.

573. Pedersen, Johs. "The Family, the Father's House and the People." In *Israel. Its Life and Culture I-II*, 46-60. London: Oxford University Press, 1926 (First published in Danish in 1920).

574. Pedersen, Johs. "The Formation of the Family." In *Israel. Its Life and Culture I-II*, 61-81. London: Oxford University Press, 1926 (First published in Danish in 1920).

575. Pedersen, Johs. "The Property of the Family." In *Israel. Its Life and Culture I-II*, 81-96. London: Oxford University Press, 1926 (First published in Danish in 1920).

576. Pelleg-Sani, Tamar. "Personality Traits of the 'Jewish Mother': Realities behind the Myth." Ph.D. diss., United States International University, 1984. 231 pp.

    The "Jewish Mother" as portrayed in the literature--does she exist? In order to find out if such a personality style does exist, 200 mothers, 100 Jewish and 100 Protestant, were asked to participate in a study. The findings of the

investigation did not support the traditional
stereotype which describes her as manipulative,
domineering, meddling, controlling through guilt,
and nurturing.

577. Peretz, David J.H. "Source Material for Sex
      Education in the Jewish Day School." Ed.D. diss.,
      Yeshiva University, 1975. 237 pp.

      This study offers resource materials in sex
      education from the point of view of the Torah. The
      purpose is to prepare a course of study in this
      subject for students in Jewish Day Schools.

578. Peritz, Ismar J. "Women in the Ancient Hebrew Cult."
      Journal of Biblical Literature 17 (1898): 111-48.

      Tries to find evidence in the Old Testament that
      all kinds of cultic activities were open to women.
      Concludes that the Semites in general, and the
      Hebrews in particular, "and the latter especially in
      the earlier periods of their history, exhibit no
      tendency to discriminate between man and woman so far
      as regards participation in religious practices, but
      that woman participates in all the essentials of the
      cult, both as worshiper and official; and that only
      in later time, with the progress in the development
      in the cult itself, a tendency appears, not so much,
      however, to exclude woman from the cult, as rather to
      make men prominent in it."

579. Peskin, Harvey, Zvi Giora, and Mordecai Kaffman.
      "Birth Order in Child-Psychiatric Referrals and
      Kibbutz Family Structure." *Journal of Marriage and
      the Family* 36 (1974): 615-18.

      A study of how the sex of the first-born reflects
      differential stress and status of the male in the
      kibbutz family and the female in the urban family.

580. Phillips, Anthony. "Some Aspects of Family Law in
Pre-Exilic Israel." *Vetus Testamentum* 23 (1973):
349-61.

Family law is another category of law in addition
to crime and tort. Under the terms of family law,
there was no recourse to the courts. Family law was
administered in the home by the head of the household
acting unilaterally. Women, children, and slaves
were regarded as personal property, and how he dealt
with members of his household who were not free adult
males, was the householder's private affair. His
domestic actions were of no concern to the courts.
Uses divorce, the institution of permanent slavery,
and adoption to illustrate his argument.

581. Pincus, Cynthia. "Other Voices: Beyond Feminist
Politics: The Israeli Woman." *School Review* 84
(1976): 564-71.

An examination of the life styles of Israeli women
compared with those of U.S. women. The findings
indicate that Israeli women manage role combining
better than the American ones. A comprehensive
network of social services for women in Israel may
contribute to this situation.

582. Piper, Otto Alfred. *The Biblical View of Sex and
Marriage.* New York: Charles Scribner and Sons,
1962. 239 pp.

583. Plaskow, Judith. "Blaming the Jews for the Birth of
Patriarchy." In *Nice Jewish Girls. A Lesbian
Anthology,* edited by Evelyn Torton Beck, 250-54.
Trumansburg, N.Y.: The Crossing Press, 1982.

Attacks the "myth" that the ancient Hebrews
invented patriarchy: "that before them the goddess
reigned in matriarchal glory, and that after them
Jesus tried to restore egalitarianism, but was foiled
by the persistence of Jewish attitudes within the
Christian tradition." Asserts that this "myth" is
developing in Christian feminist circles and that it
reinforces already existing anti-Judaic attitudes.

584. Plaskow, Judith. "The Jewish Feminist: Conflict in
      Identities." In *The Jewish Woman: New
      Perspectives*, edited by Elizabeth Koltun, 3-10.
      New York: Schocken Books, 1976.

      In this essay the identity of the Jewish woman is
      discussed. There is a conflict between being a woman
      and being a Jew. This is, in the first place, a
      conflict between communities; between the Jewish and
      feminist community. The Jewish community will not
      let the feminist feel at home in it. This, the
      author says, arises partly from the fact that
      everything in the Jewish written tradition comes
      from the hands of men. Tradition excludes women.
      Also, men have determined the words to describe
      women's reality. Women need to name anew the world
      around them in order to express the experiences of
      women. It is necessary to recover and reappropriate
      the histories of Jewish women who managed to be
      persons within the boundaries allotted to them. As
      an example, the story of Lilith and Eve is told.

585. Plaskow, Judith. "Das Kommen Liliths: Schritte zu
      einer feministischen Theologie." In *Frauen in der
      Männerkirche*, edited by Bernadette Brooten and
      Norbert Greinacher, 245-58. München: Kaiser, 1982.

      Relates the story of Lilith as a basis for a
      discussion of the possibilities of a feministic
      theology.

586. Plaskow, Judith. "The Right Question Is
      Theological." In *On Being a Jewish Feminist. A
      Reader*, edited by Susannah Heschel, 223-33.
      New York: Schocken Books, 1983.

      An answer to Cynthia Ozick (see 560), who tried to
      find the right question concerning the status of
      Jewish woman. Ozick found the right question to be
      a sociological one; Plaskow asserts that it is
      theological. Halakhic change is of no importance as
      a medium of expression and repair. Believes in a new
      understanding of Torah, God, and Israel.

587. Plautz, Werner. "Monogamie und Polygynie im Alten
     Testament." *Zeitschrift für die Alttestamentliche
     Wissenschaft* 75, Neue Folge 34 (1963).

     Monogamy is the most frequent kind of marriage in
     the Old Testament. We also find some examples of
     bigamy, a man married to two wives, and several
     examples of polygamy, three wives or more. Until
     the seventh century B.C. there is no criticism of
     polygamy in the Old Testament, but from the
     Deuteronomy onward, it was criticized and limited.
     The role of the woman in a polygamous marriage is
     discussed. Thinks that polygamy has an unfavorable
     influence on the status of women and strengthens the
     patriarchy. On the other hand: the more wives, the
     more sons, which strengthens the family and the man's
     reputation. More wives also mean more workers.

588. Poethig, Eunice Blanchard. "The Victory Song
     Tradition of the Women of Israel." Ph.D. diss.,
     Union Theological Seminary in the City of New York,
     1985. 303 pp.

     Sees the early Israel victory song tradition as a
     carrier of Israel's theology of liberation. These
     songs are ascribed to women. Examines the evidence
     for women as the composer-poet-traditioners of these
     songs and assesses the implications of the songs and
     narratives as expression of women's theological
     tradition. Concludes that the victory songs and the
     narratives point to the importance of women in early
     Israel and the victory songs celebrate not only
     Israel's victory over its external enemies but the
     importance of women to the victory of Yahweh in
     Israel.

589. Pollitzer, Anita L. "Woman and the Law." *The Jewish
     Woman* 4, no. 4 (1924): 7-8 and 45-46.

590. Pollock, Beatrice. "The American Par Excellence."
     In *Jewish Grandmothers*, edited by Sydelle Kramer
     and Jenny Masur, 105-18. Boston: Beacon Press,
     1976.

A personal account of an immigrant woman who came
to the United States from Eastern Europe. Has a good
life in America, being able to combine the values of
her native culture and the culture of her new
country.

591. Porter, Jack Nusan. "Rosa Sonnenschein and *The
American Jewess*: The First Independent English
Language Jewish Women's Journal in the United
States." *American Jewish History* 68 (1978): 57-63.

The periodical *The American Jewess* (1895-99), was
published and edited by Rosa Sonnenschein
(1847-1932). This study analyzes the magazine and
its editor and places them into the feminist history
of the late nineteenth and early twentieth century.

592. Porter, Jack Nusan. "Rosa Sonnenschein and *The
American Jewess* Revisited: New Historical
Information on an Early American Zionist and Jewish
Feminist." *American Jewish Archives* 32 (1980):
125-31.

A revision and expansion of his previous article on
Rosa Sonnenschein (see 591). The main source of his
new information is the recollections of
Sonnenschein's grandson, David Loth. The Zionist
aspect is here treated on par with the feminist one.

593. Porter, Judith, and Alex A. Albert. "Attitudes
towards Women's Role: Does a 'Jewish Subculture'
Exist in America?" *Gratz College Annual of Jewish
Studies* 5 (1976): 127-42.

A research report. The sample utilized consists of
approximately 790 white women living in the
Philadelphia area. The purpose was to investigate
the effect of dominant American culture or a distinct
subculture on sex role attitudes. The findings
indicate that a Jewish subculture does persist to
some extent, at least with regard to the dimension of
women's role. It seems to operate to some extent

within certain social structural categories to offset
dominant conservative influences created by those
structures.

594. Portrait, Ruth. "Jewish Women in Search of Equality.
     Will Moderation Sway the Rabbis?" *Jewish Observer
     and Middle East Review*, June 14 (1974): 18-19.

     About a confrontation between four delegates from
     the International Council for Jewish Women (ICJW) and
     two chief Rabbis from the Israel Chief Rabbinate.
     The delegation presented a wish for the Rabbinate
     "to find the means and interpretations in the Talmud
     and the Codes" to do something in matters concerning
     get (divorce), *chalizah* (the obligation for a
     childless widow to obtain the consent of the dead
     husband's brother before she can remarry), and
     agunah (a woman whose husband is missing without any
     proof of being dead), polygamy, and inheritance.
     There was little agreement.

595. Posen, Jacob. "Die Stellung der Frau im jüdischen
     Religions-gesetz (Halacha)." *Judaica* 41 (1985):
     142-51.

     About women's position in Jewish religious law
     (*Halachah*). The different directions within Judaism
     have different attitudes to *Halachah*. For some Jews
     Halachah is absolutely binding, for others it means
     very little. When it is complained that women are
     treated as inferior to men, this concerns especially
     family law and women's role in public religious
     services. Describes women's position in these
     spheres according to Jewish religious law and
     concludes that *Halachah* tends to refer women to the
     domains of housewife and mother but stresses that
     the position of women has improved in Orthodox
     Judaism.

596. Prais, S.J. "Statistics of Milah and the Jewish
     Birth-Rate in Britain." *Jewish Journal of
     Sociology* 12 (1970): 187-93.

Asserts that the number of male births in the
Jewish community in Great Britain during the period
1965-68 was about 2000 a year. This number is
consistent with the number of synagogue marriages
and with the number of deaths. When the number of
deaths is compared with number of births, a
deficiency of about 400 male births a year emerges.

597. Prais, S.J., and Marlena Schmool. "The Fertility of
     Jewish Families in Britain, 1971." *Jewish Journal
     of Sociology* 15 (1973): 189-203.

An inquiry was carried out in relation to a sample
of some seven hundred Jewish male births in 1971, and
the present paper discusses the results. The parents
were asked about the number of children previously
born, the date of their marriage and to which section
of the religious community they belonged. Tries to
find a correlation between the answers to these
questions and fertility.

598. Prais, S.J., and Marlena Schmool. "The Social-Class
     Structure of Anglo-Jewry, 1961." *Jewish Journal
     of Sociology* 17 (1975): 5-15.

599. Prais, S.J., and Marlena Schmool. "Statistics of
     Jewish Marriages in Great Britain 1901-1965."
     Jewish Journal of Sociology 9 (1967): 149-74.

Tries to find some reasons for the fall in Jewish
marriages by synagogue group from 1901 to 1965.

600. Prais, S.J. and Marlena Schmool. "Synagogue
     Marriages in Great Britain 1966-8." *Jewish Journal
     of Sociology* 12 (1970): 21-28.

A continuation of the study from 1967 (see 599).
Examines possible reasons for the fluctuations in
number of synagogue marriages since the beginning of
the decade and discusses expected trends and
problems in the ensuing quinquennium. The figure
for 1966 showed a sharp increase compared to the
previous year. This was followed by a small decline

in 1967 and a small rise in 1968. Suggest that in
the next few years the level of synagogue marriages
will be somewhat higher than in the earlier part of
the decade.

601. Pratt, Norma Fain. "Culture and Radical Politics:
Yiddish Women Writers, 1890-1940." *American Jewish
History* 70 (1980); 68-90.

A study of fifty women Yiddish writers whose works
were published in the United States. Most of them
wrote poetry, came from Eastern Europe, and were born
into Orthodox Jewish families. They were a part of
the radical Yiddish subculture and were on the whole
quite conscious about their problems as women.
However, they were never part of any feminist
movement.

602. Pratt, Norma Fain. "Transitions in Judaism: The
Jewish American Woman through the 1930s." *American
Quarterly* 30 (1978): 681-702.

A study of the growth in the status of Jewish women
in America. Jewish women came from different parts
of the world and stood for different spheres of
religious behavior. This determined the rapidity of
development and growth. Reform Jews from Western
Europe initiated radical innovation in the position
of woman, while Orthodox Jews, mostly from Eastern
Europe, had less freedom. However, many young women
did not remain Orthodox Jews. Conservative Judaism
attracted many second- and third-generation American
Jews of Eastern European background. Conservatives
adjusted the status of women following somewhat the
practice of Reform Judaism. Secular Judaism, which
developed in the late nineteenth century offered
women a different place in Jewish society. They
rejected most theological values and women had more
equality with men than their sisters in the Orthodox,
Conservative, and Reform movements. In the 1920s and
1930s the fear of assimilation and a growing anti-
Semitism was a strong inhibiting force among the
women themselves. There was not much development as
far as struggle for equality with men was concerned.

Not much happened until the 1970s, when Jewish
feminists pressed for new changes.

603. Prell, Riv-Ellen. "The Dilemma of Women's Equality
      in the History of Reform Judaism." *Judaism* 30
      (1981): 418-26.

      States that by making women equal, reformers made
      them invisible. "Religious reformation that denies
      gender by making all participants conform to the male
      model inevitably reinforces women's invisibility."

604. Prell, Riv-Ellen. "The Vision of Woman in Classical
      Reform Judaism." *Journal of the American Academy
      of Religion* 50 (1982): 575-89.

      Treats some of the efforts of mid-nineteenth century
      German Jewish reformers to create a Judaism that
      incorporated the best of the Enlightenment and
      eliminated those features of Jewish Orthodoxy
      unappealing to the culture. The status of women
      was one of the features they wanted to change.

605. Prell-Foldes, Riv-Ellen. "Coming of Age in Kelton:
      The Constraints on Gender Symbolism in Jewish
      Ritual." In *Women in Ritual and Symbolic Roles*,
      edited by Judith Hoch-Smith and Anita Spring,
      75-99. New York and London: Plenum Press, 1978.

606. Priesand, Sally. "From Promise to Reality." *Keeping
      Posted* 17, no. 7 (1972): 17-19.

      Recounts some of the history of Reform Judaism
      concerning the status of woman. Important changes
      began to take place well over a century ago. In 1892
      the Central Conference of America Rabbis made Jewish
      women eligible for full membership in their
      congregations, which meant full religious equality.
      The reason why so few women use their religious
      rights, he says, lies with individual Jews and their
      attitudes.

607. Priesand, Sally. *Judaism and the New Woman.* The
     Jewish Concepts and Issues Series. New York:
     Behrman House Inc., 1975. 144 pp.

     Sally Priesand was the first woman to be ordained
     by any theological seminary into the rights and
     privileges of the rabbinate. Her book examines
     Jewish tradition in terms of its view towards women.
     Points to the many ways in which Jewish law
     discriminates against women and discusses the
     relationship between being a woman and being a Jew,
     both historically and in the modern world.

608. Proctor, Priscilla. *Women in the Pulpit: Is God an
     Equal Opportunity Employer?* Garden City, N.Y.:
     Doubleday, 1976. 176 pp.

     On women in the ministry, including comments by
     some thirty women ministers and rabbis.

609. Prusak, Bernard P. "Woman: Seductive Siren and
     Source of Sin? Pseudepigraphal Myth and Christian
     Origins." In *Religion and Sexism. Images of Women
     in the Jewish and Christian Traditions*, edited by
     Rosemary Radford Ruether, 89-116. New York: Simon
     and Schuster, 1974.

     Tries to trace the origins of the concept of sin in
     the Old Testament.

610. Quart, Barbara. "The Treatment of Women in the Work
     of Three Contemporary Jewish-American Writers:
     Mailer, Bellow, and Roth." Ph.D. diss., New York
     University, 1979. 269 pp.

     The works of Norman Mailer, Saul Bellow, and Philip
     Roth are examined regarding their attitudes toward
     women. Although Mailer has come under heavy feminist
     attack, he is here regarded as the one of the three
     who expresses most tenderness, romantic passion, and
     plain need for women in his work. His rage against
     women is seen as proportionate to his great
     dependency on them. In Saul Bellow's work, women

are hardly present at all. If they are, they are
treated as threats to men or as objects of ridicule.
Roth's women are often self-righteous and
faultfinding, wielders of guilt, and the men often
feel immense rage toward them. Concludes that a
common trait in the works of all three is a view of
women as cannibals and destroyers.

611. Rabin, A.I. "The Sexes: Ideology and Reality in the
      Israeli Kibbutz." In *Sex Roles in Changing
      Society*, edited by Georgene H. Seward and Robert C.
      Williamson, 285-307. New York: Random House,
      1970.

      Asserts that progress in the area of equality
      between the sexes has been slow and uncertain. There
      remains a discrepancy between ideology and reality.
      The background, history, and current status of this
      discrepancy are the major concern of this article.

612. Rabinowitz, Mayer E. "An Advocate's Halakhic
      Responses on the Ordination of Women." *Judaism* 33
      (1984): 54-65.

      Asserts that there are no valid Halakhic objections
      to the ordination of women. Nothing in the sources
      indicate that women cannot count in a *Minyan* or serve
      as witness and wedding officiant, so there should be
      no reasons why they cannot be ordained.

613. Rackman, Emanuel. "Arrogance or Humility in Prayer."
      Tradition 1 (1958): 13-26.

      About prayer in Orthodox Judaism.

614. Rackman, Emanuel. "Ethical Norms in the Jewish Law
      of Marriage." *Judaism* 1 (1954): 221-28.

615. Raming, Ida. "Von der Freiheit des Evangeliums zur
      versteinerten Männerkirche. Zur Entstehung und
      Entwicklung der Männerherrschaft in der Kirche."

In *Frauen in der Männerkirche*, edited by Bernadette Brooten and Norbert Greinacher, 9-21. München: Kaiser, 1982.

Stresses the freedom and high status of women in the circle around Jesus and in early Christianity in contrast to their low status in late Judaism (Spätjudentum).

616. Raphaël, Freddy. "Le couple de l'image a la réalité." In *L'autre dans la conscience Juive. Le sacré et le couple. Donneés et débats*, edited by Jean Halpérin and Georges Lévitte, 233-55. Paris: Presses Universitaires de France, 1973.

About the couple. Tries to reveal the nature of the couple and the role of women in the family. The article is followed by a debate.

617. Raphael, Marc Lee. "Female Humanity: American Jewish Women Speak Out." *Judaism* 30 (1981): 212-24.

618. Raphael, Marc Lee. "From Marjorie to Tevya: The Image of the Jews in American Popular Literature, Theatre and Comedy." *American Jewish History* 74 (1984): 66-72.

Asserts that *Marjorie Morningstar* by Herman Wouk sets the pattern for the stereotype of the American Jewish woman for the whole decade. She is the virtuous American girl and also a replica of the non-Jewish world.

619. Ravven, Heidi M. "Creating a Jewish Feminist Philosophy: An Agenda and an Approach." *Anima* 12 (1986): 96-105.

Proposes the following agenda: A Jewish feminist contribution to social and political theory, to law, to ethics and ethical theory; a feminist analysis of the authority of tradition; a feminist contribution to the philosophic definition and analysis of the central beliefs and praxis of Judaism; to clarify

which Jewish beliefs and rituals are especially
important to women. Thinks that Hegelian philosophy
seems to offer feminists a systematic way of
integrating their experiences and formulation of
Judaism into Jewish philosophy.

620. Reguer, Sara. "Jewish Mother and the Jewish American
     Princess--Fact or Fiction?" *USA Today*, no. 2412
     (1979): 40-42.

     Asserts that "the Jewish Mother is a purely
     American phenomenon growing out of a long tradition."
     She is as much a stereotype as the "Jewish American
     Princess," her daughter. Both confirm to a fixed
     pattern, the mother hovering over her children,
     sacrificing everything for them and the daughter,
     the epitome of the materialistic and spoiled young
     woman who manipulates the world for her own selfish
     ends. Tries to explain these two stereotypes by
     analyzing the history of Jewish women focusing on
     the Eastern Europe areas and the "Yiddische Mama,"
     since most American Jews come from this area. The
     social circumstances and the way the properties of
     the "Yiddische Mama" were perceived in the United
     States created the stereotypes. "Fact or fiction?"--
     a combination of both.

621. Reguer, Sara. "Kaddish from the 'Wrong' Side of the
     Mehitzah." In *On Being a Jewish Feminist. A
     Reader*, edited by Susannah Heschel, 177-81.
     new York: Schocken Books, 1983.

     An account of the frustration felt by an Orthodox
     Jewish woman because she had to say Kaddish (the
     prayer recited for a deceased parent, spouse, or
     child for eleven months from the date of the burial
     and again each year on the anniversary of the death)
     for her mother in a *mehitzah* (the partition
     separating women from men used in many synagogues).

622. Reifman, Toby Fishbein, and Ezrat Nashim, eds.
     Blessing the Birth of a Daughter. Jewish Naming

Ceremonies for Girls. Englewood, N.J.: Ezrat
Nashim, 1976. 40 pp.

623. Rein, Natalie. *Daughters of Rachel, Women in Israel.*
Harmondsworth, England: Penguin Books, 1980.
182 pp.

Stresses the nonexistence of women in the history
of the Jews, in the development of Zionism as well as
in the Old Testament. Goes through the history of
modern Israel from the first wave of immigrants
(1880-95) to the 1970s with emphasis on the status of
women. Part 2 starts with the 1970s. In this decade
women's liberation movements arose in many countries
and also in Israel. It started with consciousness-
raising groups, and continued with practical work and
political activity. Feminists brought into the open
all sorts of taboo subjects: abortion, pregnancy,
birth control, prostitution, homosexuality.
Concludes by asserting that feminists have set a new
moral tone and wonders if this will continue to
flourish or has to go underground.

624. Reis, Nannie A. "The Modern Esther." *Jewish Woman*
8, no. 1 (1928): 4-5.

625. Reisman, Deborah. "Exemplary Women Leave Mark on
Jewish History." *Israel Digest* 22, no. 16 (1979):
4-5.

About Jewish women who have played an important
role in history. Mentions examples of famous female
warriors, politicians, poets, and social workers, and
concludes with praising the traditional role of the
Jewish woman in history, the role of wife and mother.

626. Remy, Nahida. *Das Jüdische Weib.* Leipzig: Laudien,
1892. 328 pp.

In order to understand the position of Jewish
women, the author, a convert from Christianity,
compares the status of Jewish women with the status
of women in other cultures. She then examines the

position of women in different aspects of the Jewish
culture. Concludes that Jewish culture and religion
are superior to any other culture or religion as far
as women's status is concerned.

627. Rich, Adrienne. "Split at the Root." In *Nice Jewish
      Girls. A Lesbian Anthology*, edited by Evelyn
      Torton Beck, 67-84. Trumansburg, N.Y.: The
      Crossing Press, 1982.

      Personal stories from different parts of the
      author's life on the subject of identity. Starts
      with mentioning a poem written in 1960: "Split at the
      root, neither Gentile nor Jew, Yankee nor Rebel."
      Describes important events in her life until 1982
      and concludes that this essay has no conclusion; it
      is another beginning.

628. Richter, Ida. "The Entrepreneur/Raconteur." In
      Jewish Grandmothers, edited by Sydelle Kramer and
      Jenny Masur, 121-35. Boston: Beacon Press, 1976.

      An autobiographical essay by a Russian immigrant in
      America. Became a success as a business woman, but
      she started to write novels in her old age.

629. Rift, Patricia Elizabeth. "Lise Meitner: The Life
      and Times of a Jewish Woman Physicist." Ph.D.
      diss., The Union for Experimenting Colleges and
      Universities, 1983. 525 pp.

      A biographical study of Dr. Lise Meitner focusing
      upon her social status at the center of twentieth
      century historical events and intellectual
      developments, while existing on the periphery of
      various cultures as a woman in science, Jew in
      Germany, and emigrant in Sweden.

630. Riff, Esther Hurwich. "Jewish Education." *Jewish
      Woman* 5, no.2 (1925): 9-12.

631. Ringelheim, Joan. "Women and the Holocaust: A
     Reconsideration of Research." *Signs* 10 (1985):
     741-61.

     Starts with asserting that Jewish women's
     experiences and perceptions of the Holocaust have
     been absorbed into descriptions by men. However,
     research on women and the Holocaust is beginning.
     This research study is based on interviews with
     twenty women who had experienced and survived the
     Holocaust. The interview schedule has a twofold aim:
     1) to recapture the Holocaust experience as a whole,
     and 2) to establish women's sense of their particular
     experience within it, what was done to them (their
     vulnerabilities) and what they did (their resources).
     Most of the women referred to feelings and
     experiences of sexual vulnerability and humiliation,
     rape, sexual exchange, pregnancy, abortion, and fear
     and grief for their children. This research was
     conducted before 1984. In part 2 of this article the
     author criticizes her own methods which she finds too
     much influenced by "unconscious use of cultural
     feminism." Thinks that a work of this kind needs a
     different political and philosophical context.
     Different questions and different interpretations of
     the replies must be made.

632. Rissi, Matthias. "Das Judenproblem im Lichte der
     Johannesapokalypse." *Theologische Zeitschrift* 13
     (1957): 241-59.

633. Ritterband, Paul, ed. *Modern Jewish Fertility*.
     Leiden: Brill, 1981. 293 pp.

     A historical perspective on eighteenth-century
     Jewish family households in Eastern Europe.

634. Roazen, Deborah. "George Eliot's Jewish Feminist."
     Atlantis 8, no. 2 (1983): 37-43.

     Asserts that "George Eliot's attitude toward her
     Jewish material (in *Daniel Deronda*) is more complex
     than has generally been allowed" by her critics or
     editors or than George Eliot understood it to be.

Eliot's attitude toward women of Jewish or alien
culture is critical, and this attitude is revealed
through Princess Halm-Eberstein, her only "feminist
figure."

635. Rochlin, Harriet. "Riding High: Annie Oakley's
      Jewish Contemporaries." *Lilith*, no. 14 (Fall/
      Winter 1985-86): 14-18.

      About the pioneer Jewish women in the American
      West.

636. Riophe, Anne Richardson. *Torch Song.* New York:
      Farrar, Straus and Giroux, 1977. 225 pp.

      A novel about a young Jewish girl who falls in love
      with a sexual pervert and her eventual degradation.

637. Romain, Sybil Sheridan. "Report on Women in the
      Rabbinate." *European Judaism* 15 (1981): 31-32.

      As a rabbi in the Liberal movement, there are no
      duties she cannot perform. Finds that she can do
      some jobs better because she is a woman and that the
      most difficult thing is to be a figure of authority.

638. Romirowsky, J. Harold. "The Jewish Understanding of
      Sex." In *Marriage and Family Life. A Jewish View*,
      edited by Abraham B. Shoulson, 51-59. New York:
      Twayne, 1959.

639. Rosen, Gladys. "The Impact of the Women's Movement
      on the Jewish Family." *Judaism* 28 (1979): 160-68.

640. Rosen, Ruth, and Sue Davidson, eds. *The Maimie
      Papers.* New York: Feminist Press, 1977. 439 pp.

      Letters written between 1910 and 1922, by Maimie
      Pinzer to Fanny Quincy Howe, a prominent Bostonian.
      Maimie Pinzer for a long time worked as a prostitute,
      but she also supported herself by such other means

as were available to working-class women of her
period. Her letters are considered a most valuable
document and source in the history of working-class
Jewish women. She was also a morphine addict and she
spent long periods in jails, hospitals, and
reformatories. Her last letter is from 1922 at
age thirty-seven. There is no information available
to document the remainder of her life.

641. Rosen, Sherry. "Jewish Intermarriage." *Midstream*
     28, no. 3 (1982): 30-34.

     About intermarriage between European-American and
     Asian-African Jews. There are many differences
     between these two Jewish groups; differences in
     living conditions, educational achievements, economy,
     and culture. Intermarriage was encouraged in the
     1960s, and the percentage of such marriages increased
     for many years. However, it has not led to the
     expected cultural mosaic but has rather been a
     cultural absorption of the Orientals by the Westerns.

642. Rosenbaum, Michael, and Sheila Shichman. "Learned
     Helplessness and Depression among Israeli Women."
     Journal of Clinical Psychology 35 (1979): 395-400.

     A psychological study attempting to replicate a
     typical learned helplessness study with Israeli
     student nurses.

643. Rosenberg, Bernard. "Women's Place in Israel: Where
     They Are, Where They Should be." *Dissent* 24
     (1977): 408-17.

     This article is an analysis of the many injustices
     to women in Israel based on sex. Reminds us that the
     Israeli population is drawn from 102 countries, which
     means special problems in the work for emancipation.
     Women are discriminated against in the labor force,
     in the family, in the army, and in politics. As for
     abortion, the Knesset passed a compromise law in
     1977. It permits abortion for girls under sixteen
     and women over forty and if pregnancy is likely to
     cause severe harm to the woman or her children

because of harsh social and family conditions. This
bill overrode a storm of protest from rabbis and
conservatives who called the new legislation "a
license to mass infanticide." In other fields women
are not much better off today than in the start of
the state of Israel. For instance, there are fewer
women in the Knesset today than in 1948. Concludes
that with Begin as a leader, there is little hope for
any improvement, tied up as he is with two political
parties whose presence can only signify a temporary
setback for women's rights.

644. Rosenberg, Joel. "The Feminine through a (Male)
      Glass Darkly: Preface to a Demythology." *Response*,
      no. 28 (1975): 67-88.

645. Rosner, Fred. "In Vitro Fertilization and Surrogate
      Motherhood: The Jewish View." *Journal of Religion
      and Health* 22 (1983): 139-60.

      An examination of the ethical, moral Jewish
      religious issues involved in *in vitro* fertilization
      and surrogate motherhood. Artificial insemination
      and sex organ transplants are also discussed.
      Stresses that according to Jewish views human life
      is sacred and medical legislation is based on this
      principle.

646. Rosner, Fred, ed. *Sex Ethics in the Writings of
      Moses Maimonides*. New York: Bloch Publishing,
      1974. 129 pp.

647. Rosner, Fred. "Test Tube Babies, Host Mothers and
      Genetic Engineering in Judaism." *Tradition* 19
      (1981): 141-48.

      The Jewish legal and moral aspects of test tube
      babies, *in vitro* fertilization, artificial
      insemination, and surrogate or host mothers are
      discussed.

648. Rosner, Menahem. "Women in the Kibbutz. Changing Status and Concepts." *Asian and African Studies* 3 (1967): 35-68.

The purpose of this article is to present an analysis of the changes that have occurred with respect to the equality accorded women in the kibbutz. It contains the conclusions reached by a larger project carried out in 1965-66.

649. Roth, Joel. "Ordination of Women: An Halakhic Analysis." *Judaism* 33 (1984): 70-78.

Asserts that nothing in the *Halakhah* makes ordination of women as rabbis impossible. Treats the subjects of legal status of women vis-à-vis *Mitzvot*, women as witnesses, and the granting of ordination per se to women.

650. Roth, Norman. "The 'Wiles of Women' Motif in the Medieval Hebrew Literature of Spain." *Hebrew Annual Review* 2 (1978): 145-65.

651. Rothman, Sarah. "The Watchmaker." In *Jewish Grandmothers*, edited by Sydelle Kramer and Jenny Masur, 18-29. Boston: Beacon Press, 1976.

An autobiographical essay about the author's life as watchmaker in Russia and in the United States. Her husband was a Bolshevik and they emigrated out of fear for his safety.

652. Rozen, Freida Shoenberg. "The Permanent First-Floor Tenant: Women and Gemeinschaft." *Mennonite Quarterly Review* 51 (1977): 319-28.

A discussion of women's roles in Amish and Hutterite communities and a comparison with women's status in Hasidic communities in Brooklyn and in kibbutzim in Israel. Though there are great differences, a common trait of all these communities is that women are subordinate to men.

653.   Rubenstein, C. "The Jewish Woman--Myself and
       Others." *Dialectical Anthropology* 8 (1983):
       181-84.

654.   Rubin, Barbara. "On Women and War: An Interview with
       Marcia Freedman." *Response*, no. 32 (1976-77):
       41-47.

       Marcia Freedman, co-founder of Israel's feminist
       movement and an independent socialist Knesset member
       (see 273).

655.   Rudikoff, Sonya. "Women and Success." *Commentary*
       58, no. 4 (1974): 49-59.

       About women who have succeeded in different spheres
       of life, some of them Jewish.

656.   Ruether, Rosemary Radford, ed. *Religion and Sexism,*
       Images of Woman in the Jewish and Christian
       Traditions. New York: Simon and Schuster, 1974.
       356 pp.

       Eleven essays "attempt to fill a growing need for
       a more exact idea of the role of religion,
       specifically the Judaeo-Christian tradition, in
       shaping the traditional cultural images that have
       degraded and suppressed women."

657.   Ruether, Rosemary Radford. *Womanguides. Readings*
       toward a Feminist Theology. Boston: Beacon Press,
       1985. 274 pp.

       Wants to create a new textual base, a new canon,
       for feminist theology. Sees the book as a working
       handbook from which such a new canon might emerge.
       The texts in this collection are from different
       cultures but remain within the context of the
       cultural matrix that has shaped Western Christianity:
       the ancient Near East, the Hebrews, the Greeks, the
       New Testament, and the marginated communities at the
       edges of Judaism and Christianity.

658. Ruether, Rosemary Radford, and Eleanor McLaughlin,
eds. *Women of Spirit: Female Leadership in the
Jewish and Christian Traditions.* New York: Simon
and Schuster, 1979. 400 pp.

Fifteen essays discuss religious women as
charismatic leaders, holy women, dissenters,
martyrs, renewers, and reformers from the early
churches to the present day.

659. Ruether, Rosemary Radford, and Eleanor McLaughlin.
"Women's Leadership in the Jewish and Christian
Traditions. Continuity and Change." In *Women of
Spirit: Female Leadership in the Jewish and
Christian Traditions,* edited by Rosemary Radford
Ruether and Eleanor McLaughlin, 16-28. New York:
Simon and Schuster, 1979.

In this introduction the authors state that the
purpose of the present collection of essays is to
recover important chapters of women's history and
the charting of the paradigms of female leadership
within theological world views.

660. Sacks, Jonathan. "The Role of Women in Judaism."
In *Man, Woman, Priesthood,* edited by Peter Moore,
27-44. London: SPCK, 1978.

This article is about women's role in social life
and customs as well as in the religious life. The
author's view is that men and women have distinct
roles. The women's role is closely related to home
and the family, but it is neither limited to it, nor
is this role something outside the concern of man.
The women are exempted from some of the commandments
but are not excluded from them. The exemption was
intended to leave them free to pursue their role.
The reason they are not allowed to conduct services
in the synagogue is largely to be understood in terms
of the different worlds of prayer that men and women
inhabit in Judaism. Concludes that "liberation can
be understood in two ways. It can be freedom from
something or the freedom to do something. The
religious Jew or Jewess does not find his or her role
as something from which to seek liberation. From the

outside, it can seem a burden, a constraint. From
within, lived, affirmed, it can itself seem the
greatest liberation. The freedom to be what one was
chosen for. The freedom of knowing that one's life
has a meaning beyond one's own arbitrary choices.
The freedom that comes from knowing that the world is
God's question and one's life the answer."

661. Sakenfeld, Katharine D. "The Bible and Women: Bane
      or Blessing?" *Theology Today* 32 (1975): 222-33.

      Asks if the Bible as a whole really does teach the
      subjection of women to men as the will of God, or is
      this a long-standing misconception? Stresses the
      point of rereading and restudying the texts with
      a real effort to set aside what we think they say
      in order to see whether they really say something
      different. Goes through the creation narratives
      with respect to the place of women. Finds that the
      status of women in Jewish culture was far less
      restricted and subordinate by New Testament times
      than it had been in much of the Old Testament
      period. Concludes with some thoughts about the
      nature of liberation and freedom. "Liberation does
      not mean that we can all do what we please. It
      means that our choices are made in the light of our
      responsibility to God's kingdom in response to social
      pressures and stereotypes."

662. Salkind, S. "The Jewish Women of Latvia: Their
      Progress in Social Work." *Jewish Woman* 3, no. 1
      (1923): 2-3.

663. Salowitz, Vivian Silver. "Sexism in the Jewish
      Student Community." *Response*, no. 18 (Summer
      1973): 55-58.

      Rejects the "myth" that young people do not have to
      cope with sexism or chauvinism. Asserts that sexism
      exists in student communities as well as in other
      contemporary Jewish organizations.

664. Sanders, Audrey, and Janice M. Steil. "Taking the
      Traditional Route: Some Covert Costs of Traditional
      Decisions for the Married Career Women."
      Imagination, Cognition and Personality 3 (1983-84):
      327-36.

665. Sasso, Sandy Eisenberg. "According to Judaism." In
      *According to the Scriptures. The Image of Women as
      Portrayed in the Sacred Writings of the World's
      Major Religions*, published by The World Young
      Women's Christian Association and World Council of
      Churches. Geneva, 1975.

      In order to develop a picture of the role of woman
      in Judaism, the author gives a short survey of the
      development of Jewish history from the Biblical
      period through the rabbinic, medieval, and modern
      ages.

666. Sasso, Sandy Eisenberg. "B'rit B'not Israel:
      Observations on Women and Reconstructionism."
      Response, no. 18 (Summer 1973): 101-5.

      About Jewish birth ceremonies. Asserts that these
      center around the birth of the boy with the father as
      the central participant. Finds a need for the
      development of a meaningful ritual also at the birth
      of a girl. Suggests a ceremony suitable for the
      birth of a daughter and calls it *b'rit b'not Israel*.

667. Satlof, Claire R. "History, Fiction, and the
      Tradition Creating a Jewish Feminist Poetic." In
      On Being a Jewish Feminist. A Reader, edited by
      Susannah Heschel, 186-206. New York: Schocken
      Books, 1983.

      A discussion of books by Jewish women writers, most
      of them feminists. Asserts that any Jewish
      feminists' attempt to create a literature of their
      own must ground itself in the area of Jewish ritual
      activity, because this is the area which is most
      immediately in need of change.

668. Scarf, Mimi. "Marriages Made in Heaven? Battered
      Jewish Wives." In *On Being a Jewish Feminist*. *A
      Reader*, edited by Susannah Heschel, 51-64.
      New York: Schocken Books, 1983.

      Asserts that Jewish women are taught that a Jewish
      family is sacrosanct and that Jewish men do not beat
      their wives. However, interviews with hospital
      personnel, psychiatrists, rabbis, social workers,
      attorneys, women at shelters for battered women, and
      other women married to Jewish men in America show
      that wife beating is as common in Jewish families as
      in any other family. Thinks that the idealizing of
      the Jewish family prevents women from seeking help.
      The women involved often deny what is actually
      happening to them.

669. Schachter, Alexander, Erna Avram, and Israel
      Gorodeski. "Cytologic Findings in Oral-
      Contraceptive Users among Israeli Jewish Women."
      Acta Cytologica 27 (1983): 142-45.

      "A group of 3317 Jewish Israeli women were studied
      to evaluate a possible correlation between previous
      and recent oral contraceptive usage and cervical
      cytopathologic findings in Papanicolaou smears. A
      positive correlation was established between oral
      contraceptive usage and the occurrence of
      inflammatory findings: the rate of inflammatory
      changes depended on the length of usage, with a time
      lapse of at least one year preceding the appearance
      of such inflammatory changes. The cessation of oral
      contraceptive usage was associated with a decrease in
      the rate of inflammatory findings. No case of
      cervical intraepithelial neoplasia or malignancy
      were found."

670. Schachter, Alexander, Erna Avram, and Israel
      Gorodeski. "Cytologic Smear Findings in Oral-
      Contraceptive Users--Population Screening in Jewish
      Women." *Acta Cytologica* 25 (1981): 40.

      Abstract from the Seventh International Congress of
      Cytology, held in Munich, West Germany, May 19-22,
      1980.

671. Schäppi, Lydia. "Die Stellung der Frau im Judentum, im Islam und im Christentum. Ein Vergleich." Part 1 in *Judaica* 32 (1976): 103-12 and part 2 in *Judaica* 32 (1976): 161-72.

   This article is a lecture given during a Kirche-Israel Studienwoche in St. Moritz, September/October 1975. Starting with a summary of women's status in "paganism" (Greek and Roman periods), she gives a comparative survey of women's status in Judaism (in part 1), Islam, and Christianity (in part 2).

672. Scher, Dena, Baruch Nevo, and Benjamin Beit-Hallahmi. "Beliefs about Equal Rights for Men and Women among Israeli and American Students." *Journal of Social Psychology* 109 (1979): 11-15.

   About an investigation of attitudes toward equality between men and women. Israeli students were more egalitarian than the American students, women more egalitarian than men, kibbutz members were not more egalitarian than others, and the more religious held the least egalitarian beliefs.

673. Schiff, Ellen. *From Stereotype to Metaphor: The Jew in Contemporary Drama.* SUNY Series in Modern Jewish Literature and Culture. Albany: State University of New York Press, 1982. 276 pp.

674. Schiff, Ellen. "What Kind of Way Is That for Nice Jewish Girls to Act? Images of Jewish Women in Modern American Drama." *American Jewish History* 70 (1980): 106-18.

675. Schlesinger, Benjamin. "Family Life in the Kibbutz of Israel: Utopia Gained or Paradise Lost?" *International Journal of Comparative Sociology* 11 (1970): 251-71.

   When the Kibbutz movement was started in 1909, one of the main aims was equality between sexes. Women were to participate in all parts of social life and not be tied to the traditional mother and housewife

role. Communal laundry, kitchen, dining room,
kindergarten, and communal education were to relieve
her of the chores of laundry, cooking, dishwashing,
and raising children alone. However, a closer look
at kibbutz life in 1970, has shown that women are not
happy in their role. They do not feel that they have
been emancipated. They are often frustrated and wish
to go back to the traditional mother and wife role.
What was right during the pioneering days of Israel
may not be right "today," and in the modern
industrial Israel a complete change in the kibbutz
family system must develop.

676. Schlesinger, Rachel Clara. "Jewish Women in
      Transition: Delayed Entry into the Workforce."
      Ed.D. diss., University of Toronto (Canada), 1983.

      A study of twenty-two Jewish over the age of
      thirty-five who have entered the workforce after at
      least five years as full-time homemakers. About how
      they achieved and understood their change process as
      they entered the paid workforce. The findings show
      a marked variety of reasons for their entering. The
      role of woman both within her family and her
      community is considered in view of the implications
      drawn from the study.

677. Schlesinger, Yaffa. "Sex Roles and Social Change in
      the Kibbutz." *Journal of Marriage and the Family*
      39 (1977): 771-79.

      This paper asks what happened to the ideology of
      equality and why men and women did revert to
      traditional sex roles in the kibbutz.

678. Schnall, David J. "Frontier Women." *Midstream* 30,
      no. 8 (1984): 32-35.

      About the Jewish settlements in Judea and Samaria.
      This conflict area in the Arab-Israel struggle has
      been held by Israel as an "administered" territory
      since 1967. Dialogue with some women about how hard
      it is for a woman to live in this area. Here is much
      violence, and women must learn to relinquish their

everyday fears and accept the danger inherent in
busing children to Jerusalem or shopping in an Arab
market. Concludes that women living in the West Bank
settlements are actively involved in its governance
and the various social, communal, or educational
committees. There is a strong female representation
in the armed forces and women have been in the
forefront as settlement activists and spokespeople.

679. Schneid, Hayyim. *Marriage*. Philadelphia: Jewish
      Publication Society of America, 1973. 117 pp.

680. Schneider, Susan Weidman. *Jewish and Female*.
      Choices and Changes in Our Lives Today. New York:
      Simon and Schuster, 1984. 640 pp.

      An exploration of the diversity of Jewish women's
      daily lives in modern society in the light of
      feminism. About the difficulties of being Jewish and
      female. Through personal stories many of these
      difficulties are elucidated. Some of the Jewish
      women's problems are specific and must be solved in
      specific ways.

681. Schneider, Susan Weidman. "Why Jewish Women Get
      Raped. Lilith Interviews Pauline Bart." *Lilith*,
      no. 15 (Summer 1986): 8-12.

      An interview with Pauline Bart on the background of
      findings in her new book, *Stopping Rape. Successful
      Survival Strategies*. Bart mentions several reasons
      and situations where women are more or less able to
      resist rape. Thinks that Jewish women are more
      likely to have the assault end in rape than women of
      other ethnic and religious groups. One reason is
      that Jews and women tend to try to talk their way out
      of potentially dangerous situations--by accommodation
      and by appeal to the mercy of the attacker. To stop
      rape, pleading is relatively useless. Physical
      resistance, yelling, and active strategies are more
      effective.

682. Schneiderman, Rose. "The Problems of Women in
      Industry." *Jewish Woman* 4, no. 2 (1924): 6-7 and
      34.

683. Schoenfeld, Eugen. "Intermarriage and the Small
      Town: The Jewish Case." *Journal of Marriage and
      the Family* 31 (1969): 61-64.

      An examination of how intermarriage can influence
      the Jewish identity of the persons involved.

684. Schwartz, Owen Gibson, and Barbara Wyden. *The Jewish
      Wife.* New York: Peter H. Wyden, 1969. 308 pp.

      A study of upper-middle-class Jewish wives.

685. Schwartz, Laura Anker. "Immigrant Voices from Home,
      Work, and Community: Women and Family in the
      Migration Process, 1890-1938." Ph.D. diss., State
      University of New York at Stony Brook, 1984.
      869 pp.

      This study focuses on the particular stories of
      Hungarian, Slovak, Polish, Italian, and Jewish
      families and provides a detailed concrete description
      of the confrontation between ethnic familial cultures
      and the exigencies of American urban life.
      Emphasizes the role of the mother who organized the
      family economy by adapting European traditions to
      American necessities.

686. Schwartz, M. R. Jewelewicz, and R.L. Van de Wiele.
      "Application of Orthodox Jewish Law to Reproductive
      Medicine." *Fertility and Sterility* 33 (1980):
      471-74.

687. Sebba, L. "The Requirement of Corroboration in Sex
      Offences." *Israel Law Review* 3 (1968): 67-87.

688. Segal, J.B. "The Jewish Attitude towards Women."
      Journal of Jewish Studies 30 (1979): 121-37.

About the contrast between the honorable state of
women in daily life and their inferiority in
religious practices and under the law.

689. Segal, J.B. "Popular Religion in Ancient Israel."
Journal of Jewish Studies 27 (1976): 1-22.

One of the main points of this article is the
question why there are so few references to the
conduct of marriage, birth, and mourning practices in
the early legislation. The reason may be that the
leading role at these occasion is played by women,
magic, and the "men of God." These three elements
stood outside the established cult and are closely
interconnected.

690. Segal, Sheila F. "Feminists for Judaism." *Midstream*
21, no. 7 (1975): 59-65.

About the work of Jewish feminist organizations.
The members of these represent the full spectrum of
American Judaism from non-religious to Orthodox. The
common aim is to find ways of expressing both their
femaleness and their Jewishness with integrity in
intellectual, social, and religious life. Finds it
important, not only for Jewish women, but for Judaism
itself that women get an equal status with men in all
parts of life.

691. Segall, Alexander. "Sociocultural Variation in Sick
Role Behavioural Expectations." *Social Science and
Medicine* 10 (1976): 47-51.

A study of seventy hospitalized Anglo-Saxon
Protestant and Jewish female patients aged eighteen
to seventy concerning their expectations in regard to
the sick role. The findings indicate that the two
groups basically held the same expectations. The
Protestant patients objected to the dependency on
others which accompanies the sick role, but both
groups accepted the sick person's obligation to try
to get well and to seek competent help.

692. Seidler-Feller, Chaim. "Female Rabbis, Male Fears."
      Judaism 33 (1984): 79-84.

      About men's fears regarding ordination of women in
      Conservative Judaism.

693. Selavan, Ida Cohen. "The Founding of Columbian
      Council." *American Jewish Archives* 30 (1978):
      24-42.

      Examines the early years of the Columbian Council
      of Pittsburgh, a local section of the National
      Council of Jewish Women, and goes through its most
      important contributions to the life of Pittsburgh
      Jewry.

694. Seligman, Ruth. "Divorce." *Midstream* 28, no. 3
      (1982): 35-37.

      Tells about *Mitzvah*, a voluntary society with the
      express purpose of helping women who are seeking
      divorce and acting as a pressure group to effect
      change within the framework of *Halakhah*. This is in
      contrast to other organizations which work for
      establishment of a parallel civil court system for
      those who do not wish to marry and/or divorce
      according to *Halakhah*. *Mitzvah* wants to bring about
      meaningful change in the religious courts through
      halakhic methods.

695. Seller, Maxine S. "Putting Women into American
      Jewish History." *Frontiers* 5 (1980): 59-62.

      About her experiences in adding American Jewish
      women to the curriculum of a survey course, "The
      American Jewish Experience" at the State University
      of New York at Buffalo.

696. Seller, Maxine S. "Reclaiming Jewish Herstory."
      Lilith, no. 7 (1981): 23-26.

      Wants material on women in an American Jewish
      history survey course.

697. Shalev, Carmel. "A Man's Right to Be Equal: The
       Abortion Issue." *Israel Law Review* 18 (1983):
       381-430.

       A discussion of the various grounds for the man's
       claim to legal protection of his interests in the
       abortion decision. Suggests that there might be
       occasion to protect the man's interest only when his
       relation with the woman is one of long-term mutual
       commitment and he desires the child to be born and
       raised within the frame of that relationship. In
       any event, a presumption should arise in favor of the
       woman, any doubt being construed in her favor and
       her position being preferred where the opposing
       interests appear balanced.

698. Shapiro, Fannie. "The Rebel." In *Jewish
       Grandmothers*, edited by Sydelle Kramer and Jenny
       Masur, 2-16. Boston: Beacon Press, 1976.

       A personal account about life in the United States
       after she arrived in New York from White Russia in
       1906.

699. Sharrow, Anita. "The Radical in Exile." In *Jewish
       Grandmothers*, edited by Sydelle Kramer and Jenny
       Masur, 76-88. Boston: Beacon Press, 1976.

       About emigration from Russia to the United States.
       Describes Russia as the country of the socialist
       revolution and the center of the people's struggle
       for a better life. Wanted to go back, and tells how
       much she misses "her country."

700. Shepher, Joseph. "Familism and Social Structure: The
       Case of the Kibbutz." *Journal of Marriage and the
       Family* 31 (1969): 567-73.

       An essay on a research project which investigated
       the extent of the association between the change of
       the children's housing system and some attitudes
       generally considered as negative according to kibbutz
       values.

701. Sheridan, Judith Rinde. "Isaac Bashevis Singer: Sex
      as a Cosmic Metaphor." *Midwest Quarterly* 23
      (1982): 365-79.

      Asserts that Singer's apparent "obsession" with sex
      must be understood in terms of Kabbalistic metaphor,
      in which sex stands for either salvation or
      damnation.

702. Shevitz, Susan Rosenblum. "Sexism in Jewish
      Education." *Response*, no. 18 (Summer 1973):
      107-13.

      About religious school education in America. The
      goal of this education is Jewish identification and
      participation, and it provides no adequate means for
      the female student to approach either of these goals.
      The girl has no possibility of directing her energy
      toward her own spiritual development. Suggests
      several means with which the girl can fulfill herself
      and participate in Jewish life.

703. Shifman, Pinhas. "Marriage and Cohabitation in
      Israel Law." *Israel Law Review* 16 (1981): 439-60.

      A discussion of the legal consequences of marriage
      vs. extramarital cohabitation. Asserts that the
      legal significance of lawful marriage is diminishing,
      whereas that of extramarital cohabitation is growing
      to the extent that the distinction is becoming
      blurred.

704. Shiloh, Isaac S. "Marriage and Divorce in Israel."
      Israel Law Review 5 (1970): 479-98.

      Marriage in Israel is based on religious precepts,
      and the Jewish law of marriage and divorce is the
      most ancient body of law in force. In spite of this,
      marriage remains in essence a business transaction,
      a contract between two parties of equal legal
      capacity. However, religious law prohibits different
      types of marriages, such as between degrees of
      affinity. Mixed marriages between a Jew and a
      non-Jew are prohibited by Jewish law and cannot be
      celebrated in Israel. Divorce is administered by the

Rabbinical Court after one of the parties has sued for divorce. A judgment of divorce by the Rabbinical Court is actually no more than an order to the husband to deliver a bill of divorcement, *get*, to his wife.

705. Shohan, Jessie Bogen. "Post-War Europe and Its Jewish Women." *Jewish Woman* 4, no. 3 (1924): 3-4, 43.

706. Shoub, Myra. "Jewish Women's History: Development of a Critical Methodology." *Conservative Judaism* 35 (1982): 33-46.

Why have women been excluded from the writings of history in general? Mostly because historical study has primarily been concerned with power elites. Remarks the scarcity of material on the methodology of women's history in general--only one magazine article on Jewish women. Discusses various methodologies in the field of women's history and suggests adaptation of these to the study of Jewish women.

707. Shulman, Gail. "A Feminist Path to Judaism." In *On Being a Jewish Feminist. A Reader*, edited by Susannah Heschel, 105-9. New York: Schocken Books, 1983.

A description of how a young woman experienced the restrictions placed on women in Jewish families. Also how she years later was able to articulate her anger and frustration with patriarchal traditions in the meeting with the feminist movement.

708. Shulman, Gail B. "View from the Back of the Synagogue. Woman in Judaism." In *Sexist Religion and Women in the Church: No More Silence!*, edited by L. Hageman in collaboration with The Women's Caucus of Harvard Divinity School, 143-66. New York: Association Press, 1974.

Stresses that it is necessary to investigate both
biblical and rabbinic writings if one wants to
understand the status of women in Judaism today.
Attacks the male definition that women are separate
but equal. The status of women in Judaism is always
that of "other" which in reality often means
inferior, unclean, or sinful. As far as property is
concerned, a woman's property becomes her husband's
when she marries. A man can easily initiate divorce.
The only grounds for a woman is her husband's denial
of cohabitation. Finds that the many references to
women's uncleanness and evilness in Jewish writings
are problematic for modern Jewish women.

709.   Siegel, Richard, Michael Strassfeld, and Sharon
        Strassfeld. "Weddings." In *The First Jewish
        Catalog. A Do-It-Yourself Kit*, edited by Richard
        Siegel, Michael Strassfeld and Sharon Strassfeld,
        158-66. Philadelphia: The Jewish Publication
        Society of America, 1973.

Talmudic law provides for three methods of
establishing a marriage and the structure of the
present-day wedding ceremony symbolically involves
all three. At the wedding ceremony the groom
presents his bride with both a wedding band and a
marriage contract. After the ceremony they retire
in private to a room for *yihud*. Describes the
wedding ceremony from the rejoicing and invitations
to the seven days of feasting.

710.   Siegel, Seymour. "Some Aspects of the Jewish
        Tradition's View of Sex." In *Jews and Divorce*,
        edited by Jacob Freid, 158-85. New York: Ktav
        Publishing House, 1968.

711.   Sigal, Phillip. "Elements of Male Chauvinism in
        Classical Halakhah." *Judaism* 24 (1975): 226-44.

This article expands an earlier article on "Women
in a Prayer Quorum" (see 712). Tries to trace why
women in classical Judaism have been excluded from
equal participation in the rites and liturgy and
excluded from equality in economic matters and in

laws of marriage and divorce. Wants to find positive
evolutionary development in *Halakhah* in the direction
of full equality for women.

712. Sigal, Phillip. "Women in a Prayer Quorum." In
     Conservative Judaism and Jewish Law, edited by
     Seymour Siegel, with Elliot Gertel, 281-92.
     Studies in Conservative Jewish Thought, Vol. 1.
     New York: The Rabbinical Assembly, 1977 (First
     published in *Judaism* 23 [1974]: 174-82).

     Argues in favor of modifying Jewish law to allow
     women to be counted as part of the *minyan*, the
     prayer quorum.

713. Sinclair, Daniel B. "The Legal Basis for the
     Prohibition on Abortion in Jewish Law." *Israel
     Law Review* 15 (1980): 109-30.

     Analyzes the biblical and Talmudic passages which
     deal with abortion and surveys the various rabbinic
     opinions as to the legal basis for its prohibition.
     States in the conclusion that abortion in Jewish law
     constitutes a tort rather than a crime and may not
     therefore be classified as a form of homicide.

714. Singer, David. "Living with Intermarriage."
     Commentary 68, no. 1 (1979): 48-53.

     Asserts that the intermarriage issue is one aspect
     of the larger problem facing American Jewry. Many
     Jews are afraid that intermarriage may lead to
     assimilation. Thinks that the real problem is the
     reverse. It is not intermarriage that leads to
     assimilation, but assimilation that leads to inter-
     marriage. Does not find it surprising that there is
     an increase in the number of intermarriages as 57
     percent of Jewish couples do not participate in any
     synagogue or Jewish organizational activity.

715. Singh, Heidi. "Roman Catholic-Jewish Women's
     Dialogue in Los Angeles." *Journal of Ecumenical
     Studies* 19 (1982):870-71.

Report from the 1982 annual workshop "Two
Traditions in Dialogue" with Jewish and Roman
Catholic women from the Greater Los Angeles Area.
The theme of this year was: "In Search of Peace:
Interfaith Perspectives" with the express hope that
an essential element in the discussion of issues
would be the search for personal inner peace and
greater attention to the idea of women as
peacemakers.

716.   Slater, Paul E., David Weiner, and A. Michael Davies.
        "Illegal Abortion in Israel." *Israel Law Review*
        13 (1978): 411-16.

In Israel the Penal Law of 1936 made it illegal to
perform or to request an abortion. In 1952 abortions
were declared permissible if performed for "bona
fide medical reasons." From 1966 it has no longer
been a crime for a woman to seek abortion. In 1977
legal standing was given to hospital abortion
committees. Describes an investigation performed
from 1972 to 1975 when abortion was requested by
480 women. 69 percent of the abortion requests were
granted. Request for abortion was denied to 149
women. Of these, 69 (46.3 percent) gave birth within
nine months. For 80 (53.7 percent) no record of
birth could be found. Probably most, if not all,
of these 80 obtained illegal abortions.

717.   Small, Sarah Leah. "Attitudes of Professional and
        Lay Leaders of Congregations in a Major
        Metropolitan Jewish Community, Chicago, toward the
        Employment of Women as Administrators of
        Congregational Religious Schools." Ph.D. diss.,
        University of Missouri--Kansas City, 1983. 151 pp.

An investigation into the attitudes of professional
and lay leaders of congregations toward the
employment of women as congregational school
administrators. The findings indicate that women
leaders are more positive than men leaders; so are
leaders under the supervision of a woman.

718. Sochen, June. "Some Observations on the Role of
      American Jewish Women as Communal Volunteers."
      American Jewish History 70 (1980): 23-34.

      About volunteer activities by American Jewish women
      in organizational work.

719. Solis-Cohen, Judith. "The Jewish Woman of Yesterday
      and Today." *Jewish Woman* 7, no. 2 (1927): 1-2.

720. Solomon, Norman. "Jewish Divorce Law and
      Contemporary Society." *Jewish Journal of Sociology*
      25 (1983): 131-39.

      A review article on *The Jewish Law Annual* 4 (1981).
      This volume presents the main issues in Jewish
      divorce law and the problems of practicing this law
      in contemporary society. This volume is virtually
      unknown to British lawyers, and women are the victims
      of their ignorance. Rabbinic courts often refuse to
      dissolve marriages without the husband's formal
      authorization. An *agunah* (the "chained" woman)
      cannot remarry if her husband refuses her a *get*
      (bill of divorcement). Thinks that lawyers in all
      countries where there are substantial numbers of
      Jews should know Jewish law on divorce.

721. Somogyi, Tamar. "Jüdische Hochzeitsbräuche in
      Osteuropa im 18. und 19. Jahrhundert." In *Die
      Braut. Geliebt, verkauft, getauscht. Zur Rolle
      der Frau im Kulturvergleich*, vol. 1, edited by
      Gisela Völger and Karin V. Welck, 172-79.
      Köln (Cologne): Rautenstrauch-Joest-Museum,
      Museum für Völkerkunde, 1985.

      A description of marriage customs among Orthodox
      Jews in Eastern Europe during the eighteenth and
      nineteenth centuries. Until the middle of the
      nineteenth century Eastern Europe, especially Russia
      and Poland, had the biggest Jewish population in the
      world, with more than 5.5 million inhabitants of
      Jewish cultural and religious unity.

722. Soskin, Rose. "The Hungry Child." In *Jewish
      Grandmothers*, edited by Sydelle Kramer and Jenny
      Masur, 32-44. Boston: Beacon Press, 1976.

      An autobiographical essay about the struggle for
      survival in a warfront town in Poland during the
      First World War and the years after, until she and
      her family left for the United States in 1923.

723. Spector, Samuel. "The Talmud on Sex." *The Jewish
      Spectator* (February 1969): 19-22.

724. Spickard, Paul Russell. "Mixed Marriage: The
      American Minority Groups and the Limits of Ethnic
      Identity, 1900-1970." Ph.D. diss., University of
      California, Berkeley, 1983. 732 pp.

      A comparative study of outmarriage by Japanese
      Americans and Jews in twentieth-century America.

725. Spiegel, Dora R. "Cooperation among National Women's
      Organizations 1. The Point of View of the Women's
      League." *Jewish Woman* 8, no. 2 (1928): 1-3.

726. Spiegler, Samuel. "Do Ten Mr.'s Make a Minyan?"
      Journal of Jewish Communal Service 50 (1973): 104.

      Reports that ten women had organized a *minyan* and
      prayed together at two *Shabbat Mincha* services. They
      did not want to break Jewish tradition but to work
      within it to make *Shabbat Mincha* more meaningful by
      active participation. Tells that several rabbis are
      working on clarifying the issue of women's right to
      organize a *minyan*.

727. Spiro, Melford E. "The Crisis in the Kibbutz." In
      Kibbutz. Venture in Utopia, 201-39. Cambridge:
      Harvard University Press, 1956.

      This chapter treats the situation of women in the
      kibbutzim. It describes dissatisfaction with
      economic roles, frustration with the maternal role,

insecurity in work, interest in clothes, sexual
conditions, and the question of emancipation.
According to the author, the women themselves are
primarily responsible for the "crisis in the
kibbutz," because of their dissatisfaction.

728. Spiro, Melford E. *Gender and Culture: Kibbutz Women
      Revisited*. Durham: Duke University Press, 1979.
      116 pp.

      This volume is the third in Spiro's series about
      the Israeli kibbutz. Presents data to demonstrate
      that in Israeli kibbutzim the "female revolution" has
      been reversed in a "feminine counterrevolution," and
      that, in shaping sex roles, "precultural" forces are
      still prepotent over cultural ideologies.

729. Spiro, Melford E. "Is the Family Universal?"
      American Anthropologist 56 (1954): 839-46.

      About marriage and family in the kibbutz.
      Concludes with suggesting the following proposition:
      "Although the kibbutz constitutes an exception to the
      generalization concerning the universality of the
      family, structurally viewed, it serves to confirm
      this generalization, functionally and psychologically
      viewed."

730. Statler, Ruth B. "The Historic Role of Women in the
      Judaic-Christian Culture." *Brethren Life and
      Thought* 15, no. 3 (1970): 117-24.

731. Stern, Arleen. "Learning to Chant the Torah. A
      First Step." In *On Being a Jewish Feminist. A
      Reader*, edited by Susannah Heschel, 182-85.
      New York: Schocken Books, 1983 (Reprinted from
      the *Long Island Jewish World*, July 31-August 6,
      1981).

      An account of how the author learned to chant the
      Torah and how she felt when she first chanted her
      portion publicly in a *havurah* (group) service.

732. Stern, Arlene L. *International Mikvah Directory.*
      New York: Armis Publications, 1979. 28 pp.

733. Stern, Elizabeth Gertrude. *I Am a Woman--and a Jew.*
      New York: Arno Press, 1969. 362 pp. (Reprint of
      1926 edition).

      A personal account of a woman caught in the clash
      of Jewish and American culture.

734. Stern, Elizabeth Gertrude. "The Job, the Home and
      Woman." *Jewish Woman* 5, no. 1 (1925): 6-8.

735. Stern, Geraldine. *Daughters from Afar: Profiles of
      Israeli Women.* New York: Bloch Publishing Co.,
      1963. 190 pp.

      A description of the lives of twelve prominent
      women living in Israel, including Golda Meir.

736. Stern, Geraldine. *Israeli Women Speak out.*
      Philadelphia: Lippincott, 1979. 222 pp.

737. Stern, Malcolm H. "Jewish Marriage and Intermarriage
      in the Federal Period (1776-1840)." *American
      Jewish Archives* 19 (1967): 142-43.

738. Stern, Norton B. "The Charitable Jewish Ladies of
      San Bernardino and Their Woman of Valor, Henrietta
      Ancker." *Western States Jewish Historical
      Quarterly* 13 (1981): 369-76.

      About Henrietta Ancker, 1835-1890, active in social
      and charitable activities in San Bernardino. She was
      one of the organizers of the Ladies' Hebrew
      Benevolent Society.

739. Stocker, Devera Steinberg. "A Jewish First at the
      University of Michigan." *Michigan Jewish History*
      22 (1982): 12-14.

A personal narrative of how the author became the first Jewish woman on the University of Michigan's intercollegiate varsity debating team.

740. Stolper, Pinchas. *Jewish Alternatives in Love, Dating and Marriage.* New York: National Conference of Synagogue Youth/Union of Orthodox Jewish Congregations of America and University Press of America, 1984. 80 pp. (First published in 1967).

"An attempt to suggest a variety of approaches for setting forth an authentic Jewish position on sex, family, and male-female relationships--the understanding of which is so crucial in preparation for successful marriage and responsible adulthood." The book is mainly based on discussions with young people and focuses especially on those specific areas that concern young people of the "dating age." Concludes that sex is a private, personal matter and when linked with love and used in accordance with the tested guidelines set forth by Torah, it can be "the greatest and most beautiful lifegiving force."

741. Strelitz, Ziona. "Jewish Identity in Cape Town, with Special Reference to Out-Marriage." *Jewish Journal of Sociology* 13 (1971): 73-93.

742. Sugerman, Anne D. "The Jewish Woman in Canada." *Jewish Woman* 6, no. 2 (1926): 4-5.

743. Swidler, Leonard. *Women in Judaism. The Status of Women in Formative Judaism.* Metuchen, N.J.: Scarecrow Press, 1976. 242 pp.

This study attempts to answer the questions: What was the status of women in the period of formative Judaism; and where did women stand in the social scale in comparison to men? The attitudes toward women in Wisdom and Pseudepigraphical Literature are discussed; so are the attitudes of major Jewish groups as Pharisees, Sadducees, Essenes and the

Rabbis; and different aspects of women's life in reaction to cult and Torah.

744. Syrkin, Marie. "Suttee at the Women's Conference."
      Midstream 26, no. 8 (1980): 34-36.

      From the U.N. conference for women in Copenhagen,
      July 1980. Attacks the conference participants for
      anti-Zionism. Thinks that they concentrated too
      much on evading responsibility for the actions of
      particular governments. The only specific villain
      to be safely named was Israel. Repression of women
      was ascribed to "imperialism," "colonialism," and
      above all "Zionism." Emphasizes that the standard of
      living of Palestinian women in Israel is higher than
      that of Arab villagers in the neighboring Arab
      countries. Her conclusion is negative, but she finds
      one worthwhile accomplishment of the conference: a
      call for increased aid for family planning projects
      and for information that would enable men and women
      to decide the number and spacing of their children.

745. Syrkin, Marie. "Woman and Blacks in November."
      Midstream 30, no. 8 (1984): 41-43.

      In connection with the presidential election in the
      United States when Geraldine Ferraro was the
      Democratic vice-presidential candidate, we are told
      about some of Golda Meir's experiences as prime
      minister. Golda Meir's experiences indicated that
      men's reaction toward women in leadership was
      initially negative. Each step in her ascent was met
      with insulting amazement at her success. In the case
      of the American vice-presidential candidate, her sex
      was an argument *for*, not *against* her election as was
      the case with Golda Meir.

746. Szold, Henrietta. "On Saying Kaddish. A Letter to
      Haym Peretz." *Response*, no. 18 (Summer 1973): 76.

      Thanks Haym Peretz for his offer to act as Kaddish
      for her mother. Rejects the offer. Traditionally
      this is done by a son, but since her mother had no

son, but eight daughters, she thinks that the
daughters should say the Kaddish.

747. Tabory, Ephraim. "Rights and Rites: Women's Roles in
Liberal Religious Movements in Israel." *Sex Roles*
11 (1984): 155-66.

A study of which religious rites women in the
Reform and Conservative movements in Israel are
allowed to perform in their synagogues and how the
male and female members feel about women performing
such rites. The findings indicate that these
questions are of little concern among the members of
these movements. Also, there seems to be little
influence from the women's liberation movement on the
demands of religious adherents in general.

748. Talmon, Yonina. "The Family in a Revolutionary
Movement--The Case of the Kibbutz in Israel." In
The Family. Its Structures and Functions, edited
by Rose Laub Coser, 550-78. New York: St. Martin's
Press, 1974.

An analysis of the interrelation between changes in
communal structure and modification of family
organization in revolutionary and collectivist
movements. The analysis is based on a research
project carried out in a representative sample of
twelve of the kibbutzim affiliated with one of the
four Federations of Kibbutzim.

749. Talmon-Garber, Yonina. "The Family in Israel."
Journal of Marriage and the Family 16 (1954):
343-49.

This article, which describes and analyzes the main
characteristics of family structure in Israel, is in
part included in a paper presented to the World
Population Conference, held in Rome, August 31, 1954.
There is a great variety of patterns of family
organization in Israel due to the fact that the
inhabitants are immigrants from all over the world.
The families are organized according to patterns
brought from abroad. In addition comes the

establishment of new types of family organization
in cooperative and communal villages.

750. Tamari, Rimona. "Working Women Still Not at the
      Top." In *Women in Israel*, published by Israel
      Information Centre, 13-16. Tel Aviv, 1975
      (Previously published in *Dvar Hapoelet*).

      About women in the labor force.

751. Tchernovitz-Avidar, Yemima. *The Daughter; The Diary
      of an Israeli Girl*. Ramat-Gan: Massada Press,
      1969. 165 pp. (Translated from the Hebrew by
      Zwi Wineberg).

      Describes the problems of conflicting claims of
      personal fulfillment and national service of a young
      kibbutz member.

752. Terrien, S. "Toward a Biblical Theology of
      Womanhood." *Religion in Life* 42 (1973): 322-33.

753. Tetlow, Elisabeth Meier. "Women in Judaism." In
      *Women and Ministry in the New Testament: Called to
      Serve*, 20-29. Lanham: University Press of America,
      1980.

754. Tetlow, Elisabeth Meier. "Religious Office in the
      Old Testament." In *Women and Ministry in the New
      Testament: Called to Serve*, 30-45. Lanham:
      University Press of America, 1980.

755. Teubal, Savina. "A Coat of Many Colors." In *Nice
      Jewish Girls. A Lesbian Anthology*, edited by
      Evelyn Torton Beck, 85-88. Trumansburg, N.Y. The
      Crossing Press, 1982.

      About identity problems. The author is a lesbian
      with British education, born into a family with a
      Syrian-Arabic father and a Jewish mother of Syrian
      heritage, raised in England. Stresses that belonging

is a form of identification and connected with
history and tradition.

756. Teubal, Savina J. *Sarah the Priestess. The First
     Matriarch of Genesis.* Athens, Ohio: Swallow Press,
     1984. 199 pp.

Even if the only source in which Sarah is mentioned
is the Book of Genesis and even if the stories
dealing with her tell very little about her, Teubal
thinks that Sarah plays an important part in Genesis.
Sarah was a "priestess" with intimate relationships
with the supernatural. Suggests further that the
particular office held by Sarah was the most elevated
in rank and status, the most sacred and most
revered--a position comparable to that of women known
as *en* and *naditu* who belong to religious orders in
the ancient Mesopotamian region of Sumer. Thinks
that Sarah is symbolic of woman's struggle against a
male culture representing a non-patriarchal system--
the first matriarch of Genesis giving us "an insight
into the potential of women's roles to affirm women."
While patriarchy as presented in Genesis emphasized
individuality and the individual, matriarchy is
concerned with the community at large. Compares the
Sarah tradition with the accounts of the other
matriarchs, Rebekah, Rachel, and Leah.

757. Thompson, Tillie S. "What is Wrong with Marriage and
     Divorce?" *Jewish Woman* 6, no. 2 (1926): 2-3.

758. Ticktin, Esther. "A Modest Beginning." *Response*,
     no. 18 (Summer 1973): 83-89.

Brings up the question of a "new *Halachah*." Thinks
that there exists a new religio-ethical
consciousness, waiting and ready to be brought
forward in clear words and deeds. There are values
unacknowledged by the rabbinic authorities, since
they are not part of the *Halachah*. Proposes four
new *Halachot* for consideration which all deal with
the issue of the entry of women into the congregation
of Israel as full and equal partners and what men
must do to help bring this about.

759. Tiger, Lionel, and Joseph Shepher. *Women in the
      Kibbutz.* New York: Harcourt, Brace, Jovanovich,
      1975. 334 pp.

      This book describes the sex roles in the kibbutz.
      Takes up the role of woman in daily life of the
      kibbutz, in politics, in education, and in military
      service.

760. Tilchen, Maida with Helen D. Weinstock. "Letters
      from My Aunt." In *Nice Jewish Girls. A Lesbian
      Anthology,* edited by Evelyn Torton Beck, 220-40.
      Trumansburg, N.Y.: The Crossing Press, 1982.

      A correspondence between Maida Tilchen and her Aunt
      Helen (D. Weinstock) starting in 1974. The letters
      deal with many items in relation with being a lesbian
      and a Jew.

761. Toll, William. "The Female Life Cycle and the
      Measure of Jewish Social Change: Portland, Oregon,
      1880-1930." *American Jewish History* 72 (1983):
      309-32.

      A comparison between family and occupational
      patterns of German and East European Jewish immigrant
      women in Portland, Oregon. Both groups were strongly
      influenced by the American way of life.

762. Tornabene, Lyn. *What's a Jewish Girl?* New York:
      Simon and Schuster, 1966. 93 pp.

      Satirical anecdotes on being a Jewish girl.

763. Tovey, Barbara, and George Tovey. "Women's
      Philosophical Friends and Enemies." *Social
      Science Quarterly* 55 (1974): 586-604.

      The views of different philosophers on the relation
      between men and women. Asserts that the Jews
      believed in the subjugation of women to men, that
      woman carries the guilt as the corrupter of mankind
      and the causes of its misery. States that Spinoza

believes that it is impossible for women to share political power with men because they do not have men's character and ability.

764. Traub-Werner, D. "A Note on Counter-Transferance and Anti-Semitism." *Canadian Journal of Psychiatry* 24 (1979): 547-48.

A description of a case where a thirty-three year-old anti-Semitic female patient is being treated by a Jewish psychiatrist. Possible countertransference motives by the psychiatrist are explored.

765. Trenchard, Warren C. *Ben Sira's View of Women. A Literary Analysis*. Brown Judaic Studies, vol. 38. Chico, Calif.: Scholars Press, 1982. 341 pp.

The book of Sirach discusses several topics in everyday life in Palestine in the second century B.C. He devotes a large amount of space to the discussion of women. Of the 1390 verses in Sirach, 105 (7 percent) deal with women. Trenchard's book treats the verses on woman as good wife, woman as mother and widow, woman as bad wife, woman as adulteress and prostitute, and woman as daughter.

766. Trible, Phyllis. "Depatriarchalizing in Biblical Interpretation." In *The Jewish Woman. New Perspectives*, edited by Elizabeth Koltun, 217-40. New York: Schocken Books, 1976 (Reprinted from *Journal of the American Academy of Religion* 41 [1973]: 30-48).

About women in Jewish literature. An examination of interactions between the Hebrew scriptures and the women's liberation movement. Looks at different exegeses of Genesis 2-3 and the Song of Songs. Wants to show that the Biblical God is not always on the side of patriarchy. For example, in the myth of the Fall, Gen. 3:1-6, the woman is the more intelligent, the more aggressive, and more sensible. Song of Songs shows "woman and man in mutual harmony after the Fall." Finds it important that biblical passages which break with patriarchy are not neglected.

767.   Trible, Phyllis. *God and the Rhetoric of Sexuality.*
       Philadelphia: Fortress Press, 1978. 206 pp.

       About female imagery for God in the Hebrew
       scriptures.

768.   Trible, Phyllis. *Texts of Terror: Literary-Feminist
       Readings of Biblical Narratives.* Overtures to
       Biblical Theology, vol. 13. Philadelphia: Fortress
       Press, 1984. 128 pp.

       Recounts four tales from the Bible: the banishment
       of Hagar; the rape of Tamar; the rape and mutilation
       of the concubine in the Judges; and the sacrifice of
       Jepthah's daughter.

769.   Trible, Phyllis. "Woman in the OT." In *The
       Interpreter's Dictionary of the Bible. An
       Illustrated Encyclopedia.* Supplementary Volume,
       963-66. Nashville: Abingdon, 1976.

       Describes woman in a patriarchal society.

770.   Tryon-Montalembert, Renée von. "Ist das Judentum
       Frauen-feindlich?" *Judaica* 41 (1985): 132-41.

       Thinks that women and men are different, and women
       cannot demand the same qualitative rights as men as
       long as they are qualitatively different. There
       cannot be any equality between the sexes because of
       their difference. Refers to Midrash which says that
       woman is related to man as the moon to the sun.
       Refers also to the Bible and the comparison between
       God's relation to his people and the husband's
       relation to his wife. A man without a female
       counterpart is as incomplete as a woman without a
       man. The couple is the fundamental reality.

771.   Tsuriel, Yeruham. "The Kedusha of Monogamy: A
       Personal Perspective." *Response,* no. 32
       (1976-77): 65-70.

772. Umansky, Ellen M. "Creating a Jewish Feminist
     Theology: Possibilities and Problems." *Anima* 20
     (1984): 125-35.

     About the possibilities and problems of creating a
     Jewish feminist theology. Part of the difficulty is
     that at times it may not be possible to harmonize
     personal experience and tradition. The most
     important source of Jewish feminist theology is
     aggada, legends and stories, and the reinterpretation
     of these.

773. Umansky, Ellen M. "The Liberal Jew and Sex."
     Response, no. 32 (1976-77): 71-74.

774. Umansky, Ellen M. *Lily Montagu and the Advancement
     of Liberal Judaism: From Vision to Vocation.*
     Studies on Women and Religion, vol. 12. New York:
     Edwin Mellen Press, 1983. 224 pp.

     About Lily Montagu, a pioneer of Liberal Judaism in
     twentieth-century England. She was inspired by the
     feminist movement and strongly interested in defining
     for herself and others what it means to be a woman
     and a Jew.

775. Umansky, Ellen M. "Women and Rabbinical Orientation:
     A Viable Option?" *Ohio Journal of Religious
     Studies* 4 (1976): 61-66.

     The possibility of ordination for women in Judaism
     has existed for a very short time and presents Jewish
     women with new challenges. Traditional sex role
     differentiation makes it difficult for many, both men
     and women, to accept women as rabbis, but a new
     consciousness among women has made several women want
     to be ordained.

776. Umansky, Ellen M. "Women in Judaism: From the Reform
     Movement to Contemporary Jewish Feminism." In
     *Women of Spirit. Female Leadership in the Jewish
     and Christian Traditions*, edited by Rosemary

Ruether and Eleanor McLaughlin, 333-54. New York:
Simon and Schuster, 1979.

Asserts that women have been excluded from
positions of religious leadership throughout most of
Jewish history. Leaders of the Reform Movement in
nineteenth-century Germany tried to increase the
participation of women within public religious life.
Although a number of liberalizing measures were
undertaken, it was not until 1972 that a woman was
first ordained from a Reform rabbinical seminary.
Maintains that largely because of the growth of
feminist consciousness and activity the status of
women within religion has been improved. New rituals
have been created, women's prayer services have been
of great importance, and a lot of literature on the
subject has enriched historical and personal
awareness of what it means to be both female and
Jewish.

777. Vaux, Roland de. "Family Institutions." In *Ancient
      Israel. Its Life and Institutions*, 19-61. London:
      Darton, Longman and Todd, 1974.

      About marriage; the position of women, widows;
      children; succession and inheritance; and death and
      funeral rites.

778. Vignola, Susan Lynn. "The American Jewish Woman's
      Socialization Process: The Study of Mother-Daughter
      Relationship as It Affects the Daughter's Future
      Choice of Husband." D.S.W. diss., The Catholic
      University of America, 1979. 339 pp.

      Two main questions are examined: 1) "What are the
      associations between an American Jewish woman's early
      life experiences and her marriage to a Jewish or
      non-Jewish man?" and 2) "What are the associations
      between an American Jewish woman's ethnic identity
      and the continuity of Jewish ethnic values in the
      home she establishes through marriage to a Jewish man
      or a non-Jewish man?" The findings show the
      following: 1) "A strong to moderate correlation was
      found to exist between maternal Jewish identity,
      maternal Jewish activity, maternal warmth and

marriage to a Jewish or non-Jewish man." 2) A
moderately strong correlation coefficient was found
between Jewish identity and marriage to a Jewish or
non-Jewish man." and 3) A strong correlation was
found between Jewish identity, marriage to a Jewish
or non-Jewish man, and Jewish activity."

779. Voolen, Edward van. "Die Jüdische Hochzeit in der
     Kunst." In *Die Braut. Geliebt, verkauft,
     getauscht. Zur Rolle der Frau im Kulturvergleich*,
     vol. 1, edited by Gisela Vögler and Karin V. Welck,
     180-85. Köln: Rautenstrauch-Joest Museum,
     Museum für Völkerkunde, 1985.

     Already in the biblical and Talmudic texts wedding
     ceremonies and wedding presents are described. From
     the end of the thirteenth century we have several
     paintings interpreting Jewish wedding ceremonies.

780. Vos, Clarence J. *Woman in Old Testament Worship*.
     Delft: N.V. Vereinigde Judels & Brinkman, 1968.
     219 pp.

     The scope of this study is woman's status and role
     as member of the cultic community as worshiper and
     possibly as cultic officiant (if women ever served as
     officiants) in the legitimate worship of Israel
     throughout the Old Testament period.

781. Waagenaar, Sam. *Women of Israel*. New York: Schocken
     Books, 1961. 47 pp. text. 112 pp. photos.

     Presents five short biographical sketches of
     Israeli women from different parts of the world, all
     speaking different languages before they learned
     Hebrew. The stories are as different as "the colors
     of their skin." The more than one hundred
     photographs illustrate the narratives.

782. Wagenknecht, Edward. *Daughters of the Covenant.
     Portraits of Six Jewish Women*. Amherst: The
     University of Massachusetts Press, 1983. 192 pp.

Presents biographical portraits of six
distinguished Jewish women of the nineteenth and
first half of the twentieth centuries, Rebecca Gratz
(1781-1869); Lillian D. Wald (1867-1940), well-known
as philanthropist; the poet Emma Lazarus (1849-87);
the anarchist and fighter for civil liberation Emma
Goldman (1869-1940); the Zionist leader Henrietta
Szold (1860-1945); and the almost unknown English
poet and novelist Amy Levy (1861-89) who committed
suicide at the age of twenty-eight.

783. Wahba, Rachel. "Some of Us Are Arabic." In *Nice
     Jewish Girls. A Lesbian Anthology*, edited by
     Evelyn Torton Beck, 63-66. Trumansburg, N.Y.:
     The Crossing Press, 1982.

     The author is a Sephardic Arabic Jewish immigrant
     of Egyptian and Iraqi parents. "Born in Bombay,
     India, I grew up stateless in the Japanese
     cosmopolitan city of Kobe." Describes her opinion
     of Jewish identity and finds no contradiction in
     being an Arabic Jew.

784. Walden, Daniel, ed. "Jewish Women Writers and Women
     in Jewish Literature." *Studies in American Jewish
     Literature* 2, no. 3, 1983.

     The whole issue contains essays on Jewish female
     authors and women in Jewish literature.

785. Wallach-Faller, Marianne. "Veränderungen im Status
     der Jüdischen Frau. Ein geschichtlicher Überblick."
     Judaica 41 (1985); 152-72.

     States that the status of Jewish woman is not
     unchangeable. Describes how it has evolved
     throughout the history. Starts with the Bible and
     Talmud and describes woman's position in family law
     and public service. Continues to the Middle Ages and
     to modern times. Concludes that the status of
     Jewish women has changed according to the spirit of
     the times (*Zeitgeist*). Most of the improvements are
     a result of women's own struggle. In Reform and
     Conservative Judaism women have a high degree of

equality today, while modern Orthodox women are a bit behind as far as equality with men goes.

786. Waskow, Arthur I. "Feminist Judaism Restoration of the Moon." In *On Being a Jewish Feminist. A Reader*, edited by Susannah Heschel, 261-72. New York: Schocken Books, 1983.

Argues that feminist-transformation of Judaism is necessary for the sake of Jewish women who have been marginalized in Jewish life; for the sake of Jewish men who have had to repress those aspects of their selves that the tradition viewed as female; for the sake of the human race which needs a renewal of Torah in order to solve the problems that it must solve to save its life; and for the sake of the Jewish people. Takes the moon as the starting point. Several Jewish texts say things about the moon, and in many religious traditions the moon is closely related to womanhood.

787. Watts, Ronald K. "Jewish Fertility Trends and Differentials: An Examination of the Evidence from the Census of 1970." *Jewish Social Studies* 42 (1980): 293-312.

788. Waxman, Chaim I. "The Threadbare Canopy. The Vicissitudes of the Jewish Family in Modern American Society." *ABS. American Behavioral Scientist* 23 (1980): 467-86.

Points to the 1970s debate about the Jewish family. There was widespread concern over the future of the American Jewish family. Thinks it is necessary for the future of American Jewry and for Jewish survival in the United States to give careful attention to the state of the American Jewish family. This means research and developing communal programs for strengthening the traditional form and character of the Jewish family.

789. Waysman, Dvora. "Women's Rights in Rabbinic Courts." *Israel Digest* 22, no. 16 (1979): 17.

About the author's experience at the first
Leadership Conference of the League for Women's
Rights in the Courts. The League is concerned with
many areas of rights for Jewish women, but the most
central item at the conference was the problem of the
aguna, a woman tied to a husband who refuses to give
her a *get*, divorce. Finds that "a pressure group
such as the Women's League for Rights in the Courts
has become a necessity in Israel to act as a
collective conscience for the plight of women
who--through no fault of *Halakhah*, but solely because
of its misapplication--have become victims of a cruel
situation."

790. Webber, Jonathan. "Between Law and Custom: Women's
      Experience of Judaism." In *Women's Religious
      Experience: Cross-Cultural Perspectives*, edited by
      Pat Holden, 143-62. London: Croom Helm, 1983.

Takes up the typical Jewish ideas of males and
females as having different domains in life even if
they are spiritually equal before God. Asserts that
the elaboration of this idea is so perfect that
Judaism is in practice a male religion, a male
culture, a male-dominated social system. Jewish
feminists have criticized the traditional Jewish
ideal. Discusses *Halachah* in connection with the
status of women, and the relationship between
Halachah and custom. Thinks that *Halachah* does not
necessarily perceive empirical social realities at
all, and, in the particular case of the question of
women, it therefore constitutes a male view of the
world in many ways.

791. Weinberg, Sydney Stahl. "The World of Our Mothers:
      Family, Work, and Education in the Lives of Jewish
      Immigrant Women." *Frontiers* 7 (1983); 71-79.

An analysis of the experience of forty Jewish
immigrant women in the United States. The subject
of acculturation is discussed.

792. Weiner, Nella Fermi. "Lilith: First Woman, First
      Feminist." *International Journal of Women's
      Studies* 2 (1979): 551-59.

      Reviews the tale of Lilith in ancient Judaic
      tradition, in folklore, and in modern feminism.
      Lilith is Adam's first wife who left him because she
      refused to lie beneath him. After this, she is
      described as a demon, killing children and seducing
      men, an outcast from the human community. For modern
      feminists, however, she is a strong woman asking for
      equality in sexual relations. She leaves Eden rather
      than submit to Adam's rule.

793. Weiss, Shevach, and Yael Yishai. "Women's
      Representation in Israeli Political Elites."
      Jewish Social Studies 42 (1980): 165-76.

      Points to data which prove that representation
      of women in Knesset, local governments, and political
      parties is extremely poor. This phenomenon persists,
      since no changes have been effected during a period
      of thirty years.

794. Weiss-Rosmarin, Trude. "Is God She? And So What?"
      Commonweal 94, no. 16 (1971): 374.

      Asserts that although God is "He" in Hebrew and in
      the religious literatures of Judaism, Christianity,
      and Islam, the symbolic language of monotheism is not
      patriarchal. In the Torah God's manifestation in
      revelation is feminine as well as God's indwelling
      and presence in the world (*Shekhinah*). There are
      several examples of the same. Thinks, however, that
      "feminization" of theological language will not help
      liberate women, and that women's liberation
      theologicians are overly optimistic in hoping that
      "feminizing" God will do away with the repression of
      women in Western society.

795. Weiss-Rosmarin, Trude. "Sexist Language." *Jewish
      Spectator* 40 (Spring 1975): 13-14.

Emphasizes that she is not one of those who are
intent upon "feminizing" God. Has no objection to
"God, the Father." Wants, however, to avoid "sexist
language" which ignores girls and women. Mentions
that linguistic sexism is prevalent in English and
other Germanic languages because nouns have no
feminine forms, as is the case in Hebrew, for
example. Finds it regrettable that American and
European women often use their husbands' names and
not their own names.

796. Weiss-Rosmarin, Trude. "The Unfreedom of Jewish
      Women." *Jewish Spectator* 35 (Oct. 1970): 2-6.

Suggests that representatives of the women's
liberation movement mistakenly think that
"liberation" requires that femininity be stamped out,
that they consider pregnancy, childbirth, homemaking
and mothering "inferior" because such is, and has
been, the masculine consensus. Thinks that women's
liberation should demand equality of "woman's work"
and work for bestowing dignity upon her work instead
of derogating it. Finds that Jewish women's
unfreedom is much due to the fact that Jewish family
law is revered as divinely revealed Torah, and thus
beyond change. The basic conviction of women is that
she is the possession of man which means that only
the husband can issue a divorce decree (*get*). Jewish
law on the whole is male-made. Concludes that she is
not a militant feminist to the extent where women's
liberation would be her only concern, "but I do
identify as a woman and the unfreedom of Jewish women
fills me with shame and anger."

797. Weiss-Rosmarin, Trude. "Women in Conservative
      Synagogues." *Jewish Spectator* 38 (Oct. 1973)
      5-6.

The Committee on Jewish Law and Standards of the
Conservative Rabbis' Rabbinical Assembly is given
credit for recognizing women as members of the *minyan*
(the quorum of ten required for congregational
prayer services). However, the Conservative marriage
contract deprives women of their basic rights as
sovereign persons. Woman is the legal possession of

the husband, and the Conservative rabbis have done
nothing to modify the marriage ritual. Asserts that
women need legal equality.

798. Weiss-Rosmarin, Trude. "Women in Jewish Law."
Keeping Posted 17, no. 7 (1972): 3-6.

Discusses attitudes toward women in biblical
narratives and in modern times. Asserts that Jewish
law is very "chivalrous" toward women and shows much
concern for women's welfare but stresses that this is
not the same as *legal equality*. Jewish law is a
typical male-oriented law, and Jewish society is
repressive of women's legal rights. Mentions several
examples of how Jewish women are discriminated against
by law.

799. Weissman, Deborah. "Bais Yaakov: A Historical Model
for Jewish Feminists." In *The Jewish Woman: New
Perspectives*, edited by Elizabeth Koltun, 139-48.
New York: Schocken Books, 1976.

The *Bais Yaakov* movement (House of Jacob) is a
network of schools and youth organizations for girls
and young women, started within the Polish Jewish
community. It still exists in many countries.

800. Weller, Leonard, Ophrah Hazi, and Orah Natan.
"Affiliative Need of First-Born Married Women."
International Journal of Sociology of the Family
5 (1975): 249-50.

An examination of 258 married women attending
classes in Tel Aviv, Israel, to find if it holds true
that first-born men and women marry earlier than
later-born men and women due to higher affiliative
needs.

801. Weller, Leonard, Orah Natan, and Ophrah Hazi. "Birth
Order and Marital Bliss in Israel." *Journal of
Marriage and the Family* 36 (1974): 794-97.

Discusses the relationship between rank of birth-
order and successful marriages. 236 women of Tel
Aviv, Israel completed a questionnaire of adjustment
to marital life. The findings indicate that the
following combinations were high: first-born husband
and later-born wife; later-born husband and
first-born wife; and middle-born husband and wife.

802. Wenham, G.T. "The Restoration of Marriage
      Reconsidered." *Journal of Jewish Studies* 30
      (1979): 36-40.

803. Wessel, Bessie Bloom. "The Jewish Girl at College."
      Jewish Woman 4, no. 2 (1924): 3-4, 33.

804. White, Ebe Minerva. "Judaism." In *Woman in World
      History. Her Place in the Great Religions*, 166-94.
      London: Herbert Jenkins, 1924.

      Starts with refuting the "general opinion" that
      womanhood is degraded in Judaism. Describes several
      aspects of women's status in Jewish laws, family,
      society and religion from the time of the Old
      Testament to "modern times." Concludes that women
      today are constantly entering new spheres and wishes
      that what is good in the old religion should be
      united to new ideas.

805. Wijsenbeek-Franken, Caroline. "The Jewish Women of
      Holland." *Jewish Woman* 2, no. 4 (1922): 6-7.

806. Wilke, Fritz. *Das Frauenideal und die Schätzung des
      Weibes im Alten Testament: Eine Studie zur
      israelitischen Kultur- und Religionsgeschichte.*
      Leipzig: Dietrich, 1907. 62 pp.

807. Willensky, Marjorie Koch. "The Effects of a Career
      Workshop on Aspects of Career Exploratory Behavior,
      Locus of Control, and Self-Concept of Jewish
      Married Women." Ed.D. diss., Boston University
      School of Education, 1979. 171 pp.

An examination of the effects of a career workshop
on the factors mentioned in the title. A treatment
group and a control group were established. It was
hypothesized that the treatment group would reflect
significantly more career exploratory behavior,
internal locus of control, and positive self-concept
at the end of the workshop than the control group
and that the workshop effects would significantly
increase thirty days after the treatment. The
findings indicate significant differences between the
two groups in career exploratory behavior scores and
locus of control scores but not in self-concept
scores. No significant differences were indicated
thirty days after the workshop ended.

808. Williams, James G. "The Beautiful and the Barren:
     Conventions in Biblical Type-Scenes." *Journal for
     the Study of the Old Testament* 17 (1980): 107-19.

     Treats various aspects of the matriarch or
     important mother figure. They are 1) the wife as
     sister; 2) the betrothal; 3) the *agon* (contest) of
     the barren wife; and 4) the promise to the barren
     wife.

809. Williams, Jay G. "Yahweh, Women, and the Trinity."
     Theology Today 32 (1975): 234-42.

     A discussion of the female element in Godhead and
     the Trinity. Asserts that throughout the whole Old
     Testament there is continuous warfare between Yahweh,
     the God of masculine power, wisdom, and judgment, and
     the goddesses of the indigenous population, Asherah
     and Anat. When Yahweh enters Palestine, Asherah and
     Anat are repudiated, condemned, and driven out. They
     are the enemy. In their place, Yahweh marries Israel
     herself. Thus, the feminine counterpart of Yahweh is
     preserved. The question of the female part of the
     Godhead has been kept alive by Kabbalists with the
     idea of *Shekhinah* as the bride of God. Within
     Orthodox Rabbinic Judaism, ideas of a feminine person
     in the Godhead has often met with strong resistance.

810. Winer, Mark Leonard. "The Demography, Causes, and
      Consequences of Jewish Intermarriage." Ph.D.
      diss., Yale University, 1977. 315 pp.

811. Winter, Urs. *Frau und Göttin. Exegetische und
      ikonographische Studien zum weiblichen Gottesbild
      im Alten Israel und in dessen Umwelt.* Göttingen:
      Vandenhoeck & Ruprecht, 1983. 748 pp.

      A study of the religious status of women and of the
      goddess in ancient Israel.

812. Wisse, Ruth R. "The Most Beautiful Woman in Vilna."
      Commentary 71, no. 6 (1981): 34-38.

      Tells about the life of her Jewish grandmother.

813. Wisse, Ruth R. "Women as Conservative Rabbis."
      Commentary 68, no. 4 (1979): 59-64.

      On the controversy over the admission of women to the
      rabbinate of the Conservative movement. Tells about
      the work of a commission appointed by the Rabbinical
      Assembly "for the study of the ordination of women as
      rabbis." The result of the commission's work was
      that a majority (11-3) recommended that women be
      trained as rabbis by the Conservative movement. Goes
      through the arguments both of the majority and
      minority. Criticizes their result on the grounds
      that it is not in accordance with tradition and
      Jewish law. Stresses that Jewish law expects
      different things of men and women and criticizes the
      commission members because the point that Judaism may
      still have something relevant to say on the question
      of sexual roles is never alluded to in the report.

814. Wolf, Mrs. Carl. "Woman and Education." *Jewish
      Woman* 4, no. 1 (1924): 10-11, 25.

815. Wolfe, Susan J. "Jewish Lesbian Mother." In *Nice
      Jewish Girls. A Lesbian Anthology*, edited by

Evelyn Torton Beck, 164-73. Trumansburg, N.Y.: The Crossing Press, 1982.

Discusses the possibility of contradiction in being at once a Jewish mother and a Lesbian, a Jewish Lesbian feminist mother of a son.

816. Wolfenstein, Martha. "Two Types of Jewish Mothers." In *Childhood in Contemporary Cultures*, edited by Margaret Mead and Martha Wolfenstein, 424-40. Chicago: University of Chicago Press, 1955.

A presentation of the picture of two mothers, one of Eastern European Jewish origin and the other of an American Jewish family. Asserts that markedly different mother-child relations appear in the two cases. Describes some of the contrasting attitudes of these two mothers and stresses that an important subject for further research would be the question of how the transition from the Eastern European Jewish to the American Jewish family is achieved.

817. Wolff, Hans Walter. "Mann und Frau. 1. Grundzüge des Eherechts 2. Das Liebesverhältnis 3. Störungen der Liebe." In *Anthropologie des Alten Testaments*, 243-58. München: Chr. Kaiser Verlag, 1973.

Discusses what the Old Testament says about marital rights; love between man and woman; and destruction of love affairs.

818. Women Workers Council. "History of the Working Woman in Israel." In *Women in Israel*, published by Israel Information Centre, 7-12. Tel Aviv, 1975.

819. Women Workers Council. "The Kibbutzim and Moshavim." In *Women in Israel*, published by Israel Information Centre, 57-64. Tel Aviv, 1975.

820. Women Workers Council. "Labor Laws and Social
      Legislation." In *Women in Israel*, published by
      Israel Information Centre, 21-31. Tel Aviv, 1975.

821. Women Workers Council. "The Women of the Minority
      Groups." In *Women in Israel*, published by Israel
      Information Centre, 49-53. Tel Aviv, 1975.

822. Women Workers Council. "The Working Woman--Cases in
      Point." In *Women in Israel*, published by Israel
      Information Center, 17-20. Tel Aviv, 1975.

823. Women Workers Council. "The Working Woman in
      Israel." In *Women in Israel*, published by Israel
      Information Centre, 4-6. Tel Aviv, 1975.

824. Wouk, Herman. *Marjorie Morningstar*. London:
      Jonathan Cape, 1955. 638 pp.

      This novel, a best-seller of 1955, is said to have
      set the pattern for the stereotype of the American
      Jewish woman, the virtuous American girl, for the
      whole decade. (See Marc Lee Raphael, 618 above).

825. Wright, G. Ernest. "Women and Masculine Theological
      Vocabulary in the Old Testament." In *Grace upon
      Grace. Essays in Honor of Lester J. Kuyper*,
      edited by James I. Cook, 64-69. Grand Rapids,
      Mich.: William B. Eerdmans Publ. Co., 1975.

826. Wurmnest, Karl Friedrich. "Die Rolle Des Individuums
      innerhalb von Familie und Ehe im alten Israel."
      Ph.D. diss., Universität zu Köln, 1979. 170 pp.

      A sociological examination of the status of
      individuality within the family and married life in
      ancient Israel.

827. Yaron, R. "The Restoration of Marriage." *Journal of
      Jewish Studies* 17 (1966): 1-11.

828. Yinon, Yoel. "Authoritarianism and Prejudice among Married Couples with Similar or Different Ethnic Origin in Israel." *Journal of Marriage and the Family* 37 (1975): 214-20.

Twenty married couples whose ethnic origin was similar and twenty whose ethnic origin was different answered questionnaires designed to measure their degree of prejudice toward the other ethnic group.

829. Yudkin, Marjorie S. "The Shalom Ideal." *Judaism* 33 (1984): 85-90.

The Shalom ideal is the ideal of wholeness. A person created in the image of God has both feminine and masculine qualities, and the one God exemplifies the Shalom ideal in unifying all polarities.

830. Yulish, Stephen. "Adam: Male, Female, or Both?" *Anima* 9 (1982): 59-62.

Discusses passages in Genesis, in *Zohar*, and in *midrah Alfa Beta de Bensira* on the first man and woman. Concludes that we have to recognize "the androgynous nature of Adam, the Godhead, and ultimately of ourselves."

831. Yuval, Annabelle. "The Israeli Woman." *Judaism* 22 (1973): 224-36.

Much about women's legal rights and about women and employment.

832. Yuval-Davis, Nira. "The Bearers of the Collective: Women and Religious Legislation in Israel." *Feminist Review* 4 (1980): 15-27.

The Israeli Declaration of Independence of 1948 rejects any discrimination on sexual grounds. In spite of this, the author claims, the legal situation in Israel is far from admitting women's equality even formally. In 1951 a law called "the law of equal rights for women" was passed in the Knesset, but with

the reservation that in questions of marriage and
divorce the principles of equal rights would not be
upheld. Jewish women in Israel are forced to abide
by Jewish Orthodox Halakhic Law for marriage and
divorce matters. Nearly every aspect of Jewish
family life is determined by Rabbinical Courts and
their judges backed by the only authoritative law in
this domain, the Orthodox *Halakhah*. The guiding
principle of this law is that a woman becomes her
husband's property in marriage. Asserts that the
only area where religious laws are incorporated into
secular legal systems is the area of personal
matters.

833.   Yuval-Davis, Nira. "The Israeli Example." In *Loaded
       Questions. Women in the Military*, edited by
       W. Chapkins, 73-77. Amsterdam: Transnational
       Institute, 1981.

       When the State of Israel was established in 1948,
       it was the first state in which women were recruited
       to serve in the army on the basis of a national
       recruitment law. States that most of the women in
       the army are occupied with office work. They fulfill
       only a small part of military roles, mostly those of
       an auxiliary nature in the rear.

834.   Zak, M. "Deification and Disdain--Literary View of
       Black and Jewish Mothers." *Journal of Psychology
       and Judaism* 3 (1979): 268-77.

835.   Zamir, Aviva. *Mothers and Daughters: Interviews with
       Kibbutz Women*. Norwood, Pa.: Norwood Editions,
       1986. 178 pp.

836.   Zeitlin, Solomon. "Personal Status in Israel."
       Jewish Quarterly Review 49 (1958): 122-32.

       The State of Israel took over the conception of
       personal status defined by the mandatory power, i.e.,
       the English law which was the law of Palestine before
       the State of Israel was established. However, the
       religious courts were authorized to deal with

matters of personal status and these often came in
conflict with the civil courts. Many cases have
arisen as a result of a collision between the two
sets of law and courts, especially in relation to
marriage, divorce, and inheritance. Refers to a book
published by a justice of the Supreme Court of
Israel, Professor of Law, Dr. M. Silberg, *Personal
Status in Israel* (in Hebrew) which analyzes many of
these cases.

837. Zingg, E. "Ehe und Familie nach den Gesetzen Moses."
      Judaica 20 (1964): 121-28.

      Discusses marriage and family law in the Old
      Testament. Stresses that law (*das Recht*) always
      will change according to culture--there is no eternal
      law. Concludes that Moses was a wise lawmaker whose
      philosophy of law in relation to order, justice, and
      peace was carried through both in private and public
      matters.

838. Zuabi, An'am. "The Arab Woman 'Twixt Tradition and
      Progress." In *Women in Israel*, published by Israel
      Information Centre, 54-56. Tel Aviv, 1975
      (Previously published in *Dvar Hapoelet*).

      About Arab women in relation to Israeli law.

839. Zu'bi, Enam. "The Changing Status of Arab Women in
      Israel." *Kidma* 7 (1975): 31-33.

      States that the Arab woman in Israel has achieved
      impressive and substantial progress in all spheres,
      at home and outside the home. The changes can be
      attributed to specific factors which Israeli
      legislation provides for: education, social security,
      minimum age of marriage at seventeen, and prohibition
      of polygamy. Furthermore, just divorce legislation
      and protection of the working woman.

840. Zuckoff, Aviva Cantor. "Jewish Women's Haggadah."
      In *The Jewish Woman: New Perspectives*, edited by
      Elizabeth Koltun, 94-102. New York: Schocken

Books, 1976 (Reprinted and abridged from
Sistercelebrations, edited by Arlene Swidler.
Philadelphia: Fortress Press, 1974).

841. Zuckoff, Aviva Cantor. "The Oppression of the Jewish
      Woman." *Response*, no. 18 (Summer 1973): 47-54.

      Asks about the nature of oppression of Jewish
      women. Both Jews and women are oppressed, so Jewish
      women are doubly oppressed. Thinks that the specific
      oppression of Jewish women is intimately bound up
      with the living in *Galut*, exile, and with how Jews
      felt about exile.

842. Zuckoff, Aviva Cantor. "Women in Israel: An
      Interview with Shulamit Aloni." *Response*, no. 18
      (Summer 1973): 178-82.

      Interviews Shulamit Aloni about religion, abortion,
      politics, women's liberation and other issues. Aloni
      came to Israel from the United States and compares
      women's status in the countries.

INDEX

The Index is divided into three parts: A Topographical Index, a Subject Index, and an Author Index.

Topolographical Index

217

Subject Index

Author Index